Otto Kuhler   THE GOLD COAST IN TRAIN LINE

Of This Limited

 GOLD COAST EDITION

1950 copies have been printed and signed by the Author.

THIS IS COPY No. 1443

The drawing-observation salon of the Pullman-built private car *The Virginia City*, rebuilt and decorated in 1954 by Robert Hanley, Inc., of Los Angeles. Originally the compartment-observation car *Golden Peak* of the Great Northern Railway, *The Virginia City* is 83 feet long, air conditioned and of solid steel Pullman-Standard construction throughout. The interior decor of the car, which was acquired after its owners had disposed of their first private car *The Gold Coast*, is Venetian Renaissance baroque. Home railroad is the Southern Pacific.

by Lucius Beebe

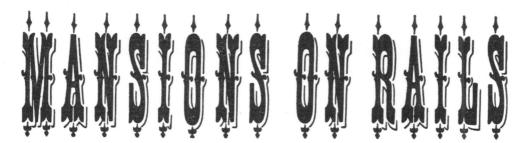

the folklore of the private railway car

Berkeley HOWELL-NORTH *California*

1959

MANSIONS ON RAILS

Published by the HOWELL-NORTH PRESS
1050 Parker Street, Berkeley 10, California

Printed and bound in the United States of America by the publisher.

Library of Congress Catalogue Card Number 59-12775

Acknowledgments

For folklore, factual detail and anecdotal and pictorial material, the author of this book is indebted to many kind and generous sources, among them Everett L. DeGolyer, Jr., of Dallas, and Arthur D. Dubin of Chicago, students of railroad transport and collectors of its mementoes who have been unfailingly helpful, to Grace Mayers of the Museum of the City of New York and to Miss Barbara Boyd of *Life* magazine for permission to reprint photographic material that originally appeared in its pages, to Howard Fogg, E. S. Hammack and Robert Richards for valued contributions of their own artistry, to Charles Hardy, Jr., and James Shea of American Car & Foundry and the Southern Pacific Railroad, respectively, for their special cooperation in the field of historic photographs and factual data from their archives, to Schuyler Livingston Parsons, J. T. Van Campen, and to many other railroads credited in their appropriate places, to Gerald Best for his time and care in reading copy and proofs and finally to Julian Graham of Del Monte Lodge for his careful processing of many old time negatives and to Samuel F. B. Morse for his provision of office space at Del Monte where this book was finally brought together. Only the princely generosity of these people has made it possible, and to all of them the author acknowledges a debt of measureless gratitude.

Because without their cooperation, assistance and interest it could not have been accomplished, this book is dedicated to these faithful stewards of the Pullman-Standard Car Manufacturing Company:

E. Preston Calvert

Nora Wilson

Melvin C. Horn

in gratitude for their patience and in appreciation
of their many generous offices.

Contents

Foreword

IT HAS NEVER OCCURRED TO THE AUTHOR of these vagrant paragraphs that the matter of private railroad cars or the official business cars that are their next of kin is of universal interest or a preoccupation of more than a handful of dedicated railroad buffs and historians of transport. Only a microscopic number of persons, compared to the daily millions who rode the steamcars in their years of ascendency, ever had personal or firsthand experience of private railroad cars, a circumstance which was one of the primary occasions for their existence at all. But the men and women who did own, ride and occupy them were largely persons whose way of life bemused multitudes who could only vicariously ride in circumstances of private grandeur. Moralists and social philosophers to the contrary notwithstanding, nothing so fascinates the many as the least available and preferably the more deplorable aspects of life among the well placed.

Not that any truly wayward character ever attached to the private railroad car other than the sagacity in worldly affairs which made owning it possible. Undeniably men of wealth attended horse races, box fights and other sporting events aboard them, playing games of skill or chance en route with painted cards and consuming spirits while doing so, but generally the character of the private car itself was blameless. It was difficult to invest with overtones of Babylonish abandon, let alone Dionysiac riot, a private Pullman containing an aging millionaire and his well upholstered wife and family on the way to French Lick to take the waters.

For every Charlie Gates or Diamond Jim Brady whose private varnish had about it associations of the boudoir, there were a score of Andrew Carnegies en route to dedicate public libraries and J. P. Morgans attending convocations of Anglican bishops. The Hollywood swimming pool and Park Avenue penthouse were far more incandescent repositories of low tumults than the private car ever became.

Compared, of course, to the oceangoing yachts of the profligate rich, the private Pullman was a citadel of monastic renunciation. The performances of specialists in the *danse au ventre* on the afterdeck which characterized the floating den of tin plate heir William B. Leeds when cruising in tropic waters had no counterpart aboard the business car of Arthur E. Still-well of the Kansas City, Pittsburgh & Gulf where attendance at divine service was obligatory for the train crew on the Sabbath. In vain would you search aboard Thomas Fortune Ryan's *Oak Ridge* for the convenience (reportedly part of the economy of a Diesel-powered mahogany love barge) through whose agency the pressure of a button from the owner's bunk dissolved a partition to find it joined on roller bearings by the bed from the adjacent cabin.

It is probable that a minimum of adultery was practiced aboard private railroad cars in America, although in the case of so prevalent and universal a shortcoming, it is difficult to imagine a premises altogether impervious to sin. Court testimony was once adduced to indicate that a Vanderbilt had erred aboard his own private varnish, but in this case the exalted status of the contracting parties themselves served to elevate the lapse well above common intrigue. There is no record of murder aboard a private car. It might occur aboard the Calais Coach of fiction, and the *Wagons Lits* of Continental usage were, of course, the stamping ground of international spy rings and assassins in the best E. Phillips Oppenheim tradition, but violence beyond the aristocratic stage of glass smashing was altogether alien to the private car mores of America.

By and large the private railroad car, and even more so the business car of railroad directors and executives, was in its lifetime a veritable cathedral of the proprieties.

Lacking any connotations of depravity other than those commonly associated with everyone who employs English servants and dresses for dinner, the private railroad car for three full generations of Americans was the supreme symbol of the uses of wealth and privilege. As Shetland ponies and St. Bernard dogs become symbols of wish fulfillment among the very young, the image of a dark green Pullman with brass railed observation platforms and sporting the name of his wife or country estate on its name boards haunted the dreams of emergent moguls in the worlds of finance and industry. That he was the architect of the gigantic United States Steel Corporation registered less in the popular imagination than that Charles M. Schwab owned two of the most spectacular private Pullmans in the record.

The time and place in the United States that saw the beginnings of private car travel and ownership was one in which the explicit fact of wealth and the possession of property aroused nothing but universal admiration. In a democracy which admired nothing so much as class distinction, investments and tangibles had all the compelling fascination that characterized ancient titles and entailed properties of land in the old world. When A. T. Stewart, a New York department store owner with nothing to recommend him to general approval save the fact that he was one of the three wealthiest men in America, died, the *New York Times* devoted seven of the eight available columns of its front page to his obituary and *Frank Leslie's Illus-*

trated Weekly Newspaper got out a special mortuary edition for the occasion. More significant in the general imagination than anything else in the world news of its day was the fortune of $105,000,000 accumulated by Commodore Cornelius Vanderbilt, founder of a notable dynasty of private car fanciers. When this amazing sum was doubled by his son William Henry Vanderbilt in his lifetime, there were occasional curmudgeons who wondered aloud how a man might usefully occupy so substantial an accumulation of worldly goods, but they were all but inaudible in the universal chorus of admiration and the resolution of every American to go and do likewise if possible.

Even conspicuous men of disaster such as Daniel Drew and Jay Gould, who were wreckers rather than builders like the Vanderbilts, Rockefellers and Jim Hills of their era, were never widely resented for the wealth they accumulated through general pillage. They were smart men; there was loot enough for all. The dominant philosophy of America in the nineteenth century urged every ambitious man to get in on it.

The idea that wealth, once accumulated, should not with complete propriety be spent for the pleasure and magnificence of the possessor never occurred to anyone. The Texas oil billionaire living without proper servants while wearing ready-made suits and affecting to be plain as an old shoe was yet in the infinitely degenerate future. Money, in 1875, was for the purpose of gratifying the tastes of those who had it, and largely they did it in uninhibited splendor that will be envied by posterity forever. The hungry yapping of the animal farm had not yet drowned out the reassuring clink of twenty dollar gold pieces.

Amidst the more impressive testimonials to resounding wealth evolved by the well-to-do in nineteenth century America, the private railway car was not a conspicuously costly or ostentatious property. Compared to seagoing yachts, whole blocks of Fifth Avenue real estate crowned with French chateaux, hunting lodges in the Adirondacks and racing stables at Lexington and Auteiul, the private car was a modest artifact and investment. Compared to the expense of securing His Grace the Ninth Duke of Marlborough as the husband for Consuelo Vanderbilt, all the Wagners and Pullmans in the Vanderbilt legend were the merest bagatelle. In a time when a million dollars for a steam yacht or pocket money to the extent of a similar amount annually for a titled son-in-law such as Anna Gould's husband, the Count Boni de Castellane, were a comparative commonplace, nobody thought twice about a private railroad car which at the outside might entail a bill of $50,000.

Yet because of the hold upon the popular imagination of railroading in the seventies and eighties and the continental dimension it had achieved, no other single property ever approached the implications of prestige of the private car and its exalted status in the general fancy.

Seven full decades of Americans were conditioned to thinking of railroads in terms of which Englishmen had for a somewhat longer period been conditioned to thinking of ships and the sea. The private car, a microcosm of all luxury contained in limited dimensions and rolling on six wheel trucks over the prairies and through the high passes of a limitless continent, was the sublimation of a national religion of railroading.

The author of these lines once knew a private car *aficionado* to whom taking a hot showerbath at three o'clock in the morning while rolling over Tennessee Pass on the Denver & Rio Grande Western Railroad aboard his own private car was the ultimate and ineffable worldly satisfaction, the gratification of the most romantic whim within the compass of fancy.

The idea has something to recommend it.

In its first fine flowering the private railroad car evoked no special reticences in its owners. The elder Vanderbilt used his private varnish as rolling advertisements for the New York Central. Railroad executives, directors and stockholders who, a few decades later were loudly to insist their conveyances be known as office cars, saw no advantage in public suffrage to be gained by distinguishing cars used for their transport as railroaders or for their private occasions of pleasure. The two were often inseparable. Where, after the turn of the century, presidents of even the most august carriers assiduously had their p.v. designated as "business cars," an uninhibited generation of directors and general managers in the nineties, such as the peerless A. A. McLeod of the Reading, had the words "Private Car" boldly engrossed on the nameboards of his car *Alexander*.

With the passing of time, however, the private railroad car became an object on the part of its owners of discretion and eventually actual secretiveness. The details of cost, construction and furnishing were closely guarded from the general knowledge where ostentations of wealth a thousand times more costly and impractical were flaunted to the world. Millionaires who had no least hesitation in permitting newspaper and magazine speculation of the prices they paid for paintings, country estates and their mistresses refused to discuss their private cars with an obstinacy that suggested a guilt fixation about what was admittedly an expensive but also highly useful possession.

It is difficult to find practical application for a racing stable, yet generations of rich men wore their racing colors as an oriflamme while hiding their ownership of private railroad cars by carrying them on the roster of a friendly or involved carrier. The coming of the motor car, which was then an expensive and wholly pointless ornament of wealth, found Vanderbilts gladly publicizing garages filled with Renaults and Rolls-Royces while shrinking from the ownership of a railroad car costing no more than half a dozen Peugeots.

The private order files of such carbuilders as Pullman Standard and American Car & Foundry during the private car years were classified matter guarded with Alamogordo precautions and in some cases, when blueprints and photographs of these properties were no longer useful and the cars themselves had vanished from general awareness, the records were deliberately destroyed rather than have them become a matter of public knowledge.

In the case of the business cars of the carriers themselves, a conspiracy of secrecy of Guy Fawkes dimensions came into being and lasted into a generation of railroaders that unhesitatingly advertised its urge toward suicide and bankruptcy through such monumental follies as Dieselization. Railroad executives shrank as from coiled vipers from the words private car. Business cars of undeniable comfort and even splendor in their internal decor and economy were purposely allowed to deteriorate with shabby exteriors and were hidden in remote parts of coach yards. Publicity about business cars, unless it concerned their complete renunciation by executives legitimately entitled to their use, was regarded as a sort of kiss of death or incitement to mob fury, for all the world as though a business car were less a necessary artifact than a drill press or switching engine.

The truth of the matter is that, from being a race of giants and empire builders whose contempt for popular approval was on a scale with their achievements, railroaders by the middle of the twentieth century had degenerated into timidity and subservience, haunted by shadows and fearful of the least breath of criticism.

These circumstances are not cited in special castigation of private car owners or of the tenants of business cars, so much they are a mere wondering commentary on a retreat into mediocrity that has made the assembling of this monograph a task to dwarf the translation of the Etruscan inscriptions. Even in a time when there were but two private railroad cars left in operable use in the United States and one of them the property of the writer at that, the words private car could send railroaders into twittering ecstasies of terror and evasion.

Although the possessors of private railroad cars seem to have regarded these properties as potentially inflammatory symbols of predatory wealth, the rabble rousers and people's friends of the private car age seem to have paid scant attention to this particular aspect of voluptuous extravagance among the aristocracy, perhaps because there were ready to hand far more costly and frivolous examples of wickedness in high places.

True, a Sunday feature writer in William Randolph Hearst's *San Francisco Examiner* in June 1905 in listing the expensive follies of the well-to-do paid passing tribute to William K. Vanderbilt's order from Pullman of a new private car at a cost of $50,000. This was *Idlehour* and the mention provides an interesting clue to the cost of the best in private varnish of the time, a cost which was to be multiplied just ten times over in the next fifty years. But the reporter had far more eye-popping extravagances to lay at the door of Newport and Fifth Avenue: Mrs. Clarence Mackay had just spent $50,000 for a bathtub carved from a single block of rare pink Carrará marble for

13

her home on Long Island; Mrs. Robert Goelet's newly commissioned ocean-going steam yacht *Nahama* and W. K. Vanderbilt's *Valiant* each represented an investment of better than $1,000,000 and Mrs. Howard Gould was building a model chicken ranch at an outlay of $500,000, an agrarian gesture which the reporter, after a brief skirmish with statistics, estimated cost the Goulds $5 for every egg served at breakfast or $60 for a soufflé for four. Then, too, James Hazen Hyde (owner of the private Pullman *Bay Shore*) had just given a costume party at Sherry's at a cost of $30,000 which had been attended by August Belmont (owner of *Oriental* and *Mineola*) and Cornelius Vanderbilt (master of innumerable New York Central business cars) and a nameless wretch, "heir to one of the proudest names of old New York's patroon society," had purchased an ermine lined motoring overcoat for her poodle. Amidst such a rich abundance of follies, a mere $50,000 railroad car was fairly small punkins.

It will be noted that this firm stand against sinful waste amongst the bloated upper classes was taken by William Randolph Hearst some years before he had commenced filling San Simeon with Cellini wine cups at $250,000 the pair and purchasing Welsh castles, Gothic refectories and zoos of African wild animals by the shipload.

An aspect of the private railroad car that at once commands attention among social historians was its durability. A ninety ton artifact of welded steel, stayed with throughbolts, braced with angle irons, riveted and annealed to withstand all but atomic concussion, was apt to be around for some time and its passage from one member of the private car club to another becomes a fascinating item of dynastic succession. The names that attached to private varnish became part of the geologic record of American society and finance, to be traced by the student of such matters as the emergence and decline of the crinoids in the Jurassic era is traced by paleontologists. The car *Alicia* of Boston moneybags A. C. Burrage ended its days as the property of Bruce Dodson, a Kansas City insurance magnate, perhaps symbolizing the westward movement not only of the society of wealth but also of its tangible properties and assets. Harry Payne Whitney's *Adios*, on the owner's death, went to his widow and thence to John Hay Whitney, later American Ambassador to the Court of St. James's. The Wagner-built car *Vanderbilt* passed from Vanderbilt *pére* to Vanderbilt *fils*, a symbolic vehicle for the conveyance of the first American fortune to total more than $100,000,000.

Similarly the epochs of national taste and fashionable decor may be traced unerringly in the photographic files of the durable Pullman Company which built so large a majority of the private cars of the great and near-great. Here one encounters the opulent splendors of Angus Archibald McLeod's first *Alexander* explicit in French *empire* furniture, swags and tassels beyond the counting, brass beds and marble handbowls all complemented by porcelain cuspidors at strategic locations. A few years later in the Columbian Exposition Pullmans there is seen a reversion to the Gothic theme first encountered in the cathedral-like Chicago & North Western's directors' car of 1868. The ceilings of *Isabella* as shown on the shores of Lake Michigan in 1893 are nearly as pure Gothic as the choir of Canterbury Cathedral rebuilt by William of Sens after the fire of 1174. Gothic to Eastlake, Eastlake to *empire, empire* to William Morris, the succession is as available to the record as the Kings of England or, more aptly perhaps, the partners of J. P. Morgan.

The saga of the private car on the steam railroads of America will be at best a fragmentary one with many of its chapters missing or merely suggested by fugitive references in folklore and the known record. Much of this scholarly confusion derives from the character of the private car itself which was at once conveyable and enduring. It changed hands, it changed home railroads and it was a fine thing to borrow, turning up at Pinehurst or Louisville at the disposal of folk in no way concerned for its original purchase or current upkeep. Thus *Cleopatra* makes an appearance at Palm Beach in the winter of 1902 occupied by S. H. Ashbridge who had no immediate or visible connection with the owning International Great Northern Railroad, but doubtless had friends there. Pullman's rental car *Idler* arrives in Florida twice in the same season variously occupied by T. DeWitt Cuyler and later by Tom Platt, the New York political boss.

On an adjacent track the Southern Pacific's *Emalita*, which only a decade ago had been the proud *Alexander I* before catastrophe overtook Angus A. McLeod and the Reading, is occupied by M. Crocker, presumably a relative of the Espee's ruling house. To compound the confusion, Charles Crocker's own car *Mishawaka* is also among those present occupied by a Mr. T. B. Harrison.

To maintain the record of occupancy by the owner, Henry M. Oliver is at Palm Beach aboard his own *Tyrone*, sentimentally named for the county of the ironmaster's birth; Thomas B. Wannamaker is sleeping in the master stateroom of *Oceanic;* William C. Whitney is master of his by now aging Wagner-built *Pilgrim,* and Frederick William Vanderbilt is in the New York Central Lines car No. 493.

But mystery surrounds many a fragrant and provocative private car recollected dimly in folklore or visible for an elusive moment on a trainsheet or in a yellowing society column. What was the pedigree of the car *Concho* which emerges occasionally from the mists of the early century at resorts of fashion occupied cryptically by "Judge Williamson"? Who was Sir J. G. Eaton for whom Pullman in 1916 outshopped a fine car according to floor plan 6-B-84, altered in the terms of Office Memo 7-24-16 to change the size of the "incased water heater"? Who was Dr. S. F. Pearson for whom American Car & Foundry built car No. 4059 from Tracing No. 77997 with one of the most provocative window arrangements in the record?

What was the car aboard which Addison Mizner rode from New York to Daytona Beach in company with Robert Graves, Louis Sherry, Samuel Untermeyer and a Mr. George Young during which Mizner was presented with "three feet of gold snake watch chain and a beautifully gold fitted travelling case" by a lawyer who wanted to meet his brother Wilson who had just married the Yerkes millions?

Or what whim dictated that Solomon Guggenheim, an Orthodox Jew of strong religious convictions, should select for his private car, assigned as its home railroad to the Nevada Northern, a name from the lexicon of most devout Buddhism? He called it *Nirvana* and it was one of the very few p.v. ever to be outshopped by Pullman to the order of a short line carrier. For a railroad with no more than 150 miles of main line, the Nevada Northern was a considerable repository of private cars, its insign appearing not only on the nameboards of *Nirvana*, but also on Colonel Daniel C. Jackling's *Cyprus* and car No. 101, the *Ely*, also Pullman-built, which ended its days as a business car on the Gulf, Mobile & Ohio.

And what rococo wonderments were lost to posterity with the disappearance of *Remlik*, the p.v. of Willis S. Kilmer, the Swamp Root King of Binghamton, New York? The multi-millionaire proprietor of this celebrated pain killer, so the late Samuel Hopkins Adams recalled, was the sporty type who attended race meetings everywhere and *Remlik* (his name spelled coyly backwards) was a splendid expression of his tastes now lost to human ken.

So here, in the private cars of the well-to-do for something like three-quarters of a century or three generations of Americans is a reflection of the society and times of which, in their way, they were the apotheosis, the ultimate expression of possessiveness and wealth which openly admired possessions and wealthy properties.

Do not patronize the private railroad car, for its social implications are those of the diamond stomacher, the opera box, steamboat Gothic mansions with cast iron stags on the lawn and membership in the United States Senate as the most exclusive club of rich men in the entire world. As James M. Barrie said of the Victorian Age, do not fail to speak scornfully of it; there will be time for meekness when you try to better it.

Perhaps the ultimate cachet of distinction was conferred upon the private railroad car in that it was never cheapened by common availability or as a property of democracy.

Unlike the ocean-going steam yacht, the private car seldom fell into the wrong hands. Unlike even Rolls-Royces, which occasionally saw servitude to undertakers and car hire agencies, the private railroad car seldom appeared on the used car lots of the land. The invasion of the private car club by arrivistes such as the Barbed Wire Gateses or Diamond Jim Brady was so infrequent as to be the exception that proved the rule. When, as was occasionally the eventual mischance, a once proud varnish car was sold south to a patent medicine spieler or dog and pony show, it achieved automatic oblivion and was forgotten, expunged from the annals of society like the member of a royal family committed to the oblivion of a monastic order. No private car in the record ever, like the homes of so many wealthy in the great cities of the land, achieved with Prohibition the status of a speakeasy. None, like declassé yachts, ever became a seagoing gambling hell.

Private cars did, to be sure, from time to time appear on used car lots and changed hands and owners, but the transaction was an elevated one, perfumed with much of the dignity with which a venerable Rolls-Royce of vintage year might find a new owner, and it may be supposed that the original owner was at pains to see that his car achieved a good home in prudent and appreciative hands.

All other barriers in the American order might fall before the insurgent tide of universal prosperity on the part of the masses and the declining resources of the *hochgeboren*, the citadel of Newport become a pavilion of jazz festivals, the automobile car, in its time of beauty and integrity a property of wealth alone, might become the most debased of national currencies, hunting lodges of a sort be available to stockbrokers, airplanes to the exhibitionism of Texans.

But the private railroad car was never, from its primeval beginnings to its ultimate disappearance from the coach yards and service tracks of the land, debased or desecrated by promiscuous ownership. It was the hallmark of millionaires, and mostly rich millionaires, at that. No private car owner of record ever imitated downgraded English nobility by welcoming tourists for a fee or entertaining sightseers at the family board. The private car remained aloof, serene and impervious to popular availability as long as it lasted. It was never outshopped in standard models as a "family car" or sold on the monthly payment plan. It was never awarded as a prize in beauty contests at Atlantic City or on radio quiz programs.

It went down the long tangent and around the final curve into history with its integrity undiminished, its radiance unimpaired as a symbol of social assurance and worldly affluence. From first to last with an irreducible minimum of exceptions, it was possessed by aristocrats alone and when the time came to make its exit, it did so in the grand manner, beyond curtain calls and in splendor.

This will be its claim to immortality in the pattern of American life and may well be its epitaph in the graveyard of remembered things. The private car was never in its lifetime anything but what its name implied.

LUCIUS BEEBE

Del Monte Lodge
1959

More Stately Mansions

THE YEAR 1911 SAW THE ARRIVAL in the United States of the high and well born Princess Lwoff-Parlaghy of Hungary. The Plaza Hotel in New York was then just four years old and there the Princess was installed in a state suite of twelve rooms where the hotel's staff of admirable servants was supplemented by her personal household: a maid, secretary, four footmen with crimson liveries and silver buckled evening slippers, a personal physician, coachman and a major domo to oversee everything. Everything included the Princess' thirty-nine trunks manufactured to her specifications by Louis Vuiton of Paris and a gold table service, even though the hotel had one of these, too.

Like many titled foreigners of the period, the Princess was well connected in the United States, one of her connections being Abbott Lawrence Lowell, President of Harvard University, and on him the Princess decided to call. For her transportation, the New York, New Haven & Hartford Railroad produced a private Pullman drawing room car which was attached to the *Shore Line Express* and there on the up trip the Princess was served her lunch off her own gold plate by her own footmen as Long Island Sound recurrently emerged and disappeared from view through the wide picture windows.

The Princess was pleased with the New Haven's arrangements and a few days later, her call on Cousin Larry ended, she asked for similar accommodations to return her to New York and The Plaza. In some inexplicable manner, however, this time the private conveyance instead of occupying the rear of the trainline, was sandwiched in between the diner and a conventional parlor car occupied by well-bred Bostonians, many of whom sought access to luncheon through the titled traveler's private apartments. A number of them mistook it for a particularly comfortable club car provided by the management and paused to read the *Boston Herald* and the *News Bureau* in its upholstered main salon. The Princess, to her credit, was first annoyed and then amused, but the major domo was still conditioned by protocol. Unable to stem the tide of democracy, he at length took his stand by the door and imposed a measure of decorum by announcing the name of each passenger as he entered. Safely back in The Plaza, the Princess managed to recover a measure of her accustomed aloofness by having the Duchess of Manchester ejected from her private elevator, an encounter which caused the Duke to inquire tartly just what she was princess of, anyway.

The little adventure of the Princess Lwoff-Parlaghy need not be taken as typical of life aboard the steamcars in the years before the Kaiser war, but it suggests the acceptance in well-to-do circles of what seems in retrospect one of the most glamorous legends of American railroading in its Golden Age, the private Pullman car.

Of all the hallmarks of wealth and distinction and of the many certifications of success in the United States in what Stewart Holbrook has called the Age of the Moguls, none was possessed of the impact upon the general consciousness and imagination of the private railroad car. None was characterized by its cachet of privilege, none represented so formidable a barrier between *hoi polloi* and worldly consequence.

There were, to be sure, many and various other ornate symbols of exclusiveness available to the well-to-do American: seats in the United States Senate, seagoing steam yachts, titled sons-in-law, estates at Palm Beach, race horses, boxes at the Metropolitan Opera, mansions on Fifth Avenue and later penthouses and cooperative apartments on Park Avenue, well publicized mistresses, seats on the New York Stock Exchange, collections of Old Masters, fleets of Rolls-Royces, Papal titles, strings of polo ponies, African safaris after big game, shooting boxes in Scotland and libraries of first editions.

James Gordon Bennett once remarked that the easiest way to dissipate a fortune was on yachts, mistresses and newspapers. He knew, having all three in abundance. In a similar vein the Elder J. P. Morgan pronounced an oft-quoted classic when he deposed that anyone who had to inquire the price of upkeep of a seagoing yacht had no business owning one. Neither Bennett nor Morgan indulged a hanker for private railroad cars, although Morgan now and then hired an entire private train of Pullmans to transport a convocation of Episcopal bishops between New York and San Francisco, much as lesser philanthropists might send a trolley load of newsboys to the country for a day. If they had had first hand experience of private railroad cars, they might well have added them to their tally of costly properties. "Every time I have the family car put in commission for a trip to Florida or the Adirondacks," the late Cissie Patterson once confided to the writer during dinner at Evalyn Walsh McLean's, "I buy it back from the Pullman Company." "The only thing that's economical about our car," Mrs. Edward T. Stotesbury told reporters, "is the solid gold plumbing. It saves polishing, you know!"

With such affidavits to its almost unearthly splendor, it must be apparent that in its times of teem nothing ever approached the private car in the realm of beauty, luxury or connotations of wealth. Nothing aroused such envy among non-possessors and so gratified owners with outrageous satisfaction. Private cars became repositories of solid platinum whimsy dwarfing to insignificance the purely utilitarian fancy which suggested to the aforementioned James Gordon Bennett that a cow be carried on the foredeck of his ocean going yacht to supply fresh milk.

An inventory over the years of private cars would disclose such items of operational and decorative economy as French chefs, Italian marble bathtubs and wash stands, deep freezes, wood burning fireplaces, antique Venetian mirrors, English butlers, crystal chandeliers, hidden jewel safes, wine cellars, silver plated trucks, Turkish baths, ship-to-shore telephones, television sets, glassed-in shower baths and gold table services from Tiffany. One private Pullman of record recreated in its drawing room an apartment from the palaces of one of the doges of Venice. On board another the footmen wore powdered wigs and knee breeches in the evening. A mushroom fancier had a miniature mushroom cellar hung on his car's undersides along with the draft gear and brake rigging. Most people of private car estate take dressing for dinner for granted. When heading for Florida for the winter Mrs. Edward F. Hutton made a practice of hiring a separate Pullman drawing room car to be attached to her own car for her personal servants. In an earlier and truly imperial age of railroading, tycoons such as Commodore Vanderbilt and Jay Gould were not satisfied with mere private palace cars, but commanded entire three and four car trains for their guests with special locomotives assigned to their exclusive service.

The private railroad car had everything, including social implications second to none.

To a certain extent it still has.

The earliest version of private railroad transport appeared in England in the 1830's and was designed to abate the prejudice, which was strong in the conservative British aristocracy, against the whole railroad business. At a number of primeval English depots, including Euston Station in London, loading docks were built, up which the coaches of the nobility and well-to-do could be driven. The coaches themselves were then fastened on flat cars as the earliest known piggy-back operation, the horses were placed in stall cars, the grooms went third class or stayed with the horses, and the lords of creation rode in specially allotted or private saloon coaches. The hitch to this otherwise admirable arrangement for placating the upper classes seemed to be their own aristocratic indifference to time and schedules of railroad operation. Baronets took to turning up ten or fifteen minutes after departure time and royal dukes as much as an hour, an attitude which caused grief to the management and eventually led to the abolition of the practice altogether. The English nobility regarded this as an insufferable affront and continued to travel by stage and private vehicles for another full decade before acknowledging progress.

The English, amongst whom privacy in travel, especially if entire families were in motion, was greatly at a premium, provided a variety of private carriages and saloon coaches on the early lines for the accommodation of the well-to-do and county families going up to London or on to the Cornish Riviera for August. These were for the most part simply leased day coaches more or less luxuriously upholstered for the accommodation of their occupants on daylight runs. They contained neither dining nor sleeping accommodations, although the British trains built for royalty and therefore no part of this brief mention were superbly appointed for both. Squire and his lady had a cold collation set out and hot tea sent in from an appropriate stopping point and were out of the private saloon the same day they embarked. The private car in the sense of a complete hotel apartment within the confines of a railroad coach owned and maintained by a private individual was unknown in England.

But Americans, to whom democratic protestations and invidious distinctions came naturally, as soon as was practicable widened the gap between the upper classes and *hoi polloi* on the steamcars by a gulf that was never to be spanned as long as railroads continued to be the dominant form of transport of the American scene. The invention of the private car put everyone concerned in his proper place, above or below the salt, and it was a barrier and manifestation of ostentatious class that was never seriously questioned or contested by anyone during its long lifetime.

This may in part have been attributable to the merging in early times of the identity of the private car owned and occupied by an individual magnate and the business or office car of the railroad official. It was an age when a great many American millionaires were also railroad owners, managers, presidents and majority stockholders, and it often became convenient to identify a private palace car as a business property in much the manner expense account entertaining was to be evolved in later years. Some of the most sumptuously appointed private cars in the record were those of railroad presidents who stoutly maintained that they were no more than frugal conveyances for the transaction of the company's business.

In a few years railroad men were to execute an abrupt about face and insist on the most meticulous definition of a business car as differentiated from a private Pullman, but as long as the institution lasted the general public refused to be instructed. A private car was a private car and a fine thing whether occupied by Averell Harriman as chairman of the board of Union Pacific or Mrs. Edward F. Hutton as queen of Palm Beach society.

Appropriately enough, since Boston at the time was still largely a cultural and economic suburb of London, the first imitation of English private car service appeared on the Boston & Providence Railroad in 1834 where a group of commuters from Dedham arranged with the management for the first club car of record. A special coach was set aside for them morning and night on the run across the Roxbury marshes to carry twenty commuters to and from their Boston places of business at a charge of fifteen dollars daily. There is no record that a bar was stocked with Lawrence's Medford rum or that cards were played en route, but the first traces of emerging private rolling stock were there and in the record for all future students of folklore of the high iron.

The private railroad car as Americans were eventually to know it seems first to have been conceived as a conveyance for heads of state. When in 1841 William H. Harrison as President-elect went to Washington for his inaugural, the superintendent of the Baltimore & Ohio Railroad asked his superiors if he should be provided with "a distinct car." The first private car with fully appointed living quarters was built during the Civil War for President Lincoln by the U. S. Military Railroad authority and was part of his funeral train after his assassination.

The private car rode to golden destinies on the flood tide of wealth and railroad expansion that followed the Civil War. It came into being as a convenience and then a social symbol of the moguls whose fortunes derived from the fantastic promotion, financing and building of the railroads that followed America westward, and its life span lasted until those railroads over which it traveled to glory were themselves in irrevocable decline.

In the beginning there was no line of demarcation or at best but an academic one between the private car of a railroad president and that of an emergent millionaire since they were in all probability one and the same person. Jay Gould, George Gould, William H. Vanderbilt, James J. Hill, Edward Harriman owned the railroad. It was immaterial whether their private car was carried on the books as property of the railroad or its president. Or whether it was called a private car or an office car.

Commodore Cornelius Vanderbilt started the ball rolling in a big way as the tycoon who brought the New York Central into being and for his pains died America's richest man with a fortune after taxes of $105,000,000. The Commodore was not one to hide his light under a bushel. His first private car was called *Vanderbilt* and was drawn by an engine named *Vanderbilt*, the former carrying in full colors on its side panels scenes from along the route of the railroad like Niagara Falls, and the latter the Commodore's name in gold lettering and his portrait, white whiskers, stock collar and all on the panels of its great headlight. To say that this promotion was a success is a triumph of understatement. From New York City to farthest Buffalo, all York State knew about the Commodore and his railroad. They envied the one and patronized the other and rival carriers recognized a good thing when they saw it and did likewise.

Jay Gould, by now Emperor of Erie, wasn't so ostentatious. He had a good solid business car that served his purpose well, but his son George Gould had bigger ideas. When the Count Boni de Castellane was courting George's sister, Anna Gould, and a very eligible heiress indeed, he recorded in his diary that aboard the Gould private train of five palace cars guests were expected to appear in full evening dress for dinner and that the servants were attired in black satin knee breeches and crimson tailcoats with gold frogs and loops past all counting.

In the far West where the completion of the Pacific Railroad had created a whole new generation of California millionaires whose extravagances and eccentricities of wealth were a byword in San Francisco, the first private car of record was the gift of Mrs. Leland Stanford to her husband, first Governor of California and President of the booming Central Pacific Railroad. Following the precedent of Commodore Vanderbilt the car was named *Stanford* and raised eyebrows by having set its donor back $20,000, a whopping sum in the hard gold currency and untaxed income of the times. Eighty years later a president of the Southern Pacific, successor to the Central, was to pay a reported $600,000 for a business car without occasioning more than passing comment among the stockholders.

The *Stanford* passed into Western folklore. With the death of the pioneer railroader, it passed to his widow and as a mark of respect to his memory was carried free over every railroad in the United States while Mrs. Stanford raised funds for the endowment of what was to become Leland Stanford Junior University, perhaps the ranking educational institution west of the Missouri River.

The *Stanford* met its end quite literally in a blaze of glory at Yuma, Arizona in 1911, while serving as business car of the late Joseph Dyer, one of the now legendary general managers of the Southern Pacific at the zenith of its fortunes. Aboard at the time was Dyer's pride and heir, Joseph Dyer, Jr., later Art Commissioner to the City and County of San Francisco but in 1911 a youth not yet in his teens. Properly to observe the impending Fourth of July, the younger Dyer had smuggled into his stateroom a generous supply of rockets, Roman candles, giant salutes and other explosives of a patriotic nature. Impatience suggested a premature assay of their combustive qualities and catastrophe ensued. The *Stanford* went skyward in a brief but impressive facsimile of the conflagration that was to be the end of so many celebrated private cars in the record.

Roughly speaking, the golden age of the private railroad car in the United States was from the early eighties to the stock market debacle of 1929, a half century that was to see its flowering in rococo splendor in a cycle of wealth largely uninhibited by either reticence or taxes.

During this period the order books of the Pullman Company, later to be known as Pullman Standard, indicated the outshopping of between three and four hundred private and business cars of varying degrees of luxury and costliness and there were other carbuilders of only slightly less celebrity: Knight, Wagner, Mann, Barney & Smith, the Worcester Car Company, Jackson & Sharp of Wilmington and its successor, American Car & Foundry, Kimball, Woodruff, the Budd Company, the St. Louis Car Company, Hotchkiss, Blue & Co., Ltd., and on the Pacific Coast both the Union and the Risdon Iron Works. Many of the carriers of the period, themselves both large and small, maintained car shops capable of turning out any sort of passenger rolling stock and well after the turn of the century such Class I carriers as Union Pacific, Central of Georgia and the Illinois Central were building beautiful business cars for the use and satisfaction of ranking executives. The private cars built or adapted by these manufactories over the years is simply not available to counting.

But whatever their source of origin and the patents covering their various devisings of convenience and luxury, the private car was never one thing and that was cheap.

Their price has varied with the years and the wealth of individual customers, but the trend in cost of private varnish may generally be described as upward. In the early seventies $20,000 bought as nice a palace car as one might wish with six wheel trucks, picture windows and Eastlake decor throughout. By the turn of the century $50,000 was the going price with Westinghouse air brakes, electric lights and king size brass beds in the master staterooms. When Charles M. Schwab replaced his *Loretto I* with *Loretto II* in 1915, the tab was popularly reported to be $150,000. By the mid twenties such magnificent private varnish as Mrs. J. P. Donahue's *Japauldon,* perhaps the finest specimen of private car building ever to come from the builder, was a bit over $300,000. By the post war years of the late forties and fifties inflation raised the cost of such fine business cars as those of Fred Gurley, President of the Santa Fe, and A. E. Stoddard of the Union Pacific to a reported half million and rumor has it that the Southern Pacific's President D. J. Russell signed a tab for something like $550,000 for the ranking office car of the country's most far flung carrier. This not counting a tidy sum said to have been spent by Mrs. Russell out of her private pocket for rare oriental furnishings from Gump's in San Francisco. Even when cars are built in the home shops of the owning railroads at considerable savings over the Pullman built article, the price is not exactly that encountered in a bargain basement. A few years ago the thrifty Illinois Central laid the underframe for a new business car for its President, Wayne B. Johnston, in its own carshops. The estimated cost was $225,000, a mere bagatelle at today's prices, but before it was rolling in mainline service, rising costs had doubled the estimated investment.

Of all the great dynastic successions of railroad builders and operators the most frugal by far, when it came to private varnish for their personal use or official cars for their executives, were the Hills, father and son. The Great Northern was evolved out of antecedent streaks of rust that were reactivated by the Empire Builder on a basis of the most stringent economies and the business cars of the St. Paul, Minneapolis & Manitoba and later of the Great Northern reflected a similarly bleak rejection of anything savoring of the voluptuary when either the Hills or their subordinates travelled abroad.

Three generations of Vanderbilts were profligate in their commissions to Pullman and Wagner for the outshopping of luxurious private cars and ordered them by half dozens at the turn of the century when the going price was approximately $50,000. It is doubtful if either Harriman *père* or Harriman *fils* ever inquired into the cost of *Arden* in the case of the former or *Avis* in the case of Averell. Certainly the last of these which was built in the Union Pacific's own shops crowded $300,000 when all the bills were in. Nothing in the record shows what the Goulds may have paid for their cars which clustered on the private car sidings of the land like leaves on Vallombrosa's surface, but none of the second generation of the family were celebrated for frugality.

In contrast to those open handed magnificoes James Jerome Hill and his son Louis were the misers of the private car club. The enormous fortune deriving from the Hill roads even now in its fourth generation of inheritors has not been altogether dissipated, and Louis Hill was celebrated in his lifetime for the baronial aspects of his social life in St. Paul, yet when he spent $7,148.40 in 1905 for a personal car that included a garage in its economy, the sum was the largest, excepting only one, listed in the records of the railroad for similar properties.

The earliest business car of any of the Hill lines, according to Bert Baker of the Great Northern's engineering department, was built for the primeval St. Paul & Pacific by Jackson & Sharp in 1879 and cost no more than $2,500. It was carried on the company books as No. A-16 from then until 1910 when it was destroyed in a snowslide at Wellington. Car No. A-3, built in 1880 by the Ohio Falls Car Company, cost $4,339.13. Official car No. A-5 rebuilt at the company shops stood the Hills only $6,250 in 1891. No. A-15 cost $1,999.16 in 1899. The first of two cars numbered A-8 built in the Great Northern's own shops in 1901 ran to $2,481.75 while A-20, rebuilt from a Jackson & Sharp sleeper came to $6,250.

The all-time high on the company's books while either J. J. or Louis Hill were alive was No. A-18 which was built by American Car & Foundry in 1900 for the personal occupancy of the Empire Builder himself and was billed to the Great Northern at $15,771.45. This and Louis Hill's automobile-bearing No. A-22 were the high water marks of extravagance.

What would have been the reaction of either Hill to a generation which ran to solid gold plumbing in its private cars, high speed roller bearing trucks which cost as much per pair as J. J. Hill's own car, and stockholders who viewed with complete equanimity the expenditure of more than half a million dollars for a presidential car for a Western carrier may best be left to the imagination.

Although the range of individual additions and improvements to private car detail is limited only by the human imagination and American Association of Railroads standards of clearance, two things were almost ritual among private car owners of the Golden Age: English butlers and concealed wall safes. From Harry Payne Whitney's *Wanderer* to Alfred P. Sloan, Jr.'s *Pheasant,* hidey-holes for jewelry and private papers sometimes protected by time locks were an invariable rule. Paderewski's *General Stanley* naturally had an upright piano as did the Pullman rented by Fritzi Scheff occupied in the years she was singing "Kiss Me Again" who added a doubtful convenience in the form of an honest to God, full length bathtub while on tour. Because it slopped ruinously when the car was in motion, Miss Scheff was constrained to taking baths only when her train was scheduled for a stop of twenty minutes or more without switching. Sometimes this was at three o'clock in the morning, an inconvenient hour.

A notable aspect of the habit of private railroad transportation is that, like drug addiction, it is difficult to cure and, like certain aristocratic diseases such as hemophilia, it is often hereditary.

Once invested with the aura of ornate elegance that derived from his car, *Vanderbilt,* nothing would satisfy the Commodore but a complementary private conveyance and he ordered the building of *Duchess.* Private cars at once became a hereditary hallmark of the Vanderbilt family and were as closely associated with them as the maroon footman's livery devised by Mrs. Cornelius Vanderbilt, Jr., to shame the powder blue of *The* Mrs. William Backhouse Astor.

Montana's Senator William Andrews Clark who lived up to the implications of the toga in every respect including a private car, the proof of whose illimitable resources of Bourbon whisky was legendary, handed on a taste for such splendid trappings to his son, Charles, who according to a well established article of Texas folklore, bought his ninety foot *Errant* so that Mrs. Clark's poodles of which she was inordinately fond, might travel with their mistress.

Acclimatized to private car travel aboard *Loretto I,* Charles M. Schwab, when it became outdated, promptly ordered from Pullman a successor in *Loretto II.* In similar vein when, having sold *Helma I,* Bruce Dodson of Kansas City discovered he couldn't live without a private car, he purchased *Helma II* from the estate of A. C. Burridge, Boston moneybags of a previous generation. Charles Clegg and Lucius Beebe, when they were minded to give *The Gold Coast* to a California historical group, retained it in their possession until after they had acquired *The Virginia City* from the Pullman Company to enable them to say they had once owned two private cars at one and the same time.

Feeling his father's *Wanderer* was too small for a growing family which included a future Ambassador to the Court of St. James's, Harry Payne Whitney presently ordered another car known as *Adios.* A. A. McLeod's partiality to cars named *Alexander* is discussed at some length elsewhere in this volume. Colonel D. C. Jackling was unable to exist without a p.v. named *Cyprus* and had two of them, while Henry Huntington, heir to the Central Pacific millions, topped the private car list with a total of five, one of them electric.

With the completion in 1869 of the Pacific Railroad at Promontory, private cars began surging over the unballasted rails of the newly opened West in all the florid magnificence of their golden noontide. Here were distances fully to justify the most ample resources of private accommodations and hotel cars with sleeping and eating facilities were a necessity to comfort as well as a symbol of privacy and ostentation. The longest distances between the cities of the East were by now no more than sleeper hops if you except the Florida resort runs which were still a quarter century in the future. But the West, with its limitless distances, its sparsity of hotel accommodations of any sort and complete absence of luxury even for travelers well able to afford the best, seemed made for private cars. Prophetically, two magnificent specimens of the new and emergent triumph of the carbuilder's art converged on Promontory as the conveyances of President Leland Stanford of the Central Pacific and Dr. Thomas Durant of the Union Pacific, respectively. Lacking later conveniences of plumbing and air-conditioning, these palaces on wheels, as they were described in the news dispatches, compensated handsomely for such minor deficiencies with ample resources of champagne and strong waters and vistas of bevel-edged French pier glasses in which a railroad director could comb his whiskers and admire the full length dimensions of a broadcloth frock coat before driving a golden spike.

Governor Stanford's radiant new car, *Stanford,* had not yet come into being (Oscar Lewis reports it as the gift of Mrs. Stanford "shortly after the completion of the railroad") and a primeval Central Pacific business car, still luxurious in the upland deserts of Utah, carried the presidential party in comfort on the long forty-eight hour haul from Sacramento. At Promontory the two-day delay consequent on the non-appearance of the Union Pacific party out of Omaha found the *Stanford* larder depleted so that the steward spent a profitable morning along the shore of Salt Lake with a shotgun and fresh plover appeared for lunch. That no serious shortage of such essentials as champagne, bourbon and foie gras was entailed seems evident from the fact that next day a bountiful luncheon was served the dignitaries involved after the Gold Spike ceremonies.

In the flood tide of Western travel that followed Promontory a great deal of private railway equipment followed the teapot locomotives out of Omaha and St. Louis and the historian is put to it to distinguish what part of it was conventional railroad rolling stock on lease or loan and what was actually recruited from the private and business cars that are properly the subject of this study. The words "private car" were used with miscellaneous abandon by reporters of the period impartially to describe Pullman and Wagner sleepers occupied by charter parties of distinguished travelers and the actually privately owned varnish cars of millionaires and well-to-do professionals. Ranking actors and other stage performers of the period such as the younger Booth, McCullogh, Salvini and Adelina Patti rented their own cars as a matter of record. Other troupes such as the Jarrett-Palmer Company occupied specially assigned Pullman hotel equipment on their celebrated "Lighting Express" across the continent.

The business cars of railroad executives were commonly at the disposal of important shippers and figures in the world of finance and politics. When John Mackay, the bonanza king of Virginia City wanted to go east he borrowed the official car of Superintendent Henry Yerington of the Virginia & Truckee. When in later years Mackay was wounded by a would-be assassin, his wife hastened to his bedside in San Francisco by trans-Atlantic steamer and the private car, *Corsair,* the loan of an Eastern carrier doing business with the Central Pacific and anxious for the good will of the richest man in the West.

When the Emperor Dom Pedro III of Brazil made the inevitable grand tour of the West after viewing the wonders of the Centennial Exhibition at Philadelphia, he went all the way aboard the Pullman Hotel Car, *Metropolitan,* placed at his disposal by the State Department. The Frank Leslie expedition of 1875 to report the Far West for the national weekly of that name occupied a succession of chartered Wagner Hotel Cars and Pullmans specially fitted with photographic dark rooms and editorial compartments for the "literary ladies and gentlemen" involved.

Both the hotel car companies and the railroads themselves maintained pools of luxury equipment not infrequently rebuilt and redecorated for important occupants and available to rental or charter. These were, with more or less propriety to be sure, referred to by the contemporary press as "private cars," but can only be a secondary consideration here.

Throughout the age of private cars beginning with Wagner Palace Car Company products long before their interests were merged and extending far into the supremacy of Pullman, the Vanderbilt family have been, as is proper to their antecedents, the greatest users, builders and admirers of private railway transport. Mention has already been made of Commodore Cornelius's first private car on the roster of the Hudson River Railroad, *Vanderbilt* and the beautiful engine *Vanderbilt* assigned to its special transport. When this conveyance proved insufficient for conveying the great man and his guests to Saratoga and other points of vantage along his ever growing railroad system, a second car, *Duchess,* was found on the Commodore's special track at Forty-second Street, a car described by Wayne Andrews, a not altogether reverent biographer of the family, as "Wagnerian" in decor as well as origin.

Loyalty to the Wagner firm, in which the Vanderbilt railroads themselves were heavy stockholders and members of the family served on interlocking directorates, lasted for another full generation and the private cars of William Henry Vanderbilt and his sons, William Kissam and Frederick William, were all outshopped by Wagner. When Dr. and Mrs. William Seward Webb, Cornelius Vanderbilt II and William K. arrived at Asheville, North Carolina, in 1895 en route to George Washington Vanderbilt's princely estate at "Biltmore," each of the three entourages occupied its own private Wagner. Originally George Vanderbilt had induced the Southern Railroad to run a branch line out of Asheville to the site of "Biltmore" to expedite building of the railroader's lodge which was copied by Richard M. Hunt after the Chateau de Blois, and his own Wagner cars arrived right on the scene during construction times, but the stub line was thereafter torn up.

Frederick William Vanderbilt was perhaps the least pretentious Vanderbilt of his generation, but he maintained a summer place at Hyde Park on the Hudson which was available either by yacht or private car on the New York-Albany mainline of the Hudson River Railroad. In the nineties Frederick W. rode to "Rough Point" aboard his personal Wagner car but with the switch of family and corporate allegiance he was shortly thereafter seen to disembark from his handsomely maintained Pullman, *Vashta*.

Dr. Webb, a Vanderbilt in-law, welcomed members of the Coaching Club, a New York group of almost unearthly exclusiveness, to his Vermont estate, Shelburne Farms near Burlington, which they achieved aboard his private Wagner *Ellsmere*. The horsey guests disembarked at Rutland and tooted their way with crimson outriders to the Vanderbilt villa. Ahead of *Ellsmere*, in the train consist were several New York Central Lines horse cars lest the animals be fatigued by the journey. "Such attentions touched the coachmen," records Andrews, "accustomed though they were to traveling on *Idlehour*, the personal Wagner car of the first Willie K."

After the Wagner Company was absorbed by Pullman, William K. Vanderbilt commanded a second *Idlehour*, this one outshopped by the successor firm. When Herman Oelrichs, a New York society headliner and friend of the family, married into the millions of California's James G. Fair, the happy bridegroom went west aboard *Idlehour I* whose name boards, to suit the occasion, had been repainted with the legend *Cupid*.

To return briefly to the Webb farm at Shelburne, it is notable that, whatever his connections with great wealth, the doctor was not unthrifty. Each week he sold 250 pounds of best Vermont creamery butter to the New York Central commissary for use exclusively on the crack flyer of the Vanderbilt network, the *Twentieth Century Limited*.

One of the most famous of all Vanderbilt private cars in the Pullman age was Alfred Gwynne Vanderbilt's *Wayfarer*, a sumptuous vehicle aboard which Gladys Vanderbilt and her husband, the Count Laszlo Szecheny, rode from New York to Newport after their wedding in 1908 at the Fifty-seventh Street chateau of Mrs. Cornelius Vanderbilt II. The conservative tastes of the Vanderbilt family are suggested by the circumstance that, although the automobile car was by 1908 accepted as here to stay and perhaps even the coming thing, the couple achieved Grand Central Station in a horsedrawn brougham with coachman and groom attired, of course, in Vanderbilt livery of deep maroon.

Although in the closing years of private car travel, the Vanderbilt family might yield the palm as champion private car patrons to the Whitneys, their pre-eminence in the field had been so long established as to be institutional.

There was sentiment involved, as well as convenience, pride and ostentation. When William H. Vanderbilt returned from one of his European trips, Chauncey Depew approached his desk with a welcoming tribute from the New York Central employees in his office. It comprised a miniature railroad car truck five by three feet in dimension with gold-plated brakes, silver brakebeams and outerframes and wheels of gilded wood labeled N.Y.C. & H.R.R. and the whole enclosed in an artistic bed of cut flowers in which damask rosebuds, smilax, mignonettes and lilies of the valley predominated.

Of less elevated social and financial implications than the conventional bond between private cars and the Stotesburys and Whitneys were the activities in the carbuilding field of New York's notorious Colonel William D'Alton Mann, editor of *Town Topics* and a blackmailer and scoundrel of actually melodramatic dimensions. Through the agency of a well organized network of servants and informers in advantageous places, Mann used his publication as an agency for blackmail and sensational exposure comparable to that to which *Confidential* and other scandal sheets were put in a more outspoken generation. In an age when the merest suggested whisper of scandal could entail social ruin, the Colonel levied toll to the extent the traffic would bear on imprudent wives, faithless husbands and the upper class careless generally. Frequently he established himself at a conspicuous table at Sherry's or Delmonico's and sent his demands for hush money to prominent patrons by a page with the suggestion that they be met with spot cash then and there. Legend maintains that he was never refused. Certainly he was never either assassinated or brought to court.

On the side Colonel Mann organized the Mann Boudoir Car Company, a concern whose corporate title either with or without conscious humor, reflected the larger interests of its proprietor. Its products were designed, at variance to the prevailing fashion in the United States of corridor cars, on the continental principal of through compartments or carriages totally isolated from one another save through the agency of a conductor's footboard on the outside of the car.

Railroads generally greeted the Mann Boudoir Car with apathy and there is no record that the design ever got off the drawing board, but along more conventional lines the firm did build a number of cars for private purchasers, one of whom was Adelina Patti, one of the beloved divas of an age when grand opera was in its fullest flower. The ornate car, uninhibitedly named *Adelina Patti*, served her well over the years and was celebrated for the profusion of gilding, murals and heraldic cherubs illustrating its interior apartments which were represented by its unsuspecting owner as authentic objects of *virtu* ravished for her from Old World sources by the devoted builder.

Alas, when the old lady died and the car was dismantled, its decor, true to the character of the Colonel, was found to be largely fraudulent. The cherubs were papier maché, the paintings spurious, the gold leaf dross.

A private car fancier in the best Eastern circles was August Belmont whose vintage private car, *Oriental*, which he had acquired in the nineties as chairman of the board of the Louisville & Nashville Railroad, attracted no small attention when early in 1958 it was finally retired to a railroad museum in the Adirondacks. Belmont was well conditioned both by inheritance and a native appreciation of the good things of life to racing stables, ornate residences and, of course, private railroad cars.

His father, the first August Belmont, had removed from Paris in the seventies to a mansion in lower Fifth Avenue where he set about paying back the social debts of a lifetime scrupulously devoted to keeping horses, women, yachts and, as a wit of the time remarked, everything but the Ten Commandments. Belmont was vexed by the parsimoniousness of his neighbors who were all recruited from old Dutch families and, especially by James Lenox, an aging moneybags who boasted that in thirty years he had served dinner in his home to none but members of his immediate family.

In the hope of inducing apoplexy in the tottering Lenox, Belmont reared a princely mansion at the corner of Fifth Avenue and Eighteenth Street, staffed it with a French chef of international celebrity and a domestic staff of sixty—butlers, footmen, valets, maids, grooms, coachmen and assorted flunkies in knee breeches and tailcoats frogged with gold bullion. When he entertained at dinner the line of carriages reached ten blocks down Fifth Avenue and the quivering Lenox, peering from behind moldy draperies in an unlit parlor, noted that special police had to be assigned to keep traffic moving. Belmont had a solid gold plate service for one hundred guests, served fifteen course dinners as the merest impromptu snack and ordered his father-in-law, Commodore Matthew C. Perry, who had opened the ports of Japan to world trade, around as a sort of personal wine steward. He also hung a huge nude by Bougeureau in his drawing room to show New York what real art was. Lenox, his reason already unseated by such extravagances, did not long survive learning that his neighbor's wine bill alone came to $20,000 a month.

Obviously, with such a father, the younger Belmont was no one to settle for anything plain in the way of railroad cars and *Oriental*, in addition to the conventional brass beds, floriated Pintsch lamps and colored glass overtransoms to its wide picture windows, boasted hat racks of solid silver fashioned like stag's horns, handbasins of rare shades of Carrara marble specially quarried in Italy and an English valet who attended his master's wants and laid out his attire for morning, business or evening as the hour required.

As part of his pattern of personal magnificence, Mr. Belmont also maintained a private electric coach in the cellarage of his Belmont Hotel in New York City to take him in comfort to the race track at Belmont Park of which he was founder and the most exalted patron. In addition to these properties of convenience and elegance, the Rothschild's American representative maintained still another conventional private car, *Mineola,* for travel on steam railroads.

In a generation when patrician birth was no obstacle to becoming a railroader and such names as Stuyvesant Fish, E. H. Harriman, George Gould and Cornelius Vanderbilt, Jr., lent elegance to operating departments, no more aristocratic chief executive could be found than Fairfax Harrison, President of the far-flung Southern. A member of the old planter aristocracy of Virginia, Harrison's tastes ran to wing collars, first editions and executive luncheons in the railroad's splendid offices in Washington where Catullus was quoted as servants passed the Rainwater Madeira.

Because it was unthinkable to Harrison to sleep under the same roof with the colored help, he took a page out of the narrow gauge business car practice of Colorado and traveled in two magnificent cars, *Virginia* and *Carolina,* operated tandem with crew's quarters forward and Harrison's personal apartments in the observation car. A brilliant railroader in whose regime the Southern flourished mightily, Harrison lacked the common touch of, say, the Union Pacific's William Jeffers who was reported to know the first name of every section foreman and station agent on the railroad. When an obscure South Carolina community petitioned the Southern to replace its beat-up depot with something more sightly, Harrison carried the offensive message into a directors' meeting at arm's length in a pair of fire tongs. "Another message from the pigpen, gentlemen," he announced.

Although others of the worldly great, including presidents in office and Robert R. Young, both before and since have died aboard business and private varnish or made their final earthly journeys in such sombre splendor, none encountered the old man with a scythe amidst such ironic trappings of vanished grandeur as did Oris Paxton Van Sweringen when he died in November 1936.

It was an age of kings dethroned and the mighty fallen, none more so than the Van Sweringen brothers whose railroad empire in its golden noontide was estimated to embrace properties worth an aggregate $3,000,000,000. O. P. was predeceased by his brother, Mantis J., by less than a year and their joint fortune was then probated at less than $200,000. Upon the death of the last of the Van Sweringens the list of railroad properties of which Oris P. was a director, president or chairman of the board filled half a col-

umn of fine type in the *New York Times* and included the Missouri Pacific
Railroad, the Texas & Pacific Railroad, the Denver & Rio Grande Western
Railroad, the International Great Northern Railroad and such Eastern carriers as the Chesapeake & Ohio, the Pere Marquette and the Nickel Plate
which were absorbed in the financial economy of the Van Sweringen's Allegheny Corporation and Midamerica Corporation. They controlled 25,000
miles of mainline railroad, and short lines, feeders, terminal facilities, industrial carriers and secondary roads almost past counting.

The empire crashed to irretrievable ruin in 1929 and in 1936 Oris P.
was en route to New York aboard the business car of Robert C. Fitzpatrick,
vice-president of the Chesapeake & Ohio, to attempt to salvage some of the
pieces in the ateliers of Wall Street.

At Buffalo the handsome C & O business car bearing the ruined titan
was sideswiped as it was being switched from the Nickel Plate to the Delaware, Lackawanna & Western for the final stage of the trip to New York.
The car foreman on duty was unable immediately to assess the damage but
he feared there might have been harm to the brake rigging and the party,
which included Van Sweringen, his secretary and personal servants, was
speedily transferred to the Lackawanna business car, *Scranton*, which was
providentially handy and provisioned.

The next morning in the Hoboken yards of the Lackawanna, the last of
the Van Sweringens complained of fatigue and retired after breakfast to
his stateroom. At 11:45 his valet was unable to rouse him, a company doctor
was summoned and twenty minutes later he was dead.

It was at first feared and the fears given space in the public prints
that the accident in Scranton yards had contributed to the financier's end
but a medical bulletin, occasioned by the rumors, attributed death to natural
causes. At the same time Thomas W. Lamont, partner in J. P. Morgan &
Company where the Van Sweringens had worked out many mighty deals,
issued a statement of regret.

Thus passed one of the last and perhaps most illusory of the railroad
tycoons. With a fine sense of the dramatic, Atropos chose to sever the skein
of the financier's life amidst the tangible souvenirs of departed greatness
and aboard the private car which symbolized at once the extent of his
earthly triumphs and the age of the moguls which was already passing.

Long before the phrase was coined in Madison Avenue the private
railway car had been established as the most resounding status symbol of
them all.

The first dinner party of photographic record to be held upon a private car anywhere in America was given by Union Pacific officials at Rock Creek, Wyoming,
early in the year 1869 that was to see the completion of the transcontinental railroad at Promontory Point, Utah. Only member of the festive group positively
known to Union Pacific archivists, and not identified in the photograph, is Cornelius Bushnell, "a New York merchant prince" who subscribed to fifty of the
original shares of U.P. stock and for whom, as a reward, the town of Bushnell,
Nebraska, was named. Ten guests in stock collars and cotton shirtwaists posed
for the cameraman on that distant day and it is safe to suppose that the toasts
they drank included "Success to The Railroad."

C & N W

Posed for its portrait against a backdrop of target switches, gas lamp standards and a grain elevator, the C&NW directors' car reeks of the atmosphere of post-Civil War railroading. In the distance is the carrier's old Kinzie Street depot, located just north of Kinzie with its east side running along the Chicago River, then as now a navigational waterway. Even the day is known when the original of this stereoptican slide photograph was taken of Henry Hull's masterpiece. It was December 9, 1867.

What could scarcely have failed of being one of the most ornate cars ever built for an American railroad was the first business car of the Chicago & North Western, depicted on these pages and built at the company shops at Fond du Lac, Wisconsin, in December 1867. Known as "The Directors Car," it was designed by Henry Hull, master carbuilder, with the floor of its central compartment two feet lower than its platforms and achieved from either end by flights of silver plated steps. Tall Gothic windows, four to a side, gave onto the cathedral-like main salon depicted below, and directors of the English-financed carrier were reminded of Locksley Hall and Stoke Poges. Aprons suggestive of later day streamlining protected the running gear, and eight wheel trucks testified to the car's unusual weight. Rich, massive Victorian furnishings gratified investors in the company's shares and for several decades the car was a celebrated property of the regions served by the railroad. Following the downward course of all business cars, it eventually was occupied by a group of construction engineers and finally was destroyed by fire "somewhere in South Dakota." Observers felt that a stately Gothic relic of railroading's primeval times had been a prey to the flames.

E. S. HAMMACK

In 1869 Piermont, on the West Shore of the Hudson, was the Erie Railroad's terminus at the New York end of its mainline to the Great Lakes. On the page opposite E. S. Hammack, the distinguished railroad artist, depicts the scene at Piermont as Jay Gould, lately elected President of Erie, follows a trusted book-keeper aboard the carrier's No. 200, one of the several private cars the great manipulator of railroad properties was to call his own before his death nearly a quarter of a century later. On this page is the interior of another Gould p.v., his *Convoy*, No. 143 of the Missouri Pacific from which he dominated the affairs of an empire of transport while rolling over 7,000 miles of his own rails that included the Kansas Pacific, Denver Pacific, Missouri Pacific, Texas & Pacific and innumerable short lines and subsidiaries. *Convoy* also housed the Gould private physician while the special Gould milk cow was safely bedded in the baggage car up ahead.

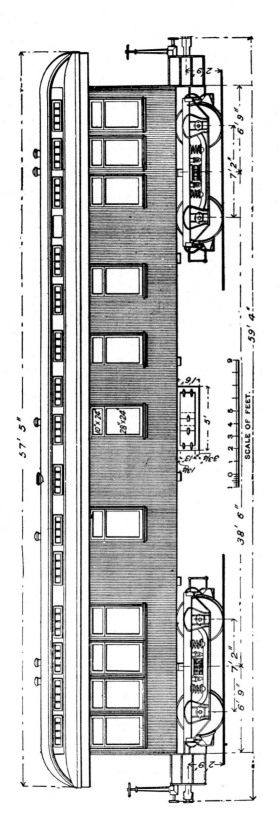

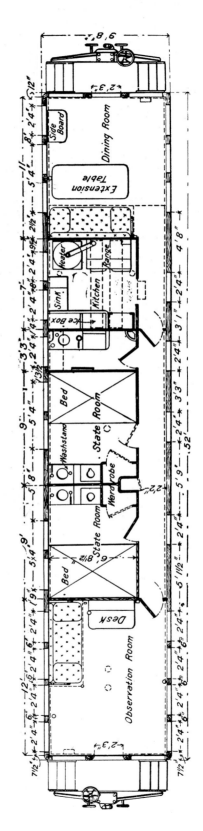

GRAHAME HARDY COLLECTION

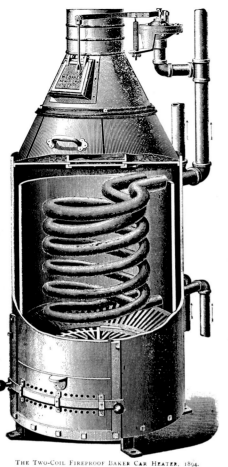

THE TWO-COIL FIREPROOF BAKER CAR HEATER, 1894.

Although lacking interior decor by Dorothy Draper, the long picture windows, air conditioning and formica panelling that was to characterize business cars of a later generation, the Chicago, Burlington & Quincy's officers' car of the eighties detailed on the page opposite, was snug against the Great Plains blizzards and might even serve for modest jollification in entertaining important shippers in Omaha and Denver. It was warmed against the elements by a Baker heater (LEFT) a patent device that for decades was to bemuse train crews, and the cook and waiter slept in the dining room located at the far end of the car beyond the kitchen. In one of the earliest of all private and/or business car interiors known to photography (BELOW) a group of Union Pacific engineers including Silas Seymour and Samuel B. Reed pose with Sidney Dillon, chairman of the board, in a midst appropriately cluttered with plans, documents and brief cases en route to a rendezvous with destiny at Promontory Point. Note the central corridor, ornate clerestory and twin pier glasses mirroring the length of the salon. The rifles and revolvers in a stand of arms above the doorway were, in 1869, by no means for ornament alone.

UNION PACIFIC

PULLMAN STANDARD

The primeval beginnings of private car travel were aboard the earliest known hotel car, the *Western World* which George M. Pullman designed and built for service on the Grand Trunk Railway of Canada in 1868. The dining compartment of this epochal conveyance is shown here, while on the page opposite are elements of Pullman car decor of ages yet to come after the *Western World* went into service. At the left is one of the handbowls of costly Italian marble, which together with satinwood paneling and silver fixtures lent luxurious overtones to Austin Corbin's palatial *Oriental* built in 1898. The 110 volt outlet for electric razors may be presumed the innovation of a later occupant. At the right is the interior of *Iolanthe*, built by Pullman in 1888 and added in that year to its pool of charter cars available to private rental.

Trans-Continental

"LET EVERY STEP BE AN ADVANCE."

Vol. 1.   **Grand Island, Nebraska, Wednesday, June 29, 1870.**   **No. 1**

The Trans-Continental.

Published Daily on the Pullman Hotel Express,
Between
Boston and San Francisco.

W. R. STEELE, *Editor.*

☞*Communications and Exchanges for this paper should be addressed,* TRANS-CONTINENTAL. 46 *State Street, Chicago.*

Notes from our Log Book.

Sunday, June 19.—All the members of the second division of the Yo-Semite party reached Knight's Ferry this evening, after riding fifty-two miles from Bower Cave, and there lodged. Before reaching the hotel, we crossed the Stanislaus river on the new covered bridge recently built, in place of the ferry formerly run by DENT & GRANT—the latter now President of the United States. The toll-keeper generously supplied the party with a basket of ripe pears from his orchard on the side of the river, as a free treat.

Monday, June 20.—The second division rode by four-horse wagons, a distance of thirty-eight miles from Knight's Ferry, to the city of Stockton, which they reached before 11 o'clock, after a cool and pleasant morning ride. There they took rooms at the Yo-Semite House, and others visited the century plant, in blossom in the Court House yard, while all roamed around the city on tours of observation. Lunch, amounting to a dinner, was served at noon, and at 1:40 P. M., all embarked on a special car kindly provided for our party through the thoughtful kindness of John Corning, the Assistant General Superintendent of the Central Pacific Railroad, and reached San Francisco before 6 P. M., after a glorious trip. Over twenty of the first party to the Yo-Semite, who reached San Francisco on Friday last, started at

4 P. M., by steamer, and over the Napa Valley branch of the California Pacific Railroad for the Geysers, and lodged this night at Calistoga Springs.

Tuesday, June 21.—The last party to the Geysers made a pleasant visit to those natural wonders. Other excursionists were in San Francisco or its vicinity, variously engaged. Many visited Woodward's Gardens, to see the flowers and wild animals.

Wednesday, June 22.—The last party to the Geysers returned to San Francisco, where nearly all the excursionists had collected, and were preparing for the start homeward Friday night. A few of the excursionists had already left for the East; a few left on Thursday, and a few will remain in California for several months. Small parties, this week, visited San Jose, the Almaden mines, Oakland, and other places, not far from San Francisco. Others visited mutual friends at their country seats in the immediate vicinity of the city.

Thursday, June 23—Was chiefly occupied in private visits, shopping, and sight-seeing at the city. During the evening, a farewell dinner, already mentioned in this paper, was given by several of the members of the excursion to gentlemen of San Francisco, who had been prominent in showing signal attentions to our party.

Friday, June 24.—This, our last day in San Francisco, was a busy one with nearly every one of the party. Many were the last things to be done; collections of photograph views, to be selected or made complete; friends to be called on, and little remembrances packed away for loved ones at home. A magnificent sunset lighted the waters and hills of the great bay of San Francisco, and lingered as a beautiful and effective final picture of the "Sunset Land" upon the memories of our excur-

sionists, and when the morning s[un] arose on the 25th, we were swiftly pres[s]ing eastward and homeward surround[ed] by all the comforts of our favorite Pu[ll]man train.

OUR TRAIN.

At Cheyenne, those of our party w[ho] had preceded us again joined our trai[n] and the Pullman drawing-room a[nd] sleeping car "Northwest" was coupl[ed] on, making one more house in our ro[v]ing village. Commencing at the engin[e] we have now—

1. Baggage car.
2. Provision car, including printi[ng] press.
3. Smoking car, including printi[ng] office, wine room, and barber's shop.
4. Commissary and dining car, "Sai[nt] Cloud."
5. Palace sleeping and drawing-roo[m] car "Marquette."
6. Palace sleeping and drawing-roo[m] car "Palmyra."
7. Commissary and dining car "Sai[nt] Charles."
8. Hotel car "Arlington."
9. Hotel car "Revere."
10. Drawing-room and sleeping ca[r] "Northwest," and we do not belie[ve] that a train equal to it in size, beau[ty] and convenience ever existed before, u[p] to this present point, in the history [of] the world. As improvement is, how[-] ever, the order of the day, what may w[e] not expect from Mr. Pullman in the f[u]ture.

—Yesterday as we journeyed acros[s] the apparently boundless Laram[ie] Plains, herds of swift antelope we[re] seen coursing with nimble feet, some[-] times keeping up with, and at othe[rs] running from our train. Grouse we[re] also seen in comparatively plentif[ul] numbers.

The junction of the Union Pacific and Central Pacific railroads at Promontory had been celebrated barely a year before the first through private train from Boston to San Francisco was chartered by a group of distinguished Easterners representing the Boston Board of Trade to cross the continent in Pullman splendor as an advertisement of the wonder and convenience of life aboard the steamcars. The train was "made up of eight of the most elegant cars ever drawn over an American railway," built to special order for the occasion by the Pullman Palace Car Company. The special departed Boston on Monday, May 23, 1870 and arrived at the Golden Gate just eight days later and a well-travelled member of the party "who had once travelled in Queen Victoria's state car, did not hesitate to say that Pullman had provided for the people of America more than was provided by the people of Great Britain for their great and beloved queen." A feature of the de luxe excursion was the party's own daily newspaper printed "on a new quarto-medium Gordon press" located in the baggage car where it shared space with "five large ice closets and a refrigerator for the storage of fruits, meat and vegetables." On the page opposite is the front page of an issue of the "Trans-Continental" with a passenger list of proper Bostonians including Hunnewells, Houghtons, Danas and Peabodys in liberal profusion.

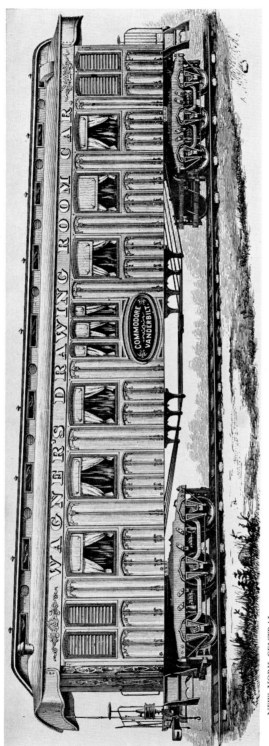

WAGNER'S DRAWING ROOM CAR

COMMODORE VANDERBILT

NEW YORK CENTRAL

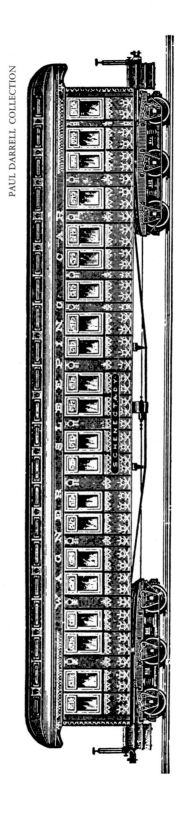

WAGNER SLEEPING CAR

SCHENECTADY

PAUL DARRELL COLLECTION

Like his father, the Commodore before him, William H. Vanderbilt was a regular and devoted patron of the United States Hotel at Saratoga Springs where he is shown on the long porch of that celebrated hostelry, surrounded by runners and lieutenants as he makes book on the afternoon races at Saratoga track. William H., along with a fortune of $105,000,000, the first of this magnitude in the United States, inherited his father's two Wagner-built private cars, *Commodore Vanderbilt* and *Duchess,* the latter an identical counterpart of the sleeper *Schenectady* shown on the opposite page. The first of these was a drawing room car designed for day occupancy only, while *Duchess* was a sleeper in case its owner should be travelling beyond the bounds of the New York Central Lines, say over the connecting and Vanderbilt-controlled Lake Shore & Michigan Southern. "Mr. Vanderbilt's car is elegantly fitted up and provided with electric bells and other conveniences," said the admiring *New York Times* in 1882. "It could not be duplicated for less than $18,000 or $20,000. He travels as fast as an engine can draw him and all other trains must keep out of the way. A special timetable is made up at least twelve hours before he starts and telegraphed along the line." In the same article *The Times* indicated that the downgrading of once sumptuous cars, so familiar to later railroad practice, was already in effect. It reported that the Commodore's once proud car *Vanderbilt* "now bears the name *Iroquois,* is owned by the Wagner Car Co., and leaves every other afternoon for Chicago at 3:55 p.m."

TWO PHOTOS: AMERICAN CAR & FOUNDRY

The ornate and stately open sections from this car in Pullman's private rental pool in the mid-nineties with permanent glass partitions between each section was the forerunner of the eventual all-room sleeping car of universal acceptance which had already been pioneered by the indomitable Colonel William D'Alton Mann with his own Boudoir Cars.

ARTHUR D. DUBIN COLLECTION

n 1873, the by then well known car building firm of Jackson & Sharp, located at Vilmington, Delaware, paused (PAGE OPPOSITE) in finishing this gleaming private ar for the President of the Pittsburgh & Connellsville Railroad to demonstrate the meaning of the word varnish when applied to passenger cars in the days of vooden rolling stock. Jackson & Sharp was eventually absorbed by American Car Foundry who, in the eighties, built the sumptuous car *Manhattan* (AT LEFT ELOW) for the Long Island Railroad. Note the legend on the door which has o truck with "business" or "office" cars and boldly says "Private."

At Denison, Texas, the Leslie party entered the Lone Star State over the rails of the Missouri-Kansas-Texas Railroad, more familiarly known then and now as the Katy.

Although the word promotion in its Madison Avenue connotation was not yet part of the American lexicon, Wagner's sleepers came in for a vast deal of favorable publicity in 1877 when the management of *Frank Leslie's Illustrated Weekly,* the *Life* of its age, arranged an extensive tour aboard the steamcars to report to its readers on the state of the American West. Although the Pacific Railroad had been open to continental travel for all of eight years and scores of newspaper and magazine writers had made the grand tour, the Leslie expedition was by far the most pretentious embracing as it did Mr. and Mrs. Leslie and a considerable staff of "artists, photographers and literary ladies and gentlemen connected with the publishing house." Among the artists were no less authentic top notchers than Harry Ogden and Walter Yaeger who stayed with the party for two years and contributed some of the best pictorial reporting of the time and place to the pages of *Leslie's.* The group departed from Grand Central in New York as depicted here on April 10 aboard a Wagner Sleeping Car redecorated for the occasion and renamed *Frank Leslie* "out of compliment to its enterprising occupant." At Chicago, after a brief stopover at the Sherman Hotel, the entourage of twelve changed to a Pullman Palace Hotel Car that had also been redesigned, perhaps along more utilitarian lines, with a dark room for the photographers and editorial space for sketch artists and writers. As far as California at least, the entire trip was reported in terms of a railroad safari aboard the Chicago & North Western, Union Pacific and Central Pacific railroads with only one notable digression to visit the Comstock mines in Virginia City. Ogden and Yaeger contributed more than 200 line drawings including this spirited recreation of the party's departure from New York, and railroad travel everywhere in the United States, but especially in the West received a tremendous impetus. Another beneficiary of the well staged promotion was *Leslie's* itself whose circulation boomed sensationally while the "literary ladies and gentlemen" remained beyond the wide Missouri.

In 1883 one of the most glittering consists of private varnish ever assembled was run by President Henry Villard over the Northern Pacific to celebrate the completion of the new transcontinental at Missoula, Montana. Among the guests aboard the special were Ulysses S. Grant and Henry Farny, the celebrated staff artist for *Harper's Weekly*. Near Grey Cliff, Montana, on the Crow reservation the train was halted one evening so that the distinguished visitors could witness a "grass dance" by more than 100 warriors in full ceremonial dress. The scene so impressed Farny, with the brightly lighted palace cars and their connotations of the ultimate in civilized travel as a background for the primitive ceremonial, that he drew one of his best known sketches of Western life shown on the page opposite.

DUNCAN EMRICH COLLECTION

In a railroad conscious age, nothing delighted readers of periodicals of the seventies and eighties more than such outrageous doings as depicted in this stirring scene from the *Illustrated Police News*, a barber shop and poolroom illustrated weekly in 1888. It affects to show the boisterous welcome accorded a private car party of Eastern dudes somewhere along the mainline of the Northern Pacific and compensates in action what it lacks in physical probability. Although it may seriously be doubted if Dr. William Seward Webb, a Vanderbilt in-law and President of the Wagner Palace Car Company, was a regular reader of *The Police News*, it was intimations of such robust disorders beyond the wide Missouri that prompted him to retain armed Pinkertons to guard his private train when he toured the West at about this time.

EDWIN FORREST.

Palace Hotel Car Edwin Forrest.

Jerome Marble, Pres. **Worcester Excursion Car Company.** Chas. B. Pratt, Treas.

THREE PHOTOS: ARTHUR D. DUBIN COLLECTION

One of the independent carbuilders whose innovations and patents were eventually absorbed by Pullman was the Worcester Excursion Car Company organized in the eighties at Worcester, Massachusetts. It specialized in the construction and rental of cars for special purposes such as theatrical companies, hunting expeditions, political campaigns and other safari of continental dimensions, its first car, *The City of Worcester*, shown at the top of this page contained extensive ice boxes for the preservation of game, gun racks, ammunition closets, a fireproof safe and a bathtub. A subsequent car *Yellowstone* improved on these facilities with a shock proof wine cellar for rare vintages. Its best known car the *Edwin Forrest*, named for the famous tragedian, was designed for hunting excursions into the Northwest and is shown in the Dakota plains in this capacity at the bottom of the page. Its name, however, attracted the attention of Joseph Jefferson, perennially on tour in "Rip Van Winkle," and thereafter it was in frequent requisition for theatrical companies on the road as shown on the page opposite. Other private cars named for stage celebrities were Lawrence Barrett's *Junius Brutus Booth*, Edwin Booth's *David Garrick* and, of course, Adelina Patti's *Adelina Patti*. In the thirties on the Chicago-St. Louis run the Wabash maintained a stately blue and gold observation car named *Helena Modjeska*. Visiting noblemen and royalties from foreign lands were especially partial to Jerome Marble's hunting cars and his patrons during the eighties included the Grand Duke Alexis of Russia, the Russian ambassador, the Baron de Streuve, and the English Duke of Sutherland whose arrival on the Comstock Lode at Virginia City was the occasion for the most magnificent party, staged by John Mackay, in the annals of Western mining.

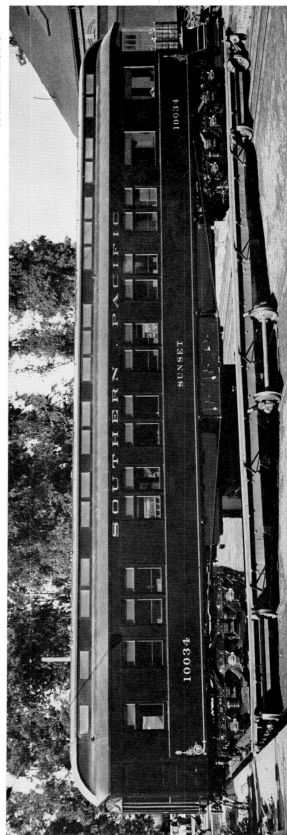

Leland Stanford indulged no nonsense about "business cars" and plainly inscribed his *Stanford* with a notice to the effect that it was a private car.

Familiar and much loved names in the California eighties and nineties were those of two of the Southern Pacific's most admired private cars Leland Stanford's own *Stanford* and the company's *Sunset*, in great requisition by San Francisco's Athertons, Popes and McAllisters upon occasions of mobile rejoicing. The chatelaine of town houses and country estates in California, New York, London, Paris and on the Riviera, Mrs. D. O. Mills was fond of remarking that from one year to the next she had no need to sleep under a roof not her own save that of a Southern Pacific private car crossing the continent. Obviously she considered this an entirely proper and even satisfactory concession.

The technique of night photography not having been evolved in the seventies, a long dead photographer took the rear platform of *Stanford* with its initialed lace curtains in the reflected illumination of a nearby arc lamp.

At once the most stylish and sumptuous pleasure dome of the Pacific Coast in 1880 was the Del Monte Hotel owned by the Southern Pacific Railroad, 145 miles south of San Francisco on the Monterey Peninsula, a resort of luxury and fashion which shortly saw the cars of Tobins, Tevises, Sharons and Crockers spotted on its private car track. Accessible only to the affluent and eligible, Del Monte was achieved every evening by *The Del Monte Express,* advertised as "The Fastest Train in the United States West of the Missouri River." Del Monte was known for the formality of its society and "the exceedingly rich, elegant and costly toilets of its ladies." Its seaside carriage drives and its multiplicity of California heiresses made it a favorite with titled foreigners and it was from the vantage point of Charles Crocker's well appointed p.v. *Mishawaka* that Prince Andre Poniatowsky, son of Napoleon III's Master of Horse and a descendant of King Stanislaus of Poland, wooed and won the hand of Beth Sperry. Shown below at Del Monte, also aboard a well-appointed Central Pacific car, is the party of President Benjamin Harrison during its Western tour. The Dundreary weepers are those of Darius Ogden Mills, powerful moneybags of the Bank of California. On the page opposite, *The Virginia City* occupies the same private car track overlooking Monterey Bay three quarters of a century later.

SOUTHERN PACIFIC

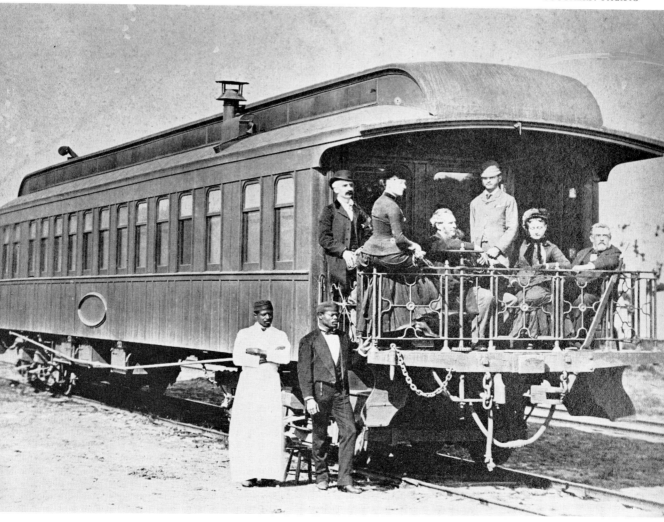

Romanée Conti

Le Faisan Perigordine

Chateau Ausone, Fromage de Brie

In 1885 Chester A. Arthur was President of the United States and Chauncey M. Depew was President of the Vanderbilt owned New York Central & Hudson River Railroad. Of practically consular dignity, since the Central was then the standard railroad of the world and one of its richest, the two men had much in common. Arthur, the most worldly of American presidents, was well born, well-to-do and accepted in the best social circles of New York and Newport. Depew was an acknowledged connoisseur of fine food and wine and the nation's leading practitioner of the oratory that was then a feature of all dinners both public and private. After a notable banquet at Delmonico's, Thomas Lamont, a Morgan partner, remarked "Mr. Depew is an institution and will become a tradition." In 1885 Saratoga Springs was the foremost resort of American finance and fashion, and it was there that Depew, aboard the New York Central's presidential car, was moved to give a small dinner for President Arthur as depicted on the opposite page. Classic years of Haut Brion, Ausone and Perrier Jouet flowed as smoothly as the periods of Depew's well-received after dinner address. Twenty years later, as shown on this page, Depew was still interested in new things and was agreeable to trying out a new make of automobile car in Fifth Avenue while a mechanic stood by in case of difficulty with the gears.

NEW YORK HERALD TRIBUNE

The lavishly beautiful main salon of *Cleopatra* shown on these two pages and built in 1888 by Pullman for the chief officer of the far-flung International Great Northern Railroad in Texas shows the economy of space which in many early private cars dictated the use of folding upper berths in dining compartments and other rooms of general assembly. Circassian walnut berth panels, bevelled edge French mirrors and Paisley portières all contributed to a sense of well-being in motion. Another International Great Northern private car, believed by students of such matters to have been *Convoy* No. 143 assigned to Jay Gould and later occupied by George Gould on the Missouri Pacific, is today a public museum at Jefferson, Texas. After many years of downgrading, during which it saw service as a yardmaster's shack at Overton, Texas, the car was recovered and restored as a souvenir of the railroad wars of the eighties. Thwarted in an attempt to secure a right of way for the I.G.N., Gould had written on the register of the Excelsior Hotel the words: "I shall live to see grass grow in the streets of Jefferson." The town survived Gould's prophesy and emplaced his one-time car as an ironic monument to his memory.

TWO PHOTOS: PULLMAN STANDARD

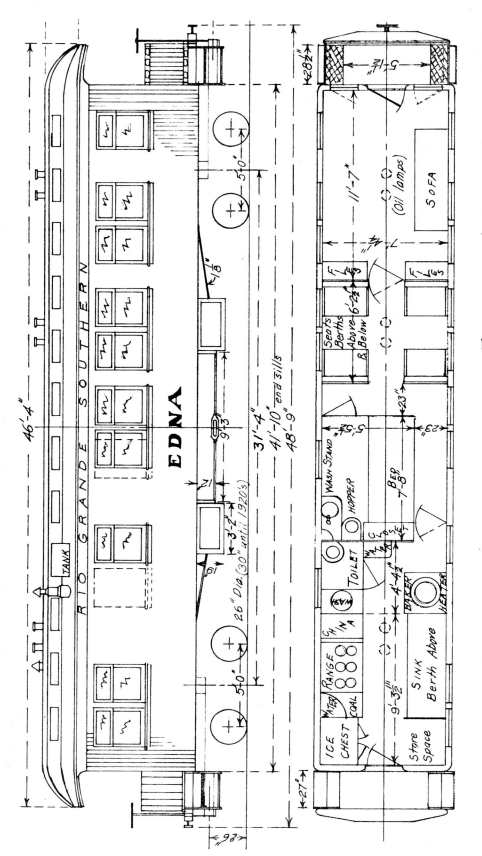

The narrow gauge business car *Edna* was acquired by the Rio Grande Southern Railroad in southwestern Colorado from the Denver & Rio Grande in 1890. It was first known as the *San Juan* and its name changed to *Edna* in 1900. It was rebuilt with additional toilet facilities and folding berths in 1925 and after the abandonment of the RGS passed to Knott's Berry Farm in Southern California in 1952.

Interior as rebuilt in 1925

DRAWN BY JOHN W. MAXWELL

Above is shown the narrow gauge p.v. *Millwood* with which Milton Latham used to pop the eyes of Northern California in the redwoods, while below is the equally three-foot gauge *Esmeralda*, sole luxury varnish of the Carson & Colorado in its lonely landfarings along the Nevada-California border in the eighties and nineties. Opulently upholstered, according to legend, at least for its time and place, *Esmeralda's* observation windows mirror a tranquil landscape of cottonwoods at Hawthorne, Nevada, at the end of the C & C's passenger train locally known as "The Slim Princess."

HOWARD FOGG

The benevolent and patriarchal appearing old gentleman in the boiled shirt and frock coat is Colonel William D'Alton Mann, designer and builder of Mann Boudoir Cars, prince of society blackmailers and a gorgeous and institutional New York character at the turn of the century. On the page opposite is shown the car *Lalee* which Colonel Mann built for Mrs. Lillie Langtry as a gift from her lover, Freddy Gebhard, a New York wine merchant and boulevardier. Unguarded remarks by Gebhard while *Lalee* was being built soon afterwards tempted the colonel, through the agency of *Town Topics* of which he was owner, to blackmail the Jersey Lily for $200,000. Mann became reasonable when the actress retained little Abe Hummel of the remarkable law firm of Howe & Hummel, who knew fully as much about Colonel Mann as the colonel knew about Mrs. Langtry. Colonel Mann at the turn of the century was a New York phenomenon. His white whiskers and rakishly worn silk top hat were one of the sights of Fifth Avenue and his breakfasts at Delmonico's were legendary. They comprised three double Southdown mutton chops festooned with baked yams and two bottles of vintage French champagne. While eating he uttered frequent gutteral cries of "Woof, Woof!" as a sign of gustatory approval. Every morning at *Town Topics* he kissed every female employee chastely and the office cat before climbing on a high editorial stool to disembowel Morgans and Astors. His secretary, whose name was actually Nevada Doody, married well and became Duchess of Oporto.

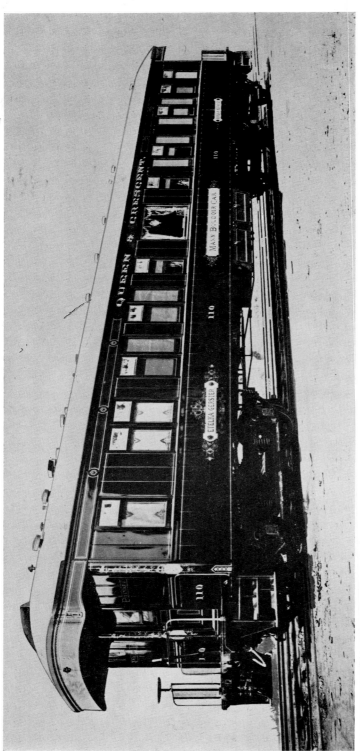

AMERICAN CAR & FOUNDRY

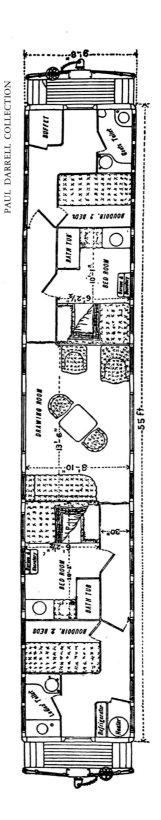

PAUL DARRELL COLLECTION

The interior of the *Adelina Patti*, described at length in an appropriate place in this volume, would have been characterized by a later generation as fussy, but it expressed the personality of a singer beloved of her time. Looped, fringed, frizzled and ferned, its rococo splendors were the tinsel stuff of grand opera itself and its decor was the essence of Victorian comfort amidst banquettes, table throws, cut flowers and decanters past counting. Its freight was not only the singer who leased it but the whole romantic legend of showmanship and the illusion of the great world, and mingled with the creaking of its woodwork on the curves were remembered echoes of "Faust" and "Don Giovanni," "Lucia" and, most appropriate of all, "The Flying Dutchman." On the page opposite the Mann Boudoir Car *Etelka Gersier* shown in floor plan and a very rare photograph from the files of American Car & Foundry, was assigned to service on the Queen & Crescent, a Deep South carrier eventually part of the Southern Railway. *Etelka Gersier* is apparently a mis-spelled tribute to Etelka Gerster, a celebrated Hungarian soprano of the eighties who was a New Orleans favorite when she sang at the old French Opera House with the Strakosch opera troupe.

PULLMAN STANDARD

No car in the roster of Pullman's private varnish available to rental was in more demand throughout the nineties and well into the new century than *Hazelmere* whose observation salon is depicted on the page opposite and whose master stateroom is shown above. Built at Pullman in 1888, a vintage year for princely private cars, *Hazelmere* paid for itself early in the game and its name came to be associated with magnificoes in the world of society and finance. Upon occasion it was leased to William Rockefeller for seasonal trips to Palm Beach and its ornate folding berth of polished satinwood shown on this page was a couch for many another name that made news in Wall Street in the age when the trusts were a-building.

Hazelmere was one of the earliest and most successful Pullman private cars to be listed in the company's rental pool for general service, having been built in 1888 and still in active availability well after the turn of the century. Its companion cars such as *Iolanthe* were more voluptuously decorated, but *Hazelmere's* substantial Gothic construction appealed to the solid men of substance of the period who occupied it and it probably made more money for the company than any other p.v. in the general service pool. Like most early private cars, it depended less on stateroom space than upon folding uppers, sofas and sections for sleeping. Its master suite, however, was both spacious and commodious as was appropriate to the moguls who rode it and as is suggested by the dressing room shown below.

TWO PHOTOS: PULLMAN STANDARD

Many wealthy Americans of the nineties well enough able to support private varnish of their own saw a sensible economy in patronizing the rental pools of Wagner and Pullman, so that in 1892 when Andrew Carnegie visited the Great Northwest over the rails of the Northern Pacific in the role of land-looker for his then expanding steel mills, he arrived aboard Pullman's magnificent charter car *Iolanthe,* whose drawing room is shown here. With him as guests were Henry Clay Frick, a Carnegie vassal and himself monarch of coke, and Dr. Andrew W. White, President of Cornell University. Unlike J. P. Morgan who delighted in the company of Episcopal bishops, Uncle Andy despised churchmen and liked the company of men of secular learning. Possibly over the years Frick tired of depending on the bounty of other millionaires for travel accommodations, for in 1910 he ordered his own car *Westmoreland* from Pullman and thereafter rolled across the country independently while the Laird roamed his ancestral glens in Scotland.

The private car *Ogontz* was built by Pullman in 1888 to the order of the Baltimore & Ohio Railroad and its handsome and masculine interior shows the disposition of sofas that might be easily convertible for sleeping purposes when guests arrived. Although gas lighting through the agency of Pintsch burners had been available for car illumination since the early eighties, the B & O put its trust in coal oil lamps which could be depended on in distant places where bottled gas was not available. Other B & O official cars excited admiration and envy in their time. "John W. Garrett, President of the Baltimore & Ohio Railroad has a car for his exclusive use, the *Maryland*," reported the *New York Times* in May 1882. "His son, Robert Garrett, the third vice president, has another, the *Baltimore*. The President of every road of consequence has a car of his own of more or less elegance, but none to compare with those mentioned."

If anything were wanting to confuse students of private car folklore in the nineties, it is the legend "Boudoir" on the upper nameboards of the charter pool Pullmans *Mayflower* and *Davy Crockett*. The word is almost wholly associated with the products of Pullman's one-time rival, the Mann Boudoir-Car Company and its use elsewhere is unique. Boudoir or not, the *New York Times* in the eighties said that the *Davy Crockett* and a companion car, the *Isaac Walton* were "hunting and fishing cars, provided with kennels for dogs and plenty large enough for parties of eight or ten." The charge was $35. a day with cook and waiter.

An upright piano aboard *Coronet* reflected the mood of the nineties with a ball fringe throw carelessly draped across its top.

FOUR PHOTOS: PULLMAN STANDARD

Such ornate and elaborate lambrequins as this one framing a stateroom window in Pullman's *Rambler* delighted private car owners and occupants of the Gilded Age.

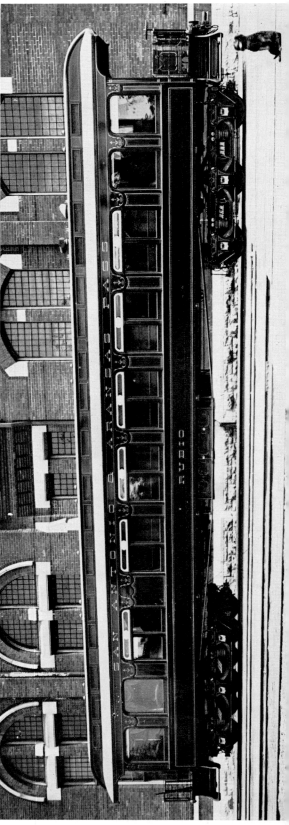

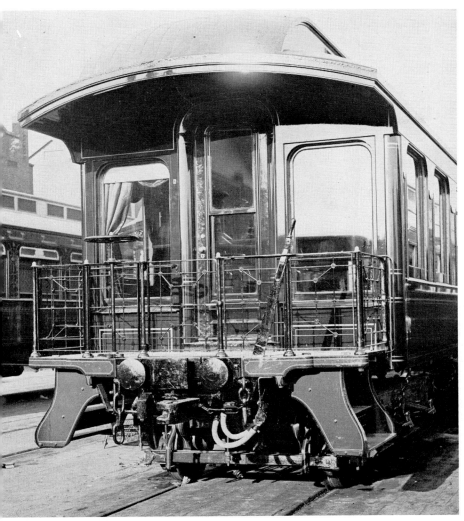

THREE PHOTOS: PULLMAN STANDARD

Few railroads in the record contrived to induce bankruptcy not only for themselves by delusions of grandeur, but also for the builders of their rolling stock as did the San Antonio & Aranzas Pass. Organized in 1885 to lay track from the capital city of its corporate name to Aranzas Bay on the Gulf of Mexico, the road early in the game began indulging the hanker for fancy properties that was to be its undoing. The stylish private car *Rubio*, a hunting car for friends and shippers, and the fine private car *Electric*, shown here and commanded for its general manager, B. F. Yoakum, were ordered from Pullman. So were several other official cars purchased from the Pecos Valley and other handy creditors. There were also munificent orders for motive power from the New York Locomotive Works at Rome, N.Y. In 1890 the S.A. & A.P. defaulted on its bonds. It failed to meet payment on its numerous debts and, as a result, the New York Locomotive Works closed its doors. Private varnish for such resounding Texas names on its directorate as Sam Maverick and Reagan Houston were attached by sheriffs. General Manager Yoakum went to the St. Louis-San Francisco Railway, and eventually the Southern Pacific picked up the pieces of the Aranzas Pass, a monument to the folly of too many directors with a nice taste in private cars. With such a title already engrossed on its name boards, Jay Gould couldn't resist picking up *Electric* for his Western Union Telegraph Company.

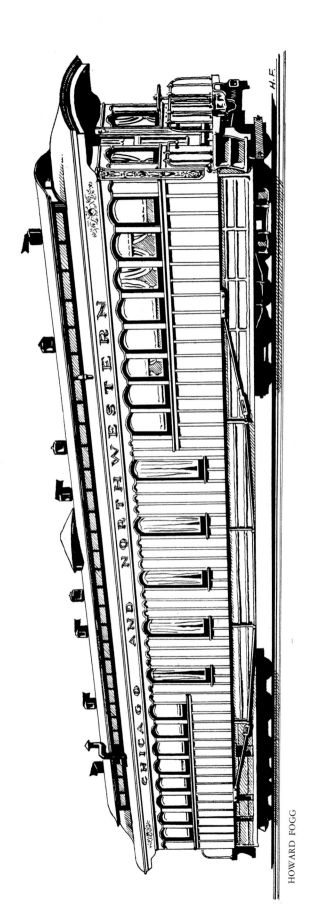

HOWARD FOGG

SOUTHERN PACIFIC

A mainline carrier of wonderful eccentricity in business cars was the Chicago & North Western whose celebrated Gothic directors' car is shown in an artist's profile on the page opposite. Below is an authentic *rara avis* among collectors of private car material: the directors' car of the Central Pacific before its absorption by the Southern Pacific and aboard which the firm of Huntington, Hopkins & Co., decided on strategems which reduced the entire state of California to the status of a feudal barony for three full decades.

GRAHAME HARDY COLLECTION

The Chicago & North Western Railway crosshatching Iowa, Wisconsin, Minnesota and South Dakota was financed by British capital, traces of which survive to this day in its left hand operations. Shown here in the nineties, perhaps aboard *Frontenac* depicted opposite, a group of English directors are making a survey of their property accompanied by members of the operating staff out of Chicago. The mustaches of the colonel at the left quiver with anticipation at a description of the low moral tone of night life in the Black Hills, while at the right a London director in a single eyeglass learns with misgivings from a dude who may well be his secretary that an attack by hostiles may be anticipated at any minute. Drawing the long bow for visiting English milords was a Western institution of long standing with the common sanction of all parties concerned.

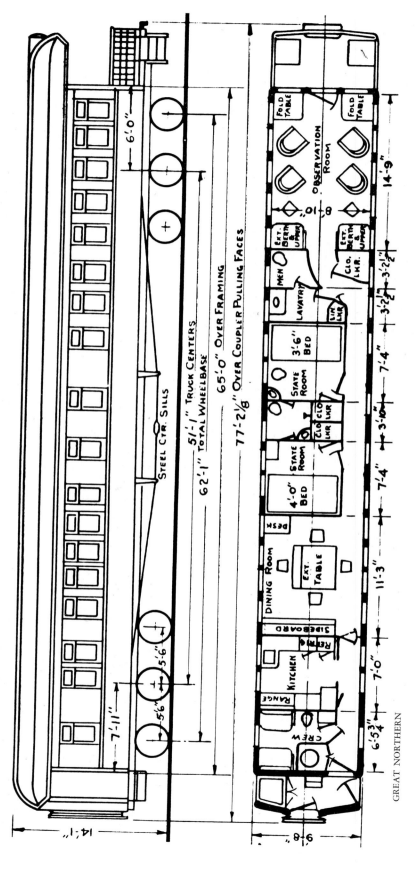

GREAT NORTHERN

Just to show the potential life span of a well cared-for business car, the Great Northern's Official Car A-9 was built for J. J. Hill's St. Paul, Minneapolis & Manitoba by Barney & Smith in 1883 and was still in service in 1953, seven decades later. It had been rebuilt in 1908 and 1923 with steel center sills and, during his lifetime, had often been used by the Empire Builder himself when his regular official car No. A-18 was not available.

Over the years between 1889 when the Louisville & Nashville's *Oriental* came from the shops at Pullman, a thing of beauty to delight the heart of any millionaire, and 1958, as shown below, the venerable car underwent many face liftings. Mostly they were at the expense of style in favor of utility, but its aristocratic origins and good breeding were apparent to the end when it went to a museum in Upper New York State to end its days in dignity and honor.

PULLMAN STANDARD

LOUISVILLE & NASHVILLE

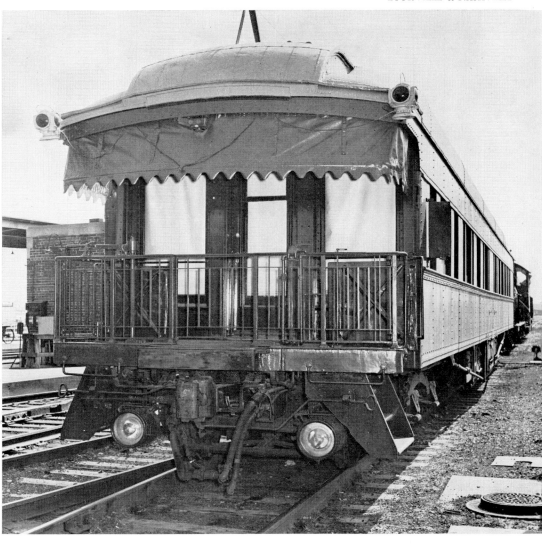

A vintage year in the production of private cars by Pullman, 1890 saw the construction of the two magnificent cars on the page opposite, the Boston & Maine's *Sorrento* and the Norfolk & Western's ranking official car where the accustomed practice of numbering presidential varnish No. 100 was varied in favor of No. 1. *Sorrento* was built to the personal specifications of James T. Thurber, vice-president and general manager of the B & M in the presidency of Frank Jones. Curiously enough the B & M's files make no mention of *Sorrento* by name although they indicate the commissioning of two "director's cars" in its year, suggesting a reticence in the matter of private cars which, even at that early date, was beginning to manifest itself among mainline carriers of the land.

A far cry from the stainless steel and gas fuel of a later generation of private car kitchens, it may be assumed that the galley of Norfolk & Western's car No. 1 still witnessed the service of much terrapin and canvasback in a generation when railroad directors and presidents were not ashamed of good living and *Flying Cloud* Madeira was still available to the frock coated owners.

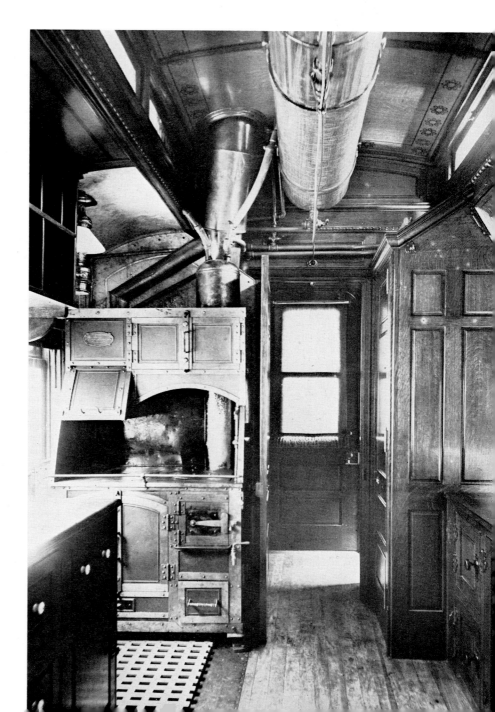

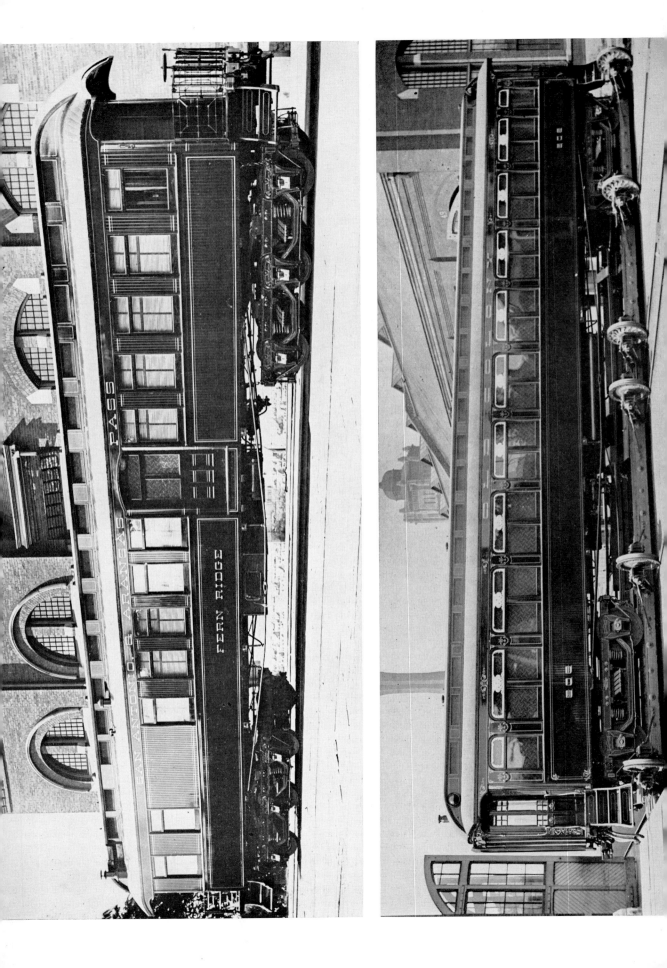

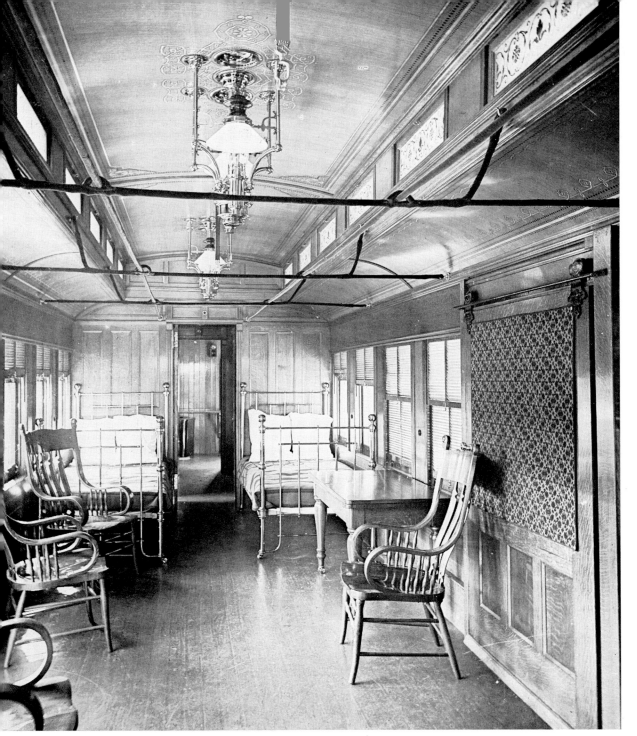

The San Antonio & Aranzas Pass' private, Pullman-built hunting car *Fern Ridge* (ABOVE AND OPPOSITE) aboard which directors and influential friends made safari in the Texas nineties was the envy and admiration of less luxuriously equipped carriers, while the fine p.v. *Electric* served upon state occasions. Even the thrifty and prudently managed Old Colony Railroad in far-off Massachusetts, a road whose dividends enriched an entire generation of proper Bostonians, relaxed sufficiently to order a handsome director's car, No. 508.

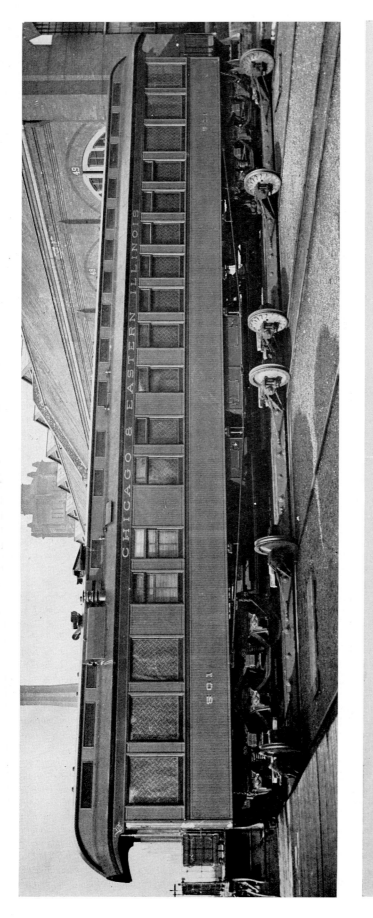

THREE PHOTOS: PULLMAN STANDARD

Pullman beauty and Pullman utility characterized the Chicago & Eastern Illinois' No. 501 and 502, built in 1891 and 1901, respectively. The equipment of No. 501, shown on this page, suggests that although Pintsch lighting had been available for two decades, the C & EI placed its trust in reliable coal oil lamps whose fuel was available everywhere and not subject to the whims of manufacturers of bottled gas.

Awnings in Arkansas, Dividends in Boston

PULLMAN STANDARD

The Kansas City, Fort Scott & Memphis Railroad, whose superbly individualistic directors' car No. 100 is shown on this and the opposite page was a consolidation of the Kansas City, Fort Scott & Springfield and the Kansas City, Springfield & Memphis and extended between the terminal cities of its corporate name a distance of 484 miles with branches. It is cheerful to know that it was from the beginning a paying proposition, entirely financed in Boston, and paid handsome dividends for many years to such eminently Beacon Street stockholders as Charles Merriam, Nathaniel Thayer, H. H. Hunnewell, T. Jefferson Coolidge, Francis Bartlett, B. P. Cheney and Abbott Lawrence. These unpacked their boiled shirts from Hewins & Hollis in the ample drawers of the master stateroom shown here and slept, perhaps with the aid of a nightcap of Lawrence's Medford rum, in its equally ample bed. In 1901 the carrier was acquired as part of the Frisco system, leaving behind it pleasant memories of four percent every quarter in the shadow of Deacon Shem Drowne's grasshopper weathervane atop Faneuil Hall.

PULLMAN STANDARD

Easily the most publicized private varnish in a railroad-conscious generation was Pullman's own car, built at Detroit in 1877 and known until Pullman's death as "P.P.C." after which Mrs. Pullman rechristened it *Monitor*. P.P.C. was used by its owner as a mobile demonstration of the Pullman product and the old gentleman toured the country entertaining railroad executives, few of whom could resist its luxurious appointments of inlaid woodwork, velvet portières, Turkey carpets and a parlor organ. Orders for private cars with equally princely decor poured into the shops and from Maine to California Pullman's salesmanship made private cars very *comme il faut* indeed. Although one of the most solvent men of his generation, Pullman was not averse to turning an honest penny on the side and the *New York Times* in 1882 reported that P.P.C. was available to private rental when its owner was not aboard. The charge was $85. a day and included services of a conductor, cook and two waiters.

TWO PHOTOS: PULLMAN STANDARD

The personal Wagner Palace Car of William Henry Vanderbilt, President of the New York Central and associated Vanderbilt carriers, was the setting for a remark, widely and maliciously quoted out of context, that was to become as celebrated in the American lexicon of quotations as "Remember the Alamo" or "Rum, Romanism and Rebellion." On October 8, 1882 William H. arrived with his sons William Kissam and Frederick William and a group of Central executives at Michigan City, en route to Chicago and the reporters came aboard as a biographer later said "for the pleasure of talking with $100,000,000." When a correspondent for the Chicago *News* asked a leading question to ascertain if one of the Central's fast trains wasn't maintained for the public benefit, Mr. Vanderbilt gave his famous reply: "The public be damned. . . . Railroads are not run on sentiment but on business principles and to pay." Without quoting the entire interview, newspapers all over the world quoted the now famous line to suggest callousness and rapacity in the conduct of railroads generally. A few days later the above caricature of Vanderbilt appeared in the New York *Daily Graphic,* showing the magnate at ease in his private car studying an auction catalogue of paintings and a treatise on trotting horses, sly digs at the Vanderbilt penchant for collecting foreign art on an extravagant scale and his favorite race horse, "Maude S." Outside the window a Vanderbilt train is shown in a wreck which was also malicious as the Vanderbilt lines were among the safest and best managed of their era. *The Daily Graphic* not too subtly associated itself with the great and powerful, however, by showing that its own editions were read by Vanderbilts.

Westward the Course of Empire

HE FIRST PRIVATE VARNISH, of a sort anyway, to eliminate time and distance in the Far West antedated the coming of the railroads by several years but in it were clearly discernible the elements that were shortly to compose the private Pullman cars of the old bearded kings of get. This was the special thoroughbraced Concord coach built to the order of energetic Ben Holladay, doyen of the staging business west of the Mississippi and one time proprietor of the great freighting and postal firm of Russell, Majors & Waddell. Ben's private Concord had an extension seat, the direct forerunner of the lower Pullman berth, so that its occupant could stretch out and catch forty winks as the vehicle thundered across the Great Plains. A cunningly devised reading lamp served during the dark hours and there were built-in food lockers to eliminate having to stop at the dreadful and infrequent eating houses along the Great Central Overland Route to California. Outriders rode ahead of Holladay to alert stocktenders and have changes of horses ready and he once covered the distance from the Missouri River to California in twelve days, ruining several expensive teams on the way.

The private railway cars in which the engineers and executives of the Pacific Railroad rode variously toward Promontory had their common ancestor in Ben Holladay's ingenious private stagecoach.

Ironically enough it was only a few years later that the private varnish car hauled by steam caught up with the rough diamond, ex-stage driver plutocrat whose family was now ranked with the upper tendom of San Francisco society. Following in the footsteps of many another Nob Hill matron, Mrs. Holladay hankered for recognition by Old World aristocracy and took their two eligible daughters to Paris in the search of suitable husbands with listing in the Almanach de Gotha or at least Burke. One day the telegraph brought word to old Ben as he was hoisting a Pisco in Duncan Nicol's Bank Exchange that his daughters, now the Comtesse de Pourtales and the Baroness de Boussière, respectively, were heading westward across the Great Plains aboard the Wagner private car *Wanderer*. Horrified beyond speech at the implications of this intelligence, rugged old Ben Holladay whom no Indian war party could dismay, made strangled sounds in his beard, clapped on his tall silk hat without even finishing his Pisco, and disappeared into the wilds of Oregon, never to return to the drawing rooms of San Francisco.

Ruin of a sort had come to the greatest of the stagers aboard the private car he had pioneered.

The long procession of private cars which surged Westward after the completion of the Pacific Railroad at Promontory Point in May, 1869 was inaugurated, excepting for the business cars of officials and private varnish of Eastern capitalists that had followed the construction of the line by an eye-popping private train of eight specially built Pullman Palace cars that comprised the transcontinental safari of the Boston Board of Trade in May, 1870.

The safari and its personnel were carefully planned to promote travel on the steamcars generally and on the Union Pacific - Central Pacific link with California in particular, and no detail was spared by its sponsors to highlight the resources and expedition of overland travel. So successful was this handsomely mounted showcase for Pullman luxury that for three ensuing decades a trip West for recreational, social or business purposes aboard private cars and, indeed, entire private trains was something of a must among people of wealth and established position.

The Board of Trade private train departed Boston on May 24 and reached San Francisco without strain, mishap or excessive effort just eight days later, a time which was immediately and widely used for editorial purposes in the press of the nation to contrast with the weeks and months previously consumed by wagon transport over the Great Plains. Its personnel were Bostonians and railroad officials of standing and importance and the entire undertaking was attributed to nicely calculated promotion and publicity before these words were known, at least in their Madison Avenue connotation.

The train itself left little to be imagined in the way of comfortable appointments and the ornate decor dear to the heart of a Victorian age. A baggage car had also abundant accommodations for food under refrigeration and carried a small printing press on which was published a daily newspaper chronicling the progress of the expedition. There followed a smoking car with the paper's editorial compartment, a wine room that today would be designated a cocktail lounge and "a beautifully furnished hair dressing and shaving salon." Two specially designed and fitted hotel cars *Arlington* and *Revere* led to two saloon cars, *Palmyra* and *Marquette*, while the entourage was completed by two commissary and restaurant cars, *St. Charles* and *St. Cloud.* From time to time as the scenery suggested, notably on the Central Pacific leg of the trip across the High Sierra, "cars of observation" with open platforms were attached, vantage points from which gentlemen passengers in frock coats and Deerstalker travelling caps appraised the various tangible resources of the regions traversed and their ladies commented on the Indians encountered.

Among the devisings of luxury carried for the first time aboard the steamcars were "two well stocked libraries, replete with choice works of fiction, history, poetry, etc." and two improved Burdett organs which supplied music in an age innocent of radio or Ampex. "The entire train was equipped with every desirable accessory that might tend in the least degree to promote the ease of the passengers — elaborate hangings, costly upholstery, artistic gilding and beautifully finished woodwork marked every portion of their arrangements." A stroke of pure genius was the daily newspaper *Trans-Continental* with dispatches of special arrangement with the Associated Press. Everyone agreed that it would be hard to improve on this evidence of progress and sent hundreds of copies home.

The gleaming varnish cars of the Board of Trade headed westward as far as Albany over the right of way surveyed and constructed for the Western Railroad forty years earlier by the father of James McNeill Whistler, to Buffalo over Commodore Vanderbilt's New York Central & Hudson River Lines and thence to Chicago over the Michigan Central, whose splendid locomotive *Ruby* was "most tastefully decorated with flowers, and on her head was painted a large medallion with 'Welcome Boston Board of Trade.' Her tender was covered with panoramic landscapes of the trip from Boston to San Francisco, including views of the cities on the line. On either side, between her driving wheels, the arms and shields of Massachusetts and California were painted and a picture of the President of the Road (who happened also to be Commodore Vanderbilt) surmounted the headlight."

All along the way the party was received with great interest and open handed hospitality. When they departed Chicago over the Chicago & North Western, one member tarried so long in the tap room of the Sherman Hotel with new found acquaintances that the cars went on without him and he was forced to charter a special engine to rejoin them at Council Bluffs. At Omaha a turnout of the finest carriages in town met the train by private arrangement and carried members of the party to the homes of first citizens to savor the bounty of the Great Plains. At Ogden President Brigham Young and a delegation, including George A. Smith and Apostles Orson Pratt, George Q. Cannon and Brigham Young, Jr., dined on the cars and fascinated the proper Bostonians with the intelligence that President Young had sixteen wives at the moment and forty-nine living children.

It was while in Utah that the Trans-Continental carried the cryptic squib: "The late Mr. Morse and the barber have been restored to us." Conjecture would indicate that Mr. Morse and the man of lotions had ventured ashore at Green River and looked too long on the wine at the Switch Key Saloon.

A side trip to Denver at the invitation of B. B. Styles, the mayor, had to be refused, but at Reno Governor H. G. Blasdel of Nevada made a welcoming oration of impressive proportions and the trip came to a climactic conclusion at San Francisco in a blaze of oratory, banquets and civic receptions. The fortunate Bostonians who made the grand tour had something wonderful to talk about all the rest of their lives.

With such auspicious precedent, it wasn't long before the private cars of Easterners were rolling out of Chicago and St. Louis in such profusion as to be almost commonplace.

One of the first *bona fide* or simon-pure private cars ever seen west of the Missouri River was the *City of Worcester* which had been specially built to the order of a wealthy resident of Worcester, Massachusetts, named Jerome Marble to accommodate a hunting party of eighteen on a three months' shooting safari with headquarters at Bismarck, S. D., on the then building Northern Pacific Railroad. So satisfactory were its special features which included gun rooms, ammunition lockers and a sort of primeval deep freeze for the preservation of game that Marble went home to form the Worcester Excursion Car Company which built and rented private cars to parties of important sportsmen until the Pullman Company, by now a near monopoly of sleeping car patents, put it out of business in 1894.

Probably the pinnacle of splendor in private car travel across the Great Plains was that achieved by the family of Dr. William Seward Webb of New York in 1889. Dr. Webb, as has been mentioned elsewhere, was a Vanderbilt in-law, having married a daughter of William Henry Vanderbilt I, and he was also President of the Wagner Palace Car Company which supplied sleepers, hotel cars and private varnish to the New York Central and other Vanderbilt lines to the great mutual profit of all concerned.

At once a man of means and of learning, Dr. Webb was of no mind that his family and guests should suffer the deprivations of the Mormons while crossing the Great Plains a third of a century earlier or of the ill-fated Donners whose peculiar dietary habits were by now well established in Western legend. To this end he assembled a private train of four cars serviced by a staff of approximately twenty domestics and other retainers not counting the train crew, fitted out an armory in the combination car and installed a number of alarm gongs connected between cars by an elaborate system of bell-pulls which could sound the tocsin in the event of attack by hostile Sioux or the Rube Barrows gang, "even though hold-ups by desperate border ruffians are not very common in the present stage of Western civilization." A semi-military guard of two riflemen was organized under the command of "Colonel Oscar Eastmond, late U.S.A.", and west of Kansas City, which evidently represented to Dr. Webb the final frontier for any dependable social order, Pinkerton detectives armed with Winchesters rode the car platforms between the hours of dusk and sunrise.

Himself a qualified surgeon, Dr. Webb felt able in his own person to take care of gunshot wounds and other casualties in anything short of Little Big Horn proportions.

The train itself comprised a combination car with space for baggage and sleeping quarters for the kitchen staff, the arms room, a bath, a smoking room complete with an extensive library and Chickering piano for occupancy by the masculine members of the expedition, and a wine cellar whose key reposed in the pocket of Dr. Webb.

Then came "Buffet Car No. 60" which the resourceful Doctor had borrowed from President John Newell of the Lake Shore & Michigan Southern Railroad, a Vanderbilt subsidiary and accommodating, and the private Wagner *Mariquita* which had been extensively remodeled to suit its present occupants as a nursery car for the three Webb children, two nurses, and Mrs. Webb's personal maid.

Last came Webb's own private car, the Wagner *Ellsmere* with suites for the owner, Mr. Julian Kean, Mr. Frank Webb and Mr. George Bird who were guests on the well upholstered landfaring. There were two chefs and eight porters in addition to the various domestics mentioned above, guards, train crew and guests.

That the Webb entourage was prepared not only for survival in the face of pioneer hardships, but equipped also with the latest conveniences of a scientific age is evidenced by the presence in the lead car of a primeval dictaphone. "The chronicler of the expedition had *talked* into a phonograph a diary of the experiences that had befallen the party since starting from New York," Webb wrote later. "The cylinders containing the material were included in the outgoing mail (Pueblo, Colorado) to be translated by a clerk back in New York 'into every day English.'"

Thus provided against every contingency of violence or mischance and with rifles at a metaphorical ready, Dr. Webb and his party braved the howling wilderness of the West in 1890. It was not until their arrival at Del Monte on Monterey Bay where they discovered Tevises, Crockers and McAllisters going abroad unarmed that they were able to relax their vigilance.

It was in the eighties, too, that Ernest Ingersoll, a member of one of the early Federal geologic surveys of the West, brought his family to Colorado and leased three narrow gauge private cars from the Denver & Rio Grande Railroad for a summer in the more remote Rockies. "Roughing it within reasonable grounds," he explained, "is the marrow of this sort of recreation." His sentiments were shared by a surprising number of Easterners over the years and the railroad made a good thing of its three foot luxury equipment on lease to Bostonians who felt that a Baker Heater represented just the right degree of removal from the by now crowding precincts of Nahant and Pride's Crossing.

The chapter that concerns itself with narrow gauge private cars in Colorado opens with sound and fury on the theme of the first of all three foot luxury cars in the Rocky Mountain region pleasantly named *Nomad* and built to the personal specifications of General William Jackson Palmer, father of the Denver & Rio Grande Railroad. General Palmer's "house car," as he was pleased to describe it in a letter to the future Mrs. Palmer, was built by Jackson & Sharp at their St. Charles shops to serve as the general's home on wheels as the infant carrier was laying its forty pound iron out of Denver toward epic but as yet unsuspected contests with the Santa Fe for a continental dimension, and one of its pioneer innovations was hot and cold running water under pressure and piped to the general's washroom. To date, only cold water had been available aboard the cars in this part of the world, induced by hand pumps. The railroad-minded *Rocky Mountain News* in due course reported the hot water as an example of the conveniences that might soon be expected aboard the steam cars everywhere, but General Palmer had a low boiling point and chose to regard as a hostile or critical attitude a news story that was in fact no more than filled with admiration. He waxed ferocious over the innocent squib and made horse-whipping motion with his cane when he encountered newspaper reporters in Larimer Street. The item was an invasion of his privacy and, besides, it reflected on the general's Spartan virtues as an old campaigner. He ordered the hot water disconnected and wore his hat at a more fiercely rakish angle than ever.

Probably by reason of the endearing diminutive of the narrow gauge itself, as well as the romantic associations of the little railroads of Colorado's bonanza years, the folklore of the three foot private cars that rolled to Leadville, Silverton and Telluride lays a particular hold on the imagination. Here was luxury in microcosm, champagne and pheasant, brass beds and the silk tile hats of the nabobs all within the ensmalled dimension of three foot operations. Rich doll houses rolled through the high passes.

Legend in the Rocky Mountain region to the contrary notwithstanding, there seems no evidence for the belief that any of the carbonate moguls of Leadville or Silverton ever themselves owned or maintained anything that might properly be designated as a private car, but there was a generous complement of narrow gauge business cars on the Denver & Rio Grande, the Rio Grande Southern and the Denver, South Park & Pacific. These were generally available to such silver kings as Charlie Boettcher, Horace A. W. Tabor, Tom Walsh and David Moffat for their private and personal occasions. The Colorado millionaires were important shippers and in many cases themselves directors of the railroads in an age innocent of the Interstate Commerce Commission and there was no impropriety in their appropriating the business cars of presidents and division superintendents when occasion demanded.

The indignation over General Palmer's hot water aboard his richly furnished little *Nomad* has already been mentioned. It was aboard this car, too, that Ulysses S. Grant rode in triumph at the end of the Rio Grande's first train into the howling bonanza community of Leadville to be greeted by Lieutenant Governor Tabor and a gorgeous multiplicity of brass bands. An office car of the Colorado Central was also bespoken by Tabor when he wished to transport his then mistress, Baby Doe, who later became the second Mrs. Tabor, between her sumptuous apartment in the Windsor at Denver and an equally ornate suite reserved for her at the Teller House in Central City.

The carbonate kings of Leadville frequently occupied South Park business cars attached to the overnight run between Denver and the mining community that was the source of their wealth, and legend envisions them in all-night poker games for heady stakes with the piled double eagles toppling to the floor in golden cascades as the little cars hit the stub switches at Como and Jefferson in the small hours. On the Rio Grande Southern, Otto Mears, "Pathfinder of the San Juan," maintained a luxuriously appointed narrow gauge business car, the *San Juan*, on which he delighted to entertain notables on tours of his remote and desolate mountain domain.

When, now in his eighties, Mears bowed to the Colorado winters and went East to live, one of the several RGS business cars went with him and ended its days as a modest residence on the outskirts of Washington.

Common practice on the Colorado narrow gauges dictated the use of business cars in tandem. A forward car was occupied by dining salon, kitchen, offices and quarters for the crew while the rear car contained bedrooms and an observation salon for occupancy by officials and their guests. As late as 1947 two of these diminutive palace cars were maintained in a state of mint preservation by the Denver & Rio Grande Western at Alamosa and the writer has ridden them to Durango and Silverton in company with the then general manager of the railroad, Al Perlman, who shortly went on to greater destinies as president of the mighty New York Central System.

No record exists of any business car on the roster of the Florence & Cripple Creek narrow gauge to the Cripple Creek diggings in the closing years of the nineteenth century, but the "Golden Circle Route," as the wealthy short line was known, possessed a specially comfortable caboose that was at the disposal of officials and their guests for the run up Phantom Canyon.

In time the wheel of the narrow gauge business car came full circle and General Palmer's *Nomad*, so long a railroad property and officially designated as a business car, reversed the more general practice and passed into private hands, to become what is probably the only narrow gauge private car of all time in the strict sense of the word. Refurbished with red plush and gold ball fringe curtains, its fine mahogany paneling restored to its original estate, *Nomad** belongs to a group of well-to-do Coloradans with oil interests in the San Juan region. Serene and aloof on the private car track in Durango, it establishes continuity with the romantic past when the narrow gauge ran everywhere in the Rockies.

Far to the west of Colorado and for years in service on the narrow gauge Carson & Colorado Railroad, a subsidiary of the opulent Virginia & Truckee, were two three foot gauge business cars of a simplicity in keeping with the economical policies which governed the building and operation of the carrier itself. The C & C had been financed by Darius Ogden Mills' Bank of California to serve the then emergent mining regions in Nevada's Southern Desert. Its business cars were just that, severely utilitarian conveyances for operating officials and devoid of the overtones of splendor that characterized the parent bonanza railroad to the Comstock. Briefly after the discoveries at Tonopah and Goldfield, the C & C's private varnish knew the presence aboard of such names that made news as Tasker Oddie, Key Pittman and George Nixon, Nevada silver nabobs of the moment, but largely their destinies were without the glamour of wealth and power.

Perhaps, if the official biographer of California's redwood railways, Gilbert H. Kneiss, is to be credited, the most sumptuous of all narrow gauge private cars was built to the special order of Milton S. Latham, a perfectionist in the amenities of living who was the guiding genius in its formative years of the North Pacific Coast Railroad, later incorporated in the fabric of the mighty Southern Pacific. The N.P.C. ran north out of Sausalito across the bay from San Francisco and eventually formed one of the segments of the Redwood Empire's Northwestern Pacific Railroad.

"To use the *Millwood,* as Latham's private car was known, (wrote Kneiss) as a business car seemed on a par with standing the Venus de Milo in a drugstore window wearing a display of trusses. The parlor, flanked by a roomy observation platform, was paneled in rare inlaid woods, draped with heavy damask, and hung with a few of the sybaritic president's own smaller canvasses. Relaxed on sofas and easy chairs, he and his guests watched countless redwoods broader than the car itself as the track picked its way through the groves, while steward Wan Sin padded back and forth from his culinary department forward with refreshing potables. Soon the China boy would spread a gourmet's banquet for them in the saloon. The rumbling wheels hushed by deep carpets, only the crystal chandeliers tinkling around the curves, and an occasional whistle from the locomotive mingled with discourse on arts and

---

*General Palmer's original narrow gauge *Nomad* was followed on the Rio Grande rolling stock roster in April 1902 by a second, standard gauge business car of the same name acquired from the Rio Grande Western. The seventy-three foot car was equipped with a Baker Heater, Pintsch gas and electric lighting fixtures, an observation room, three staterooms, a toilet and a kitchen. It contained over-all accommodations for fifteen passengers and two attendants, and the new owners added such equipment as an air signal, six wheel trucks and National couplers. Second *Nomad* was renamed *Denver* in 1903 and in 1911 retired and was replaced by *Weldon,* but it was a car of wide circulation in its lifetime and appears on the list of private cars hauled to Palm Beach by the Florida East Coast and its connecting lines during the winter season of 1894.

letters as they savored Milton Latham's gracious living on the narrow gauge. Afterward, a 'flick of the wrist' converted the saloon into four staterooms — as for the president, he had a master bedroom amidships, complete with four-poster and red marble commode."

To haul this noble vehicle there was a special engine with domes, bell and other trim of German silver, its cab solid burnished mahogany. To match the car, it bore the name and monogram of Milton S. Latham in solid gold leaf without other identification on its nameboards. To see the *Millwood* drawn under a canopy of patrician soot by the *Milton S. Latham* as it threaded the fields and uplands of Northern California was one of the great sights of the Old West's most spacious times.

Still another private car that must have enjoyed factual existence but which with the years has become the stuff of legend, emerging like the Flying Dutchman, briefly from a cloud wrack of folk myth only to disappear again, is one built for President Brigham Young of the Latter Day Saints upon the completion of the Ogden & Salt Lake Railway later the Utah Central which the Mormons chartered after the Union Pacific had been surveyed through Ogden rather than the City of the Saints.

The Mormons had done contract labor on the U. P., so runs the rune, to the extent of more than $1,000,000. In the absence in the treasury at Omaha of anything resembling cash to meet this claim, arbitration was resorted to and a committee of Saints headed by Joseph A. Young settled for $600,000 worth of equipment which the transcontinental carrier had absorbed from some now forgotten operation to the east.

One of the first things the Mormons did on receipt of the rolling stock was to rebuild the most available coach into a private car suitable to Brigham Young in his joint capacity as Chief of the Utah State and President of the Church. Angels were painted on the ceiling, so folklore holds, and gilt and scrollwork appeared in wildest profusion. When finished the car combined the best features of business office and episcopal palace and aboard it the bearded patriarch travelled extensively and splendidly over the then existing railroads of Utah surrounded by his wives, bishops of the church, elders and other peers in saintliness until his death in 1877.

"It was a very fancy affair," recalled a veteran in a newspaper interview many years ago. "I rode in it often and was rather dazzled by the gilt and glitter of the interior. I recall there was a frieze of cherubs and flowers all done in gaudy colors, while painted angels trailing diaphanous garments fluttered above the heads of the passengers on the oilcloth roof."

Whatever the angelic theme of its interior decor, the car disappeared from human ken toward the turn of the century. Claims were made to have seen it in secular service and converted form on the White Pass & Yukon Railroad in Alaska. Other chroniclers maintain it was purchased by Augustus F. Heinze, the Montana copper satrap, for use on a railroad he was building to Rossland in the shadow of Red Mountain on the Columbia River. Still another version had it on a plantation railroad among the Cuban canebrakes.

Sufficient to the historian that it vanished to be seen no more, one with the Sword Excaliber and Charlie Ross, to become the stuff of folklore in the roundhouses and switch shanties of the Western land.

Only naturally, the Big Four of the Central Pacific Railroad went in for private varnish in a big way. Mention has been made elsewhere of Leland Stanford's handsome *Stanford,* a present from his wife, and the more ordinary business car in which, before *Stanford* had been built, he went to Promontory, Utah, for the Gold Spike Ceremony in 1869. Charles Crocker's *Mishawaka* was for several decades a West Coast institution plying between San Francisco and the Southern Pacific's exclusive hotel development at Del Monte, while Collis Huntington went his partners one better when he commissioned Pullman to build for him not one but two cars to be used and occupied en suite. *Oneonta,* named for the town in upper New York State where he had spent his youth, was a conventional millionaire's palace with the fringes, flounces, potted palms and marquetry fashionable at the time. *Oneonta II,* also Pullman-built, was an auxiliary designed to supplement first *Oneonta.* It contained a baggage compartment in the fore end, storage space for the owner's trunks and other luggage, and simple sleeping arrangements for servants or overflow guests from the main car of the entourage.

There is no record that Mark Hopkins, fourth partner of the Big Four, ever had a car built to his special order or one assigned to his private occupancy by the railroad, but he had the distinction, shared many years later with Oris P. Van Sweringen, of dying aboard a business car while inspecting the Southern Pacific's newly completed Sunset Route through Yuma. Uncle Mark's body was returned to San Francisco in the car in which he had met his end, another mortuary honor shared this time with his partner Charles Crocker who was the first guest to die at Del Monte and was himself returned to San Francisco aboard *Mishawaka.*

One of the most swaggering and battle scarred of all the old bearded kings of get who dominated the West in the mineral years was William Andrews Clark, who as a young man of twenty-five had entered the wilderness of Montana with an ox-team and left it at last for the Senate of the United States aboard a private car that was to be the hallmark of his success. Clark acquired in the cut-throat competition for copper in Butte and Last Chance Gulch, as Helena was known when he first saw it, one of the truly massive American fortunes and had the distinction of being able to reply when Senator Robert LaFollette listed him as one of the one hundred men who owned America that no single share of stock or bond issue had ever been printed by any of the enterprises with which he was connected. He was a lone wolf of the curly variety who, when once the Senate at Washington refused to seat him on grounds of corrupt campaign practices, returned to the fray and eventually achieved the toga to the cheers of the entire West.

Senator Clark's interest in railroads was not restricted to his Pullman outshopped to his private order and modestly carried on the rolling stock roster of the Northern Pacific as No. 2001. He and his brother J. Ross Clark almost unaided had built the San Pedro, Los Angeles & Salt Lake Railroad which now is the Los Angeles division of the far-flung Union Pacific, and one of the allied projects of this desert carrier was a railroad-financed township which is today the gambling capitol of the known universe at Las Vegas in the Nevada wasteland.

At Las Vegas, Clark also originated his Las Vegas & Tonopah Railroad which was planned to tap the borax deposits of Death Valley and at the same time connect with the boom towns of Beatty and Rhyolite in the Southern Deserts of Nevada and with the Bullfrog & Goldfield Railroad which connected in turn with the Northern Camps. Everywhere in the West from the Amargosa Desert to Butte and from Salt Lake to San Francisco, the senator's palace on wheels was an oriflamme of big business backed by aggressive millions ravished from the deep mines under Butte.

Senator Clark's influence even extended to short lines such as the Butte, Anaconda & Pacific, but socially he is best remembered in upper New York state where his son-in-law, Dr. Lewis W. Morris, was owner of the pastoral Unadilla Valley Railroad. The senator's private car jaunts in the East made a sort of triangle tour between Washington when Congress was in session, New York where he had built a splendid Fifth Avenue mansion in the best Vanderbilt-Gould tradition and Butternut on the U. V. where No. 2001's fantastic resources of Bourbon and champagne were the wonder and amazement of the surrounding countryside.

Of truly epic stature among butlers associated with the folklore of private cars is the figure of Neilsen who superintended the domestic economy of *Errant*, the property of Charlie Clark, son of Senator William Andrews Clark. *Errant*, ninety feet long and one of the heaviest private cars ever outshopped by Pullman, was extensively used in her travels by Mrs. Clark who had misgivings about speed, a sentiment shared by President F. D. Roosevelt who never encouraged the presidential train to exceed thirty miles an hour and liked to look at the scenery. One of the duties of Neilsen, a splendid and capable fellow who later became a capitalist in his own right and retired to California, was to go forward at frequent intervals with a box of Prince de Galles cigars and advise the engineer of Mrs. Clark's sentiments in the matter of speed. Often this complicated the schedule of transcontinental trains with eighty-five mile an hour carding on the tangents, but it is a testimony to the tact of the incomparable Neilsen that more often than not Mrs. Clark's wishes were accommodated.

A crisis that temporarily shattered Neilsen and perhaps hastened his retirement occurred when *Errant* arrived in Chicago one below-zero morning on the end of a Chicago & Eastern Illinois train from the Deep South and the major domo, imprudently attired in his shirtsleeves and striped waistcoat of office, descended to procure a copy of the *Tribune* for his master. He had not been advised that a close connection was scheduled with a Chicago & North Western train for California leaving shortly from the North Western depot two miles across the city. Returning from the newsstand, Neilsen was confronted with an empty track and the bitter necessity of crossing the city in a taxicab and his shirt sleeves. The incomparable butler's account of this hardship froze the marrow of listeners and dwarfed to insignificance the sufferings of the Mormons crossing the Great Plains. Intimates reported that never again did he appear on the platform of *Errant*, much less set foot to earth without his morning coat tightly buttoned and composure intact.

The year 1876, Centennial Anniversary of American Independence, witnessed brave doings in the railroad world. Where but a century before, delegates to the Continental Congress had foregathered in Philadelphia by stagecoach, diligence and on horseback, hundreds of thousands of visitors now attended the Centennial Exposition riding in almost unearthly splendor and in good solid comfort aboard Pullmans and Wagners fringed, carpeted and upholstered in rare fabrics, panelled in costly woodworks and aboard ordinary day coaches, if the word could be used to describe vehicles only slightly less ornate in their resources of plush, plate glass and silver finished hardware.

There were fine things to see at Philadelphia, exhibits by all the important car builders and locomotive works, narrow gauge, standard gauge, coaches, business cars, diners, sleeping cars, mail vans, baggage cars and, reigning supreme among the exhibits of the railroads, examples of private varnish that glittered with the elegances of decor of an age uninhibited by the functional and happily innocent of the *moderne*. From distant California came the private varnish car of Peter Donohue, San Francisco speculator and railroad builder. Jackson & Sharp, who didn't have so far to come being located at nearby Wilmington, showed diminutive business cars destined for the Denver & Rio Grande out Colorado way. So did Billmeyer & Smalls who specialized in three foot equipment up in York, Pennsylvania.

But the prize exhibit of the railroad pavilion was the personal car that had been built that year by Jackson & Sharp for Dom Pedro II de Alcanta, Emperor of Brazil, if for no other reason than that Dom Pedro himself came to Philadelphia as a joint attraction with his car, named as was the custom of the time, *Dom Pedro*.

Like his car, which bore on its name boards the title, "Companhia Sao Paulo e Rio de Janeiro," the emperor glittered. His uniforms and decorations, his manners, speech and even his beard were all anyone could ask of the first actually reigning royal personage to set foot in the democratic United States. The car, aside from the splendor of its owner, was of special interest to the lady editors of women's magazines as its interior decor had been supervised by Mrs. W. S. Auchincloss, wife of the President of Jackson & Sharp and a nineteenth century predecessor of Dorothy Draper. The salon attracted widespread attention for "its lavishness combined with the most irreproachable taste."

Dom Pedro left Philadelphia for San Francisco aboard the hotel car, *Metropolitan*, which the Department of State and Pullman arranged for his occupancy. He wanted to see the Palace Hotel where he was to be the guest of Governor Leland Stanford, but on the way he got black looks from natives of Virginia City atop Nevada's Comstock Lode. Everybody in those days who was anybody visited Virginia City to marvel at the deep mines which were making millionaires by the score and raising startling mansions on San Francisco's Nob Hill. It was expected that Dom Pedro would have the *Metropolitan* cut out of the Central Pacific's *Overland Express* at Reno and routed to the Comstock over the swaggering Virginia & Truckee, and John McCullough, the actor, who chanced to be a house guest of John Mackay at Virginia City, was sent down the hill to Reno to meet the emperor and escort him to the International Hotel.

The Comstock suspected treachery when the imperial personage failed to appear and it was learned that McCullough, recreant to his trust, had not only failed to persuade Dom Pedro to stop off, but had actually joined him and gone on to San Francisco amidst the rococo splendors of *Metropolitan*. Nevadans felt better when they learned that the emperor and the Judas of the footlights had stepped down from their conveyance while the train made its conventional pause at Cape Horn in the Sierra and been left behind when the engineer whistled off for the descent to Colfax. Served them richly right was the opinion voiced in Virginia City's teeming C Street.

But the progress of even enthroned royalty through the American countryside of that now distant year was nothing to the excitement generated by the transcontinental race against time of the Jarrett & Palmer *Lightning Express*.

Hailed by the press of the nation as "incomparably the most dramatic event of the Centennial Year," the *Lightning Express* was the inspiration of Henry C. Jarrett, one of the proprietors of the Booth Theater in New York where Lawrence Barrett and his company were just coming to the end of a long and successful run in Shakespearean repertory. The curtain was due to ring down on the concluding scene of "Henry V" on a Wednesday night and the company was contracted to open their San Francisco season with the same drama the Monday evening following.

Travel by the steamcars between New York and California was only seven years old and the regular time occupied by the 3,000 mile passage was a full seven days and nights. A project to cut this time to an incredible four days such as was dreamed up by the resourceful Jarrett set the entire American people by the ears. The play must go on, thundered Jarrett over the wire services of the time. He hinted at ruinous forfeitures and penalties if Barrett wasn't on stage when the curtain went up at the California Theater. Shakespeare, the steamcars and continental distances all added up to a pattern of excitement and publicization that Barnum might have envied.

The details of the race occupied the attentions of the press for days in advance. Along the routes and at division points of five connecting railroads between Jersey City and San Francisco, trainmasters, division superintendents, maintenance of way men and dispatchers toiled over running cards, stop schedules and operational expertise that would give the train green over every mile of track from the Hudson River to the Golden Gate.

First leg of the sprint was to be over the Eastern Division and then the lines west of the Pennsylvania and its recently acquired trackage on the Pittsburgh, Fort Wayne & Chicago Railroad, west to Council Bluffs on the trackage of the Chicago & North Western, built with English capital and British ideas of operations, and out of Omaha via Union Pacific and its connecting line at Ogden, Utah, the Central Pacific. Assigned to the first leg of the journey was the Pennsylvania's fleetest American type eight wheeler, the *Governor Tilden* (it was an age when even the great Eastern trunk lines still named their locomotives). There was a baggage car, then the hotel car, *Thomas A. Scott*, not to be confused with Mr. Scott's own car as president of the railroad, No. 120, and finally the Pullman sleeper, *Yosemite*.

Especially interested in all these details which were spread for its readers in column after column of pica and long primer was James Gordon Bennett's *New York Herald*, perhaps the most promotion-minded newspaper on Park Row. *The Herald* planned, on the evening of May 31 when the train was scheduled to leave, a special edition under the next morning's dateline to be sold on the streets of San Francisco four days later. A print order of 15,000 copies was rushed from the pressroom unfolded as it came from the rollers, to be folded in the baggage car as the train sped west.

No such precipitate haste could, however, be induced in playactors of that stately era. After the final curtain had been rung down at the Booth, the company must repair to a late supper at the Astor House with the speeches, toasts and congratulations without which no successful run could terminate. By the time their cabs rolled off the Jersey City ferry close to one o'clock, the mail, the *Herald* and everyone else was aboard and waiting and the conductor fretted, watch in hand, to give the eagle eye his highball in the *Governor Tilden* up ahead.

From then until the end of the ride four mornings later scarcely a brake-shoe was changed or a sandwich eaten aboard the *Lightning Express* but its every detail was known to the farthest reaches of the land. A reporter for the *Herald* who also represented the Associated Press tossed off breathless dispatches as the cars swayed into the night, and outside newspaper offices in Boston, New Orleans and Manhattan crowds cheered the bulletins which appeared at feverish intervals. Chop whiskered bankers in Ohio and farmers in Indiana stayed up beyond curfew to clock the flyer as it streaked over spiked switches and through yards cleared of traffic until it had passed.

Between Chicago and Council Bluffs the *Express* met and passed no fewer than thirty-seven other train movements on the North Western's single track. Four engine changes were made and one stop to repair a broken air line. The fastest time achieved was 62.2 miles an hour and the average for the run was 42.6.

Aboard the cars the distinguished passengers were unable to avail themselves of the comforts and facilities of the *Thomas A. Scott* and *Yosemite* save on a limited basis. Hot food, it soon appeared, was out of the question as the cars rocked so that cooking was impossible. So was anything but the most primitive toilets and masculine members of the company arrived in California with four full days' beard. To have attempted a shave with the straight razor of the time would have been suicide. Few got much sleep and bit players and starred performers alike clutched at their seats and resolved to use their return tickets, which were embossed in silver filagree and guaranteed their round trip to New York, on less impetuous excursions.

Those who undertook to retire to their berths did so without benefit of clean linen as the porters were unable to free both hands at the same time to spread the sheets.

A short distance out of Ogden on the Central Pacific leg of the run, a hot-box developed on the baggage car and a C. P. roadmaster who was riding head-end knelt on the car step to cool the running parts as the train was in full progress across the Utah desert. Holding on with one hand he succeeded with the other in prying loose the patent journal box and getting fresh waste and lubricant on the sizzling brasses. When an air line broke and the brakes were rendered inoperable, the train never slackened but went on under what control was available through hand braking.

At Promontory, only seven years earlier the scene of the joining of the transcontinental rails, the prostitutes and gamblers who were by now its only inhabitants got out of bed at high noon, a most unaccustomed hour in their professions, to cheer the train through.

Its most spectacular entry was at Reno where Mr. Jarrett was minded to "go through like a streak of lightning to justify the train's name." A magazine of red fire was precariously carried to the top of the swaying tender and Roman candles in abundant quantities were distributed to the passengers. At the outskirts of town every window flew up, the fireworks were ignited "and into Reno went the train, flames rolling from the smokestack, an immense red fire burning on the tender and hundreds of balls belching out of the Roman candles. The whole town was up and the train passed to the thunder of cannon."

From the operational standpoint the run of 879 miles from Ogden to San Francisco was the most spectacular. With a single engineer at the throttle of a single engine, Hank Small with No. 149, the *Black Fox* for the entire run, it was a test of human and mechanical endurance out of the ordinary. The descent of the western slope of the High Sierra without air alone was a feat of daring and skill that thrilled the nation. The direct route of the Southern Pacific from Sacramento to Oakland had not been built and the train was routed via Stockton and Niles. "On the finish from Livermore to Oakland," reported the *San Francisco Bulletin,* "there was a fine exhibition of speed . . . a run of four miles was made in four minutes."

The players were received in San Francisco with transports of enthusiasm. The passage from ocean to ocean had been accomplished in one minute fewer than eighty-four hours and copies of the *New York Herald* were indeed on sale in Montgomery Street the fourth day after publication. A cannon thoughtfully mounted by the management on the roof of The Palace Hotel sounded a thirteen gun salute. As the line of hacks sped up Market Street at a dead gallop they turned into the Great Court of the hotel and Mr. Jarrett was able to sign the register at just two minutes short of eleven o'clock.

Having left New York stuffed with foie gras and champagne and endured for better than 3,000 miles on cold chicken and bottled beer, nothing would do but that a state breakfast must be served the survivors. The light collation run up for the occasion by Warren Leland, the manager, included the following snacks:

Salmon Grille à la Maître d'Hotel
Tom Cod Frit, Sauce Tartare
Cucumber Salad
Filet de Boeuf, Sauce Bearnaise
Cotelettes d'Agneau, Sauce Soubise
Escalope de Veau à la Guennoise
Pomme de Terre, Maître d'Hotel
Rognon Sauté au Champignons
Poulet Grillé a la Cresson
Oeufs Brouillés au Point d'Asperges
Oeufs Frits en Temben
Pré-Salé
Apricots, Raspberries, Strawberries, Cherries

After that everybody went to bed until curtain time the following evening. Lawrence Barrett himself was credited by local wits with saying he was unable to get to sleep in his apartment at the Palace until he had retained the services of a bellhop to throw handfuls of cinders in his face and at intervals shake the bed while shouting, "Omaha next stop, next station is Cheyenne."

Jarrett & Palmer's *Lightning Express* made railroad history and the fine hotel car, *Thomas A. Scott,* was almost as good as new after three weeks in the backshops.

The year 1880 saw outshopped by Pullman for Nevada's well-heeled Senator William Sharon a private car that lived up to every suggestion and overtone of the staggering wealth of the Comstock Lode at Virginia City where the Senator had made an enormous fortune and many enemies. After the death of the ill-fated William Ralston, cashier of the Bank of California, Sharon had taken over most of the unfortunate man's assets including the glittering Palace Hotel in San Francisco, his palatial villa at Belmont and his share in numerous profitable Nevada properties including the Virginia & Truckee Railroad. Like many of his peers and contemporaries, Sharon hankered for the toga and set about achieving election from Nevada by methods which, even in a time when brass knuckles were standard political equipment, caused the Virginia City *Territorial Enterprise* to denounce him as "a hyena in human form who deserved to be lashed naked from the haunts of civilization." Sharon answered by purchasing the newspaper outright and installing in office an editor of more charitable attitude. Two years later he won the election.

Senator Sharon's Pullman aroused universal envy and admiration for its appointments which were hailed as "a miracle of convenience and comfort" and its two improved sleeper sections with sliding walls which recessed into the sidewalls of the car when not in use.

"Even the Queen of England does not travel as royally as this silver satrap of the Sierras" proclaimed the *Detroit Free Press* invoking the then comparative standard of all opulence in the person of Victoria Regina. The writer grew ecstatic over rare woods, bronze fittings and leather chairs with silver headed upholsterers' tacks from the deep mines of the Comstock not to mention silver plumbing fixtures, door knobs, bell-pulls and other hardware.

"In the galley," said the reporter verging on pure poetry, "the fire glowed in the range and shone on polished pots, pans and porcelain utensils in the cutest of kitchens as clean as a holystoned deck . . . Pudding and jelly molds, skewers, steamers and saucepans as bright as silver hang on the hooks of the dresser. Stores of delicate china are nestled in snug closets, crystal and silverware crown the oaken buffet in the adjoining room."

Aside from his reprehensible politics and generally larcenous inclinations, Sharon was an amateur of the fine things of life on an exalted plane. His chefs were imported direct from Delmonico's in New York, his wines were chosen with the knowing expertise of a practiced oenophile and the Senator played a superb game of poker. The advent of his car in Virginia

City, San Francisco or Washington was hailed by acquaintances who knew its resources of entertainment to be limitless and princely and who forgave Sharon his shortcomings under the influence of Terrapin Maryland and magnums of Otard Dupuy Cognac of the magic vintage of 1845.

During the closing decades of the nineteenth century one of the great magnificoes of San Francisco commerce and society was James Ben Ali Haggin, many times a millionaire, the financial peer of Darius Ogden Mills, Senator William Sharon and Lloyd Tevis, partner in the swaggering Pacific Mail Steamship Company, director of Wells Fargo and owner of celebrated stock farms for race horses at Sacramento and Lexington, Kentucky. Haggin's princely hospitality, Lucullan table, his thoroughbreds and his Corinthian porticoed mansion on Nob Hill were the hallmarks of a Renaissance personality. To travel in comparable magnificence between California, his Kentucky estates and his equally opulent New York town house at 587 Fifth Avenue, Haggin in 1890 ordered from Pullman one of the most sumptuously designed private cars of all time. *Salvator's* galley was in charge of a chef from Foyot's in Paris; its table service was gold from Shreve's, and the details of its decor were executed by W. & J. Sloane who had opened a San Francisco branch of their New York shop to furnish Senator William Ralston's then-building Palace Hotel. Frequent guests aboard *Salvator* in its transcontinental landfarings were William C. Whitney and James R. Keene, sportsmen and in their own right members of the private car club, and such San Francisco luminaries, Del Monte-bound via the Southern Pacific, as Hall MacAllister, Charlie Crocker and Sir Thomas Fermor-Hesketh, seventh baronet, who was to forge gilt-edge bonds of matrimony in California by marrying Flora Sharon.

Much of the discovery of the American West by adventurous Englishmen, a process continuous from the time of the Mountain Men until approximately the closing of the open cattle ranges, was accomplished in something approaching splendor aboard privately chartered and handsomely appointed special trains of Pullmans and Wagners operating out of Chicago. Such resorts as the overpowering Windsor Hotel in Denver and the heiress preserves of Del Monte and Colorado Springs, were liberally populated with Dundreary weepers, single eye-glasses and Norfolk jackets which found everything most extraordinary, not the least of it the private charter cars on which they achieved the howling wilderness. The visiting Britons provoked wonder, mirth or respect as circumstances might dictate. Mostly they were highly intelligent travellers, appreciative of the hospitality made available to them, but sometimes superciliousness got a comeuppance, and as late as 1898 a dude type in a quilted smoking jacket who appraised the peasants through a monocle from the observation platform of Will Crocker's private car in the Southern Pacific depot at Phoenix was lassoed and dragged to the platform by outraged waddies.

A description of the consist of such a de luxe tourist train has been left us by William Hardman, who published the story of his American adventure in London in 1884.

Our departure from Chicago was the real commencement of our journey into the great Northwest with the eventual destination of Yellowstone, he wrote. It was then that we found ourselves for the first time in the railway train which was to be more or less our home for the next three weeks . . . Immediately behind the engine was a capacious car for our luggage and for stores of fruit, vegetables, cases of champagne, claret, Apolinaris and lager beer and other necessities for the luxurious existence we enjoyed. Next came the dining car with kitchen, pantry, storeroom and ten tables, five on a side to accommodate four persons each. After that followed four Pullman sleeping cars and after them the private car of Mr. John C. Wyman, the orator of our party, a gentleman of remarkable eloquence and geniality, always amusing us with some fresh joke or story. Finally, at the tail of the train, is what is called an observation car, a platform at the end where such passengers as did not mind the dust might sit and enjoy the scenery as we passed along. . . . Punctually at 7:30 A. M., the serving of breakfast began, at one o'clock we had lunch and the dinner hour was six. The colored attendants who acted as chambermaids began making up the beds soon after nine and by eleven o'clock everyone was fast asleep. It was a very strange sight to see these darkies at the bedmaking. Their rapidity and dexterity are marvelous. Their civility and attention, too, are beyond praise.

This was the private train of well-to-do Englishmen on a conducted grand tour of the West. Foreigners of more exalted station, Boni de Castellane or the Grand Duke Alexis, might ride in truly imperial splendor aboard the private varnish cars of Goulds and Harrimans where dinner dress and gold table service were taken for granted.

During the golden age of steam railroading in the United States hundreds of special trains, many of them involving private equipment of one sort or another, rolled across the landscape at the behest of necessity or whim on the part of affluence, usually in a hurry. Specials were frequently commanded to transport medical specialists to the bedside of important patients, a case in point being a hastily assembled special on the Southern Pacific to take physicians from San Francisco to the bedside of Charlie Crocker at Del Monte in 1888.

The Santa Fe, being a railroad noted for its fast track across the continent and the expedition of its operations generally, was the scene of a number of cross country scurries by people who wanted to be some place else quickly. Over this route in 1900 A. R. Peacock, a director of Carnegie Steel & Iron, took a small party aboard a Santa Fe business car from Chicago to Los Angeles in fifty-seven hours, fifty-six minutes. For a Mr. H. P. Howe of the Engineering Company of America on special assignment in the West, the same carrier ran a coach and hotel car from Dearborn Street to the Old Pueblo a few years later in fifty-two hours and forty-nine minutes. When Collis P. Huntington, a guest on the Santa Fe aboard his own two *Oneontas,* wanted to get from Pueblo, Colorado, east to Chicago, a reverse record of sorts was established. Huntington disapproved of night travel as well as speed and his special took three full days and nights on the way.

Most celebrated of all fast runs on the Santa Fe was, of course, the *Coyote Special* commanded in 1905 by Walter Scott, better known as Death Valley Scotty, a show-off and self-promoter of purest brass serene. For the sum of $5,500 the Santa Fe put Scotty into Chicago aboard a three-car train with nineteen engine changes in forty-five hours and forty-five minutes. A publicity expert for the railroad dropped dispatches for the Associated Press along the way and the dash achieved fantastic newspaper space for all concerned. The diner that was part of the consist remained open on a twenty-four hour a day basis, and part of the time Scotty spent eating caviar sandwiches and Porterhouse steaks, rare. The *Coyote Special* piled up speed records all along the line, at one time hitting 106 miles an hour for a world's record. At division points where a change impended, Scotty climbed forward over the coal in the tender, to give the head-end crew a twenty dollar gold piece each. Word of this extravagance preceded the special via the magnetic telegraph, and beyond Trinidad there was at all times a division superintendent in the engine cab. Twenty dollars gold meant something in those days.

Throughout the closing years of the nineteenth century in the golden age of steam railroading, the private cars of the lords of creation were a familiar property from the high passes of the Rockies to the fashionable resorts of California. They clustered thick as autumn leaves on Vallombrosa on the private car tracks at Colorado Springs and foregathered annually for the statelier sarabands of San Francisco society at Del Monte on the Monterey Peninsula. Titled foreigners and mining millionaires rode grandly up to the Union Depot in Denver where the arrival of nabobs was recorded for posterity in the Denver papers by youthful reporters including Eugene Field and Gene Fowler.

Both the Burlington and the Union Pacific regularly hauled the splendid private varnish of the great cattle ranchers to Cheyenne where their occupants, many of them proprietors or managers of such vast foreign-owner spreads as the Prairie Cattle Company of Edinburgh or the Swan Land & Cattle Company of London, gloried and drank deep in the sacrosanct premises of the Cheyenne Club, one of the richest private clubs in the entire world. Its affluent members bought up entire vintage crops of French champagnes that took their fancy and because they dined in full evening dress waited on by liveried footmen, they were popularly designated as "The Penguins." The U. P. private car track at Cheyenne flowered with the incongruity of silk top hats and opera cloaks on the Great Plains.

From the brass-bound observation platforms of private varnish of powerful Eastern carriers such as the New York Central and Pennsylvania names that made news, including J. Pierpont Morgan, Lady Randolph Churchill, William K. Vanderbilt and Prince Louis of Savoy, en route to California watched the antelope grazing on the Wyoming uplands and marvelled at the vastness of the land.

In the closing years of the long saga of precious metals in Colorado, the carbonate kings of Cripple Creek, Bert Carlton, Daniel Jackling and Spencer Penrose indulged a nice taste in private cars which had their focus in Colorado Springs over the trackage of the Fort Worth & Denver City, the Colorado Midland, the Rio Grande and the Santa Fe. Here, too, Pennsylvania's lordly Senator Boise Penrose one morning long ago arrived in a Pennsylvania Railroad business car shared with Colorado's equally patrician Senator Edward O. Wolcott. Penrose had just invented an infusion of fresh peaches in bourbon whisky which was later commercialized as Southern Comfort and he wanted to share the secret with his younger brother Spencer. The expedition was a resounding success throughout "Little Lunnon" and old-timers to this day speak in hushed voices of the carnage occasioned around the Antlers Hotel by the Senator's invention.

It was on this occasion, or at least a similar senatorial safari, that Wolcott stopped over in Denver long enough to lose $22,000 in an evening of poker at Ed Chase's gaming rooms, a circumstance that was charged against his character by the opposition when he came up for re-election. "It's nobody's God damned business but my own," roared the bold old man in the columns of *The Rocky Mountain News*, "and besides, I had won the money the day before at the races."

Eccentric individualism achieved an all-time high among members of the private car club in the person of Arthur E. Stillwell, President of the Kansas City, Pittsburgh & Gulf Railroad, a carrier eventually destined to become the Kansas City Southern. In 1897 Pullman outshopped for its rental pool of private cars a magnificently furnished private varnish known as *Campania* and placed in service that year with its companion car *Lucania*. Among the properties of *Campania* was a parlor size mahogany-finished organ and this it was which caught the eye of Arthur Stillwell who promptly bought the car. On Stillwell's business cars, when he was away from home, divine services were held and attendance was required of the entire crew. The car was spotted on a convenient siding or passing track and conductor, brakeman, eagle eye and tallow-pot convened to sing "Rock of Ages" and "Lead Kindly Light."

Stillwell was even less conventional in business affairs. His properties were ordered in accordance with dreams and revelations from the spirit world, and astrologers, necromancers and seers of assorted mysteries for a time guided the destinies of the K. C. P. & G. with ghostly train orders. One day Stillwell, who wore close-cropped side whiskers, read in George

Ade, a popular philosopher of the day, the line: "It's a man's own fault if he wears sideburns." The sentiment haunted him and he brooded over its implications. A few nights later, as he sought repose in the master state-room of *Campania*, which was now simply known as Car No. 100, the spirits came and gave Stillwell the word. Next morning he shaved off the sideburns.

But more practical realities than those of a spiritual nature were involved in the affairs of the K. C. P. & G. One of them was John W. (Bet-A-Million) Gates, the dough-heavy barbed wire king who was majority stockholder in the carrier and took a dim view of Stillwell's commerce with the soothsayers. After a brief but spirited proxy battle Stillwell found himself out of a job, although he later went on to the promotion of the Kansas City, Mexico & Orient Railway, and the Texas City of Port Arthur, named for him, stands as his memorial to this day.

Car No. 100 stayed with the K. C. P. & G. and its new occupant was John W. Gates who had small use for spirit messages and still less for parlor organs. Low company became the order of the day where formerly the Godly had foregathered for Sabbath worship. There were high stake poker games with James R. Keene, the hatchet man of Wall Street and other of Gates' cronies as participants. Empty bottles filled the wastebasket and claro Havana cigars clouded the atmosphere where once an odor of sanctity had obtained. The temple was profaned on a twenty-four hour basis and there were money changers in loud pajamas in the upper berths. Arthur Stillwell, by now busy conning Porfirio Diaz into a subsidy for the Orient Railway, was far away and salvation a distant thing.

In the end *Campania* went to glory in a fire in the yards at Kansas City in comparatively recent years. It remained a property of the Kansas City Southern as the business car of minor executives who claimed it smelled agreeably of brimstone to the end.

The last of the great continental gold rushes in the United States excepting only the final appearance of precious metals at Tonopah and Goldfield, Nevada, in 1905, was at Cripple Creek, Colorado. Cripple and its social and residential suburb at Colorado Springs produced its crop of members in the private car club, some of them men of bounce beyond the average.

Nabobs of resounding implications of wealth through their association in the Golden Cycle Mine at Cripple Creek and later the Golden Cycle Mill at Colorado City were Charles Tutt, Spencer Penrose and Charles McNeill. Penrose, as remarked above, a brother of Pennsylvania's formidable Senator Boise Penrose, was to achieve his most lasting fame as builder of the Broadmoor Hotel at the Springs. McNeill was the discoverer of the great Daniel C. Jackling of copper celebrity everywhere in the West, and Tutt was to outlast the entire generation of his peers as administrator of the Penrose estate and that of Penrose's closest friend, Albert Eugene Carlton. A shadowy figure on the fringes of the Colorado private car club was Henry

M. Blackmer who eventually left Colorado to become involved in the Teapot Dome scandals of Wyoming and to die in exile from his native country.

In 1912 the Colorado Springs & Cripple Creek District Railway running between the terminals of its corporate title was proud possessor of a business car, the *Colorado*, No. 99 which was jointly and severally used by Penrose, McNeill, Blackmer and Carlton for purposes of pleasure and finance throughout the Rockies. Because the car had a wooden underframe, it was generally denied access to trunk line interchange outside the state, but it figured largely in Cripple Creek's most scandalous and hilarious moment, of which more presently.

The Midland Terminal Railway, heir to the abbreviated destinies of the once transcontinental Colorado Midland, inherited from the C. M. a steel-sheathed car, named the *Cascade*, No. 100, which for structural considerations not available to the record was acceptable for interchange and often took Bert Carlton and his family and friends to New York and other destinations both in the East and in California. "It was a wooden car with steel underframe, very ornate and comfortable with Pintsch lamps," recalls Mrs. Albert Carlton, "but I was afraid of it in mainline trains where the speed was high. One time I was left to arrange for its hauling over the Santa Fe between Chicago and Colorado Springs via Garden City, Kansas. Nobody understood how it happened, but it was put on the end of the *Fast Mail*, the fastest train on the line. Talk about crack-the-whip, I was black and blue for weeks afterward."

Charlie McNeill had a modern, all-steel car called *Mather* which he kept stored at the Short Line yards and later with the Colorado Midland at the Springs, but its wheel base was so long as to render it inoperable over the sharp curves of the C. S. & C. C. D. and it was eventually sold to an Eastern carrier as a business car. Just why he owned a car that, locally at least, was something of a white elephant has never been properly explained in the body of Colorado folklore, but legend has it that he won it in a poker game from Charles Boettcher, venerable Colorado pioneer and owner of the Brown Palace Hotel in Denver.

Unlike many of his mining contemporaries in the private car club, Daniel C. Jackling did not achieve wealth through the agency of precious metals. True, he had started out at Cripple Creek where, as a partner of Spencer Penrose and Charles Tutt, he had built a highly successful reducing mill for Cripple Creek ores at Canyon City, but his obsession was a process for recovering copper from low yield ore and in 1904 at Bingham, the Utah Copper Company was born. Tutt and Penrose had grubstaked Jackling and were in on the ground floor when Utah Copper began paying the dividends which have amounted to more than $500,000,000 over the years. Tutt was pocketing $100,000 a month out of his share of the deal; Penrose double that amount and Jackling himself was obviously a nominee for the private car club in a big, emphatic way. His first *Cyprus*, built by Pullman in 1909, was sold shortly afterwards to Julius Fleischman and thence, as *Hopedale,* passed to the Pittsburgh & West Virginia as one of its two office cars, both of them with aristocratic antecedents. The P. & W. V.'s other car had been Henry Clay Frick's *Westmoreland* and retained this name in its latter ownership. Come 1913 and Colonel Jackling ordered a second *Cyprus* from Pullman which for three decades was a landmark on private car tracks and sidings in Utah, Nevada and Montana, wherever copper was mined, milled or rumored. In 1938 Gilbert Kneiss took a photograph of second *Cyprus* at San Jose, California, at which time its nameboards showed its home carrier to be the Nevada Northern, a copper railroad serving the vast open pit mines at Ely, Nevada.

Of special interest, however, were the smaller initials at each end of the venerable varnish car of the Bullfrog & Goldfield and the Las Vegas & Tonopah, railroads long since vanished from the *Official Guide* in which Jackling had been interested at the turn of the century. Their rights of way had long been reclaimed by Death Valley and the Nevada desert, but their initials went with *Cyprus* as souvenirs of departed things in the golden annals of Western mining.

Bert Carlton's private varnish which he maintained as biggest mine owner of Cripple Creek and largest single stockholder in the Colorado Midland Railway was the direct agency and beginning of one of the most hilarious controversies in the annals of the centennial state and one whose details are still recounted with gusto by old-timers around the bar in The Players in Gramercy Park where both the participants were members in their lifetime.

In 1914 an artist-reporter team on the staff of *Collier's Weekly,* now vanished but then an important periodical of fact and opinion, were Wallace Morgan and Julian Street. Morgan was a fine pen and ink sketch illustrator of the type even then all but displaced by photography and the halftone and Street, a thirty-five year old feature writer with a national reputation.

On a swing-around of the United States for a series commissioned for *Collier's* by its editor, Mark Sullivan, Street and Morgan arrived at Colorado Springs to profile "Little Lunnon" for the magazine's large circulation and were, in the natural course of events, entertained by Carlton, Spencer Penrose, Charlie Tutt and other millionaires whose fortunes derived from the mines of Cripple Creek across the shoulder of Pike's Peak. Having seen one side of the medal among the stylish homes and clubs of the Springs, Street voiced an interest in seeing the fabled mines from which such splendors derived, and Carlton promised that next day his car, *Colorado,* would be at Street's and Morgan's disposal to go up the mountain over the Colorado Springs & Cripple Creek District Railroad which was also a Carlton property. The car boasted an impeccable English butler and limitless resources of rye which was then the accepted wine of the Colorado countryside.

Next day Carlton was preoccupied and Street and Morgan made the trip alone, sampling the cellar and marveling at the scenery of the Short Line run which, a few years earlier, had prompted President Roosevelt to say it was "a ride that bankrupts the English language." The Carlton car was a strain on the Short Line's motive power, the trip was slow and its distinguished passengers arrived in what might be described as impressionable condition. Next day when Street consulted his notes and prepared to send in his weekly dispatch to *Collier's*, his entire recollections of Cripple Creek seemed to center about Myers Avenue and its professional residents. Myers Avenue was the town's red light district and its inhabitants were exclusively soiled doves. Street's story, which appeared shortly thereafter, apprised the nation that Cripple Creek had the biggest red light district in the West and practically nothing else.

The *Collier's* spread occasioned grief and indignation when it reached Cripple Creek. Its substantial residents, according to Marshall Sprague, the district's official historian, "sprang to its defense with the fury of the farmers of Lexington." Back in New York Sullivan was deluged with demands for an apology. The *Cripple Creek Times* spoke disparagingly of Street as "a phantom-brained murderer of truth" and hinted that the reporter had simply followed his own debased inclinations in exploring the town.

Sullivan stood by his reporter and no retraction was forthcoming. Cripple seethed with frustration and the incident received a resounding national press. All America was enchanted with the uproar. But Cripple had the last laugh. At the next meeting of the town aldermen, a brief statement was handed the local stringer for the Associated Press, and from Bangor to San Diego the nation was convulsed next morning with inextinguishable laughter.

The A. P. dispatch read:

TONIGHT THE CITY COUNCIL OF CRIPPLE CREEK, COLORADO, APPROVED UNANIMOUSLY CHANGING THE NAME OF MEYERS AVENUE TO JULIAN STREET.

Street never lived it down and blamed his undoing until his dying day on Bert Carlton and the rye aboard the Colorado Midland's car No. 99.

A private car anecdote that has been firmly established in the folklore of the Southwest concerns the time Judge Roy Bean, "Justice West of the Pecos" and the peer of Big Foot Wallace and Sam Houston in the regional mythology of Texas, flagged down the special train of Jay Gould. Judge Roy Bean was, of course, a national character of the time whose courtroom decisions combined frontier common sense and eccentricity to such a picturesque degree that they frequently made the wire news and Judge Bean was almost as well known in New York as in West Texas and perhaps more favorably.

Judge Bean greatly admired personal publicity and he read the newspapers of the day assiduously, so that he was apprised well in advance that

Jay Gould, who at the time controlled the greatest railroad empire in the world, would pass through Langtry on the Southern Pacific where court was holden by Judge Roy Bean. Bean sent to San Antonio for a case of the best champagne and when Gould's special train of private varnish slowed for orders at Langtry depot, he thoughtfully waved a large red bandana where the engineer couldn't help seeing it. It wasn't a formal or recognized train signal, but it suggested danger and with Jay Gould, his cow, personal physician, members of the family and assorted railroad brass ranging from the general superintendent of the Missouri Pacific to the receiver for Erie, the hogger couldn't be too careful. The train ground to a stop. The rear shack hastened down the line with torpedoes and fusees. The Gould private cow mooed up in the baggage car. Miss Helen Gould, the old gentleman's daughter, came out on the platform of her own car *Stranrear*, and Gould himself raised a window in the salon of *Atalanta* to see what was toward. This was nothing more than an order board stop and Gould knew it. He knew all about railroads, his own and other people's.

Through the open window Judge Bean introduced himself. "You must be Jay Gould," he said looking pleased. "I'm Roy Bean. Happy to make your acquaintance."

Like all the rest of the world, Gould had heard tell about the Justice West of the Pecos and he imagined it would do no harm to the Southern Pacific if the train paused long enough for a visit to Bean's courtroom saloon. Followed by his doctor and daughter, the tycoon descended. Judge Bean, always thoughtful, had plastered his abode of justice with newspaper photographs of Jay Gould and when he suggested a nice glass of chilled champagne Gould was enchanted. It was the one drink his physician allowed him and he sent the steward for a plate of ladyfingers from the galley of *Atalanta*.

The station agent by now joined the party and a good time was had by all with Jay Gould laughing heartily, a thing he didn't do often, at Judge Roy Bean's comical ways and everybody drinking Judge Bean's good French champagne. Pretty soon Gould looked at his Hamilton and allowed they had better be on their way before the division got tied up. The engineer whistled off and the station agent returned to his office where the circuit from San Antonio was smoking with urgent inquiries from the chief dispatcher: "Where Gould special? Where Gould? Due Langtry three hours, due Del Rio two hours. What in hell goes on here?"

To which the unruffled man of dots and dashes sent the answer that has become a classic, forever enshrined in the folklore of the Lone Star State: "Jay Gould, Roy Bean, Me spending afternoon drinking champagne, eating ladyfingers. Champagne, Gould special both gone."

As Robert J. Casey says in telling the story in "The Texas Border," that was one day when Roy Bean made the front pages all across the country.

PENNSYLVANIA RAILROAD

SPECIAL TRAIN

CONVEYING

H. R. H. PRINCE HENRY OF PRUSSIA

PULLMAN DINING CAR "WILLARD"

WINE LIST

CHAMPAGNES

PIPER-HEIDSIECK, SEC, WHITE LABEL	MOET & CHANDON, BRUT IMPERIAL
G. H. MUMM & CO., EXTRA DRY	POMMERY & GRENO, VIN SEC
POMMERY & GRENO, VIN NATURE	RUINART, BRUT IRROY, BRUT

GERMAN CHAMPAGNE
RHEINGOLD

VINTAGE CHAMPAGNES
PIPER-HEIDSIECK, BRUT

AMERICAN CHAMPAGNES
COOK'S IMPERIAL, EXTRA DRY   GOLD SEAL, SPECIAL DRY   GREAT WESTERN

CLARETS
ST. JULIEN   PONTET CANET   CHATEAU LAFITTE, 1881   MEDOC

SAUTERNES
GRAVES, DRY   CHATEAU LATOUR BLANCHE, 1886   CHATEAU YQUEM

BURGUNDIES (RED)
BEAUNE, 1889   POMMARD, 1889   CHAMBERTIN, 1881

BURGUNDIES (WHITE)
CHABLIS, 1887

SPARKLING WINE
CABINET MOSELLE

RHINE WINES
DEIDESHEIMER   NIERSTEINER   LIEBFRAUMILCH, 1891

MOSELLE WINES
ZELTINGER   ERDENER TREPPCHEN

CALIFORNIA WINES
LA ROSA, ZINFANDEL, RED   CABINET RIESLING, WHITE
UNFERMENTED GRAPE JUICE, CRYSTAL BRAND

SHERRY WINE
AMONTILLADO PASADO

BRANDIES
OTARD DUPUY & CO., 1878   V. S. O. P. COGNAC, 1840
G. F. CHAMPAGNE COGNAC, 1811

RYE AND BOURBON WHISKIES
WILSON   HUNTER   OLD CROW   PEPPER   EXTRA OLD RYE

SCOTCH AND IRISH WHISKIES
JOHN DEWAR'S SPECIAL   JOHN DEWAR'S EXTRA SPECIAL
KING WILLIAM V. O. P.   JAMESON'S IRISH

ALE
BASS & CO.'S PALE ALE, WHITE LABEL

BEERS (IMPORTED)
PILSNER   CULMBACHER

BEERS (DOMESTIC)
PABST'S BLUE RIBBON   MAERZEN (HEINRICH)   ANHEUSER-BUSCH

MINERAL WATERS
WHITE ROCK   APOLLINARIS   LONDONDERRY LITHIA   POLAND SPARKLING
GERMAN SELTZERS   DELATOUR SODA   SYPHONS   HATHORN
CLUB SODA   GINGER ALE, CANTRELL & COCHRAN
CHAMPAGNE CIDER

ARTHUR D. DUBIN COLLECTION

Menu on Pennsylvania special train for Prince Henry of Prussia shows that, before the 1914 war, visiting royalty fared well aboard the steamcars of the democracy.

AGREEMENT, dated this 4th day of May, 1916, between THE PULLMAN

COMPANY, hereinafter called the same, and MR. H. E. HUNTINGTON OF LOS ANGELES,

CALIFORNIA, hereinafter called the Purchaser.

The Pullman Company will construct, sell and transfer to the

Purchaser

——————————— One (1) Steel private car,——————————

                                        to be built in accordance

with Pullman General Specifications dated March 14, 1916, and reissued May

4, 1916 (and drawings mentioned therein), attached hereto and made a part of this

agreement, and will deliver the same at Chicago, Illinois, at the earliest

practicable date, for the sum of Forty one thousand ($41,000.00) Dollars; this

price being inclusive of all equipment enumerated in paragraph #90 of attached

specifications, including kitchen and pantry equipment, glassware, silverware,

crockery, chinaware, bed and table linen.

Terms of Payment — Cash in New York or Chicago funds as car is

delivered, as above.

Car to be subject to inspection and acceptance by an authorized

representative of the Purchaser at the Works of The Pullman Company, Pullman,

Illinois.

Executed in duplicate the day and year first herein written.

                        THE PULLMAN COMPANY,

                By _____
                            Manager Sales Department.

When the Prince of Wales, later King Edward VII, visited the United States in 1868, he arrived from Canada aboard a car specially built for the occasion by the directors of the Grand Trunk Railroad, and the youthful heir to the throne of England is shown in its drawing room on the page opposite. The sketch appeared in the *New York Illustrated News* which achieved reflected respectability by association on the center table with the *New York Times* and *New York Tribune*. With him are the Duke of Newcastle and General Williams. When the Prince's younger brother, Prince Arthur of Conaught arrived in New York ten years later aboard a car furnished by the Hudson River Railroad (BELOW) the most elegant equipment available still had a wood stove in its state apartment.

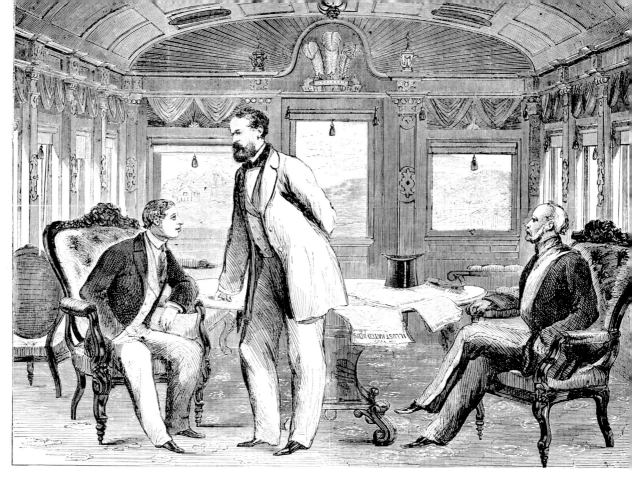

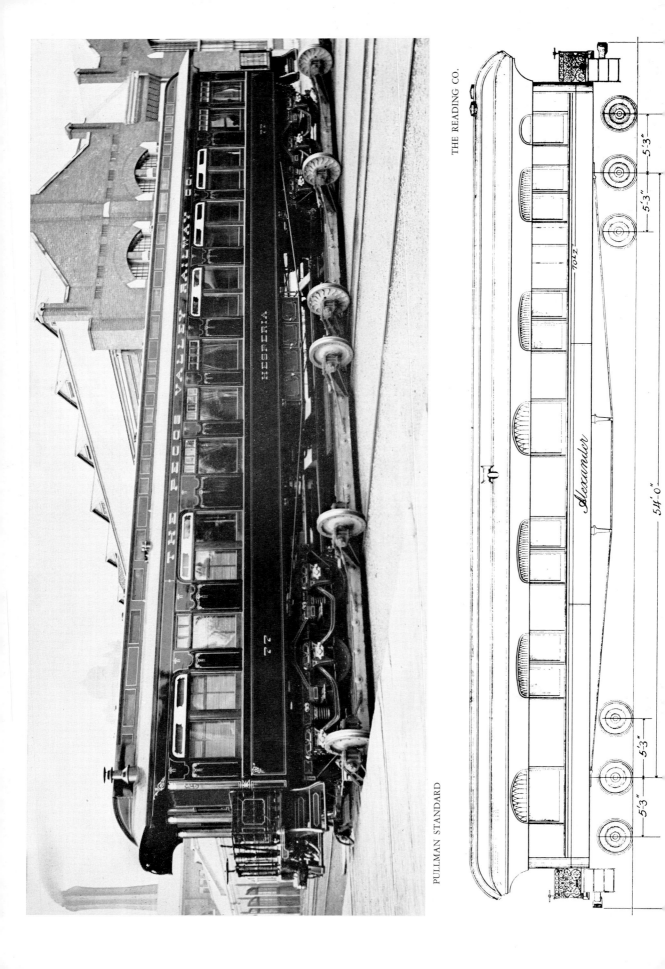

PULLMAN STANDARD

THE READING CO.

PULLMAN STANDARD

Superb examples of private varnish in the era of open platforms at both ends are *Alexander* and *Hesperia*, shown on the page opposite, the latter for the order in 1892 of the Pecos Valley Railroad in the golden age of railway expansion in Texas. On this page is represented a neighboring carrier, the San Antonio & Aranzas Pass, known to history for the expensive tastes in rolling stock and locomotives which led to its eventual bankruptcy. The handsome interior of its private car *Electric*, Pullman built in 1889 for General Manager B. F. Yoakum, contributed to its eventual insolvency.

Most celebrated of the private cars of California's millionaires of bonanza days was James Ben Ali Haggin's *Salvator,* built by Pullman in 1890. Aboard it San Francisco society had memorable moments at Del Monte and its owner regularly visited his stock farms in Kentucky and his New York town house within its luxurious confines. On these two pages are various views of *Salvator.* Not shown are its gold dinner service from Shreve's, its French chef from Foyot's in Paris or its magnificent patron who, according to Gertrude Atherton "Always entered a room looking as though he hated someone."

A familiar property on the private car sidings at Del Monte, at Yosemite and wherever else fashionable San Franciscans foregathered in the opulent nineties was the private car of Charles Crocker, the *Mishawaka* which had been built to the rail tycoon's personal order by Pullman in 1890. Aboard it Tevises, Haggins, Sharons, Fairs and other owners of everything in sight in California attended the stately weddings which characterized the San Francisco decade, drank Pisco punch and displayed the latest Paris frocks as occasion might demand, so that *Mishawaka* in time became very much a local institution among well bred residents of Nob Hill, one with opening nights at the California Theater and private supper rooms at the Poodle Dog.

Three views of the private Pullman of Charles Crocker, named *Mishawaka* after the Indiana town where Mrs. Crocker, the former Mary Ann Deming had been born.

THREE PHOTOS:
PULLMAN STANDARD

ALEXANDER

The Ineffable Alexanders

On these and following pages are shown aspects of two successive cars named *Alexander* built by Pullman for Angus Archibald McLeod, President of the Philadelphia & Reading Railroad.

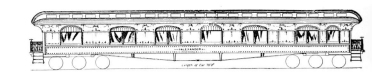

Archetype and supreme example of the carbuilder's *expertise*, the first *Alexander*, outshopped by Pullman in 1890 to the exacting specifications of Angus Archibald McLeod, President of the Philadelphia & Reading Railroad, was perhaps the most beautiful of all private cars in an age when owners of such properties aspired to perfection. Shown on an earlier page on the transfer table at Pullman, it reflected the lavish personal tastes of an affluent connoisseur with the means for their gratification. The first of McLeod's two *Alexanders* was assigned to the Reading as its home road, but the record shows that it was an entirely personal property and not carried as a company car. Depicted below is the master bedroom of first *Alexander;* on the page opposite the same apartment on second *Alexander* opening directly off its French Empire furnished drawing-observation salon. McLeod's second car boasted a more satisfactory compartmentation, electric illumination and other improvements over its predecessor in an age when competition in the elegance sweepstakes was of cut-throat proportion among railroad tycoons everywhere in the United States.

Neither compromise nor spurious modesty were any part of the formidable A. A. McLeod, the Pennsylvania perfectionist, and when in 1892 he ordered from Pullman a second *Alexander* incorporating improvements over his original p.v. of that name, he had the nameboards engrossed with the legend "Private Car." The ground plan of *Alexander II* shows the progress achieved by 1892 in making private varnish a self-contained microcosm of luxury and convenience.

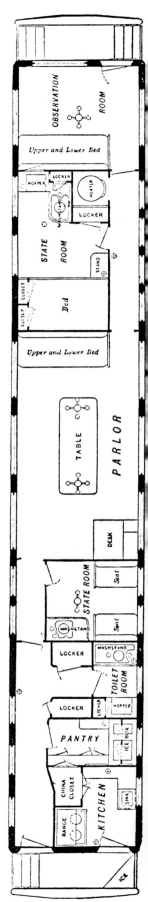

Autocrat, perfectionist and a swaggering tycoon of the frock coat age, A. A. McLeod was also well connected socially and *Alexander II* was a familiar property on the private car tracks of the land from Palm Beach to Louisville wherever the sidewhiskered moguls of transport foregathered to bow to each other from brass bound observation platforms of overpowering magnificence. Here a corner of the dining salon provides a suggestive glimpse of one of the sumptuously furnished master staterooms beyond.

One of Pullman's masterpieces of private car design was *Virginia* built in 1892 to the personal specifications of E. R. Bacon, President of the Baltimore & Ohio South Western Railroad and shown on this and the opposite page. Bacon demanded and received a varnish car to which he could point with pride and aboard which he could ride in unabashed comfort and splendor in an age when railroad presidents delighted to enter their private conveyances in wildly competitive elegance sweepstakes. It was an age that unabashedly admired excellence and elegance in private cars and in 1882 the *New York Times* commented rapturously on "three private cars recently built by the Pullman Palace Car Company that are indeed palaces on wheels. One was constructed for Hugh J. Jewett, President of Erie; another for Henry Villard, President of the Oregon Railway & Navigation Company; and a third for T. W. Pierce, President of the Sunset Route in Texas . . . All are handsome in the extreme. That of Mr. Jewett, the *Ramapo*, is heavily inlaid with costly woods and magnificently upholstered. They cost about $20,000 each." As an indication of what private cars might do to a man, Robert Garrett for many years prior to his death suffered from the delusion that he was the Prince of Wales. Thousands of dollars were spent by his family to humor this whim. An expert on heraldry and English court etiquette was imported and actors were hired on a permanent basis to impersonate court officials and pose as ambassadors and archbishops. Scots bagpipers played him to dinner and he dressed daily in the uniform of a different British regiment. If private car grandeur led to this misfortune, few of Garrett's contemporaries heeded the warning.

The best of everything went into the building and furnishing of *Virginia* whose dining salon is shown here, and to keep time in its observation room Pullman commissioned Seth Thomas in Waterbury, Connecticut, master clockmaker to the American people, to design the ornate and handsome timepiece reproduced on the page opposite.

The super-plush Pullman exhibit train from the Columbian Exposition of 1893 comprising five cars of superlative varnish with a diner, library car, barber shop and lounge car of breath-taking magnificence (PAGE OPPOSITE) was just the ticket for such archmillionaires as Jay Gould's son George when he wished to cross the continent in style. It was aboard this string of p.v. splendor that the younger Gould acted as matchmaker for his sister Anna when she was being courted by the French adventurer and titled deadbeat, the Count Boni de Castellane. Anna became the Countess de Castellane and, after her husband had spent $6,000,000 of her money, most of it deriving from Erie, Missouri Pacific and other Gould railroads, she divorced de Castellane and married his cousin and thus became the Duchess of Talleyrand et Périgord. Other well placed Americans occasionally retained the Pullman Exposition Train, but none in such style as the Goulds who required full evening dress of their guests *en route* and had them served off gold plates by footmen in knee breeches. The footmen, de Castellane noted in his diary, wore full formal house livery with tailcoats and ruffled shirts precisely as was required of waiters in French luxury travel of the time of the Compagnie International des Wagons-Lits et des Grands Expres Européens. de Castellane felt at home with the Goulds.

E. S. HAMMACK

Either Harry Ogden or Walter Yaeger sketched "The Chef in His Glory" for *Frank Leslie's Illustrated Newspaper* in his capacity as staff artist on Leslie's celebrated expedition aboard the cars to report the American West. In a generation that drank Hock and Champagne for breakfast in the diner, the chef was monarch of all he surveyed from the Plutonian region dominated by what the car-builder's catalogues of the period described as a "Director's Car Model Range & Hot Water Heater." On the page opposite, travellers found eye-popping details of magnificence aboard Pullman's diner *La Rabida* on view at the Chicago World's Fair of 1893. *La Rabida* was available for private rental to parties whose requirements ran to an entire private train of five of the most stylish cars ever produced by the car building industry in the United States, and its lessors included such notables as George Gould and J. P. Morgan the Elder.

PULLMAN STANDARD

The observation drawing rooms of *Isabella* (PAGE OPPOSITE) and *The Virginia City* show the different possibilities of treatment and decor of similar private car apartments six decades apart. *Isabella* with a Romanesque overall decor and a Gothic ceiling that might have been copied from William of Sens' choir at Canterbury was built by Pullman as the showpiece of its five-car private train exhibited at the World's Columbian Exposition at Chicago in 1893. *Isabella* was classed as an observation-sleeper and had eight sections of upper and lower each, and a bathtub. In later years it ran in general service and available to the public. The also Pullman-built p.v. *The Virginia City* was rebuilt and decorated by Robert Hanley of Hollywood sixty years later in Venetian Renaissance Baroque with marble topped tables, Venetian glass chandeliers and a ceiling of applied gold leaf.

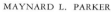
MAYNARD L. PARKER

Under a dome of many colored glass and enthroned in a Koch's Patent barber chair, nabobs who chartered Pullman's princely five car private train might have their whiskers curled and singed aboard the combination baggage and club car *Marchena.* On one occasion when crossing the continent to attend a conference of Anglican bishops in San Francisco, J. P. Morgan, Sr., ordered wine racks built in the baggage compartment to ensure safe transit for his favorite Rhinewine.

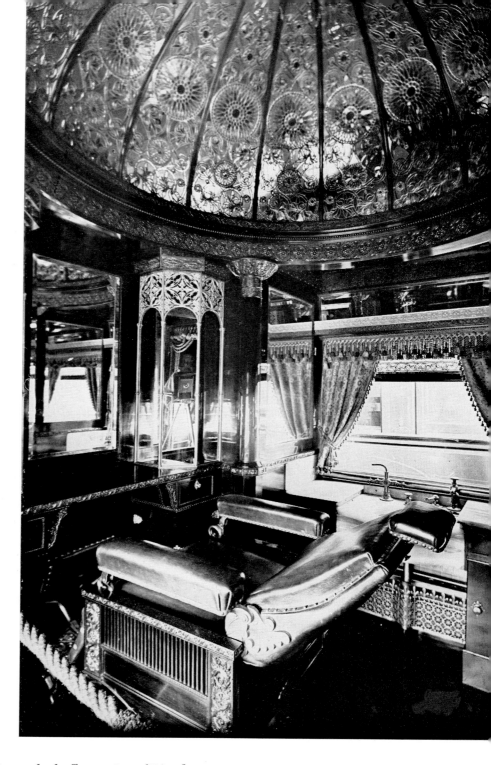

Opposite is shown the buffet section of *Marchena* where guests of J. P. Morgan the Elder and George Gould smoked Prince des Galles fancy tales and discussed the destinies of United States Steel. After venison steaks and Mumms in the diner *La Rabida* they could retire to silk sheets in the sleeper *America,* all for $500 a day including a complete staff of porters, valets, chefs and waiters.

Just what effect the decor and appointments of the Columbian Exposition Pullman diner *La Rabida* may have had on the digestion of its occupants isn't recorded but the car was universally felt to be about as stylish as anything could be. Aboard it, when its train was chartered by George Gould, the Count Boni de Castellane recorded that all the guests dressed scrupulously in full evening attire.

More austere than *La Rabida* was the Burlington's business car No. 200 aboard which during his long presidency of the system (1881-1901) Charles Elliott Perkins, a Boston Brahmin of perfumed ancestry, rode literally hundreds of thousands of miles across Western America. If his party was larger than could comfortably be accommodated aboard this venerable car, there was No. 100, affectionately known as "Old Hundred" which could be used en suite. If schedules were inconvenient, the cars ran as a special train movement, and with Perkins in those halcyon times rode members of his family, business acquaintances and friends, Buffalo Bill Cody among them, to far places of an as yet untamed continent. Perkins kept a log of No. 200 covering its years of faithful service with such pleasant entries as "After dinner we adjourned to 'Old Hundred' where Miss Woelfle (the governess) much to the enjoyment of all, played on the zither." Ah, far away and long ago time!

Wine cellar aboard the *Oneonta* was designed for vintage wines that matured in the nineties and were fit for the table of a California arch millionaire: the Musignys and Richebourgs and Romanee-Contis of '78, '81, '84 and '86, Champagnes of '80, the splendors of claret in years now forgotten save in ancient cellar-books and, perhaps, the greatest of all wines of the entire nineteenth century, the epic Lafite '64, a magnificence of Bordeaux that was alive and potable for sixty years to become legendary in the annals of France.

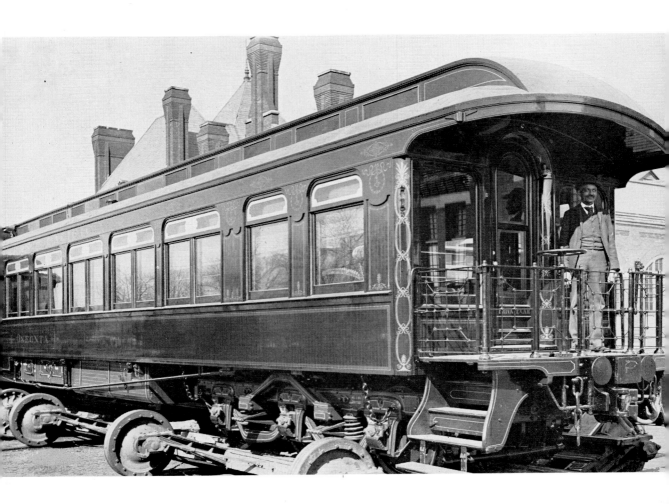

Although few would have accused Collis P. Huntington of sentimentality, three pieces of railroad rolling stock, a locomotive on the roster of the Central Pacific and two private railroad cars built for his personal use *en suite* and assigned to the Southern Pacific, were named for the upstate New York community in which the future man of millions made his first business stake before coming West. The below photograph shows the sitting room of the master apartment aboard the first *Oneonta* with its dressing room and stateroom beyond. Aboard *Oneonta* and *Oneonta II*, the empire builder rode thousands of miles to supervise the affairs of the all-powerful Southern Pacific system and, by indirection, the state of California which it all but owned.

PULLMAN STANDARD

The builders of Collis P. Huntington's *Oneonta* were liberal with washroom and dressing room space for the comfort of the powerful old moneybags of the Southern Pacific. The handbasin and commode, shown in the foreground of this photograph, gave a man room to turn around aboard his own private car while rolling over his own railroad through the California countryside which, in a manner of speaking, was his own private feudal domain.

The master suite of *Oneonta*, reaching in a vista of sleeping compartment, dressing room and private sitting room is shown here across the somewhat rumpled berth of the owner. The car's profligate use of interior space and grand disregard for economy of compartmentation is explained by the circumstance that the old gentleman usually rode abroad on company business without his family and that secretaries and other functionaries could be accommodated less handsomely.

TWO PHOTOS:
PULLMAN STANDARD

TWO PHOTOS: PULLMAN STANDARD

A *rara avis* in the category of simon-pure private cars with no company overtones about it was Collis P. Huntington's *Oneonta II* in that it was, in a matter of speaking, a private car second class. As supreme arbiter of the affairs of the Southern and Central Pacific Railroad, Huntington traveled in style between California and Washington where he dominated the railroad lobby in the national capital. *Oneonta II* was designed to supplement *Oneonta* in the matter of the owner's luggage, servants and occasional overflow of guests. Access from one car to the other was through enclosed vestibules, one of the earliest instances of this practice in private cars. Thus accommodated in two cars *en suite*, the old gentleman rode at prudent acceleration across the continent, the entire distance being traversed over his own or their subsidiary lines. Like other members of the private car club including President Franklin Roosevelt, he seldom went faster than thirty miles an hour.

Built at Pullman
1894
For B. C. Berens, Esq.

WEST VIRGINIA CENTRAL & PITTSBURGH

KATHARYNE

Distinguished for a classic purity of line and refinement of decorative treatment, the private car *Katharyne* with no business car nonsense about it rests on the transfer table at Pullman with the venerable Pullman clock tower for background. *Katharyne* was built in 1894 to the specifications of R. C. Kerens as his personal property and assigned as its home railroad to the West Virginia Central & Pittsburgh of which its owner was a director and important stockholder. Kerens was also a heavy investor in the St. Louis, Iron Mountain & Southern, a vice president of the St. Louis-Southwestern and finally was associated with Montana's peerless Senator William Andrews Clark in the incorporation of the San Pedro, Los Angeles & Salt Lake Railroad, now the Los Angeles Division of the Union Pacific. Over all these far-flung interests *Katharyne* transported Kerens and his friends in expedition and comfort, sometimes pausing at the four towns named for its owner in Texas, Arkansas, West Virginia and California, a geographic immortality accorded few other railroaders.

PULLMAN STANDARD

In the painting by Howard Fogg on the page opposite is shown the Southern Pacific's Wagner-built and splendid private car *San Emidio,* available to directors of the company and friends in high places among the well-born and well-to-do of San Francisco before the fire. Assured of both of these qualifications is its occupant of the moment, William Sanders Tevis, son of patrician old Lloyd Tevis, one of San Francisco's aristocrats from the Deep South whose association in such profitable ventures as Wells Fargo & Company and the mines of James Ben Ali Haggin had made him rich as well as socially impeccable. William Tevis and his family are en route aboard *San Emidio* to the Tevis summer estate at the south end of Lake Tahoe, a property recently acquired from another California notable, Lucky Baldwin. *San Emidio* is depicted rolling over the Southern Pacific's single track of the time at Emigrant Gap with the High Sierra for a backdrop. In his galley, luncheon is being prepared by the Tevis chef, William Henderson, a notable practitioner even in San Francisco of 1902.

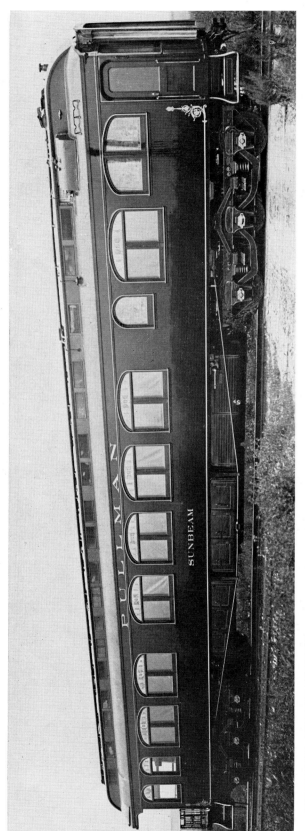

TWO PHOTOS: PULLMAN STANDARD

Symbols of an age of established order and tangible properties, the Prince Albert frock coat, the silk top hat and the open platform private railway car met for a photographic moment in 1895 at Cleveland as William McKinley, shortly to be President of the United States, boarded his Big Four private car for a campaign tour of the Middle West. Beyond the Missouri he rode aboard the Union Pacific's No. 100, whose interior is shown at the left. Approximately a decade later the golden age of private cars reached its apotheosis in *Sunbeam* and *Santa Susana*, each added to the Pullman private car rental pool in 1906.

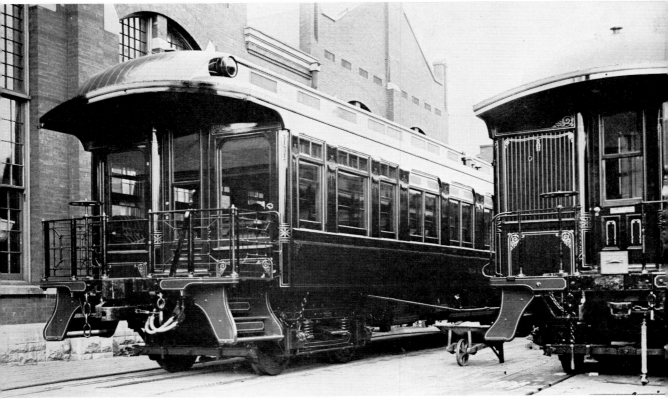

A churlish observer or one conditioned to the austerity of twentieth century *moderne* might take exception to the decor of one of *Mohaska's* drawing rooms as highly over-embellished, but the well-to-do of 1895 who chartered the car from Pullman's private car pool for $50 a day considered it fetching in a conservative sort of way. On the page opposite is the rarely beautiful observation platform of the Southern Pacific's first *Golden Gate* and (BELOW) the Denver & Rio Grande's *Ballyclare* for the personal occupancy of General William Jackson Palmer. In 1890 when *Ballyclare* was delivered, the Rio Grande was in transition from narrow to standard gauge and still adhered to light equipment with four-wheel trucks.

GEORGIA NORTHERN

MOULTRIE

M. WAKEFIELD

Few cars in the p.v. record have the long history of Henry M. Flagler's *Rambler* that came into existence as No. 100 of the St. Johns & Indian River Railway, one of the antecedent companies that was eventually absorbed into the Florida East Coast. The car was built in 1886 by Jackson & Sharp at Wilmington, in the bright May morning of private varnish and lasted on its trucks and in operating order for sixty years until the sun was declining on railroading everywhere. The initials of its first owner, H.M.F., were incorporated in the decor of the observation salon near the ceiling, and in 1934 when it was purchased from the Florida East Coast to become the personal conveyance of Charles W. Pidcock of the Georgia Northern, the silverware still bore the monogram of the St. Johns & Indian River. As the Flagler car it had been in the consist of the first train to cross the causeway to Key West in 1912 and photographs show Flagler descending there from its open platform amidst a sea of silk hats. Renamed *Moultrie* on the Georgia Northern, it was a familiar sight on the Pidcock network of Georgia short lines that included the Albany & Northern and the resoundingly named Georgia, Ashburn, Sylvester & Camilla. When an end came to its travels in 1947, it passed into the possession of a railroad man and was set on the ground at Harrisonburg, Virginia, as a summerhouse for D. W. Thomas, President of the Chesapeake Western. Full of years and honors, it passed to an estate of *otium cum dignitate* among the rose gardens of the Old South.

GEORGIA NORTHERN

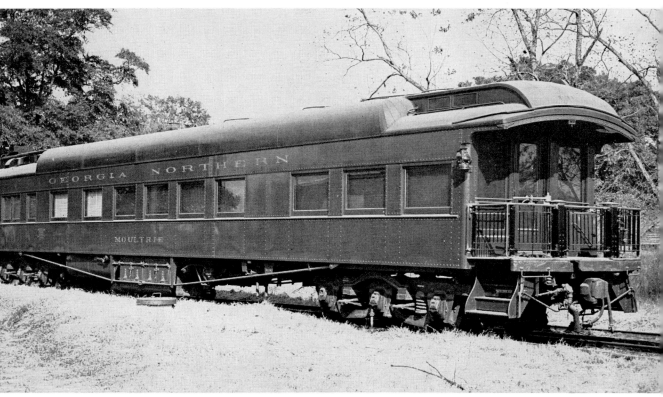

Finding that, after all, he needed a business car and tiring of borrowing them from the Central of Georgia and other connecting carriers, Charles Pidcock of the Georgia Northern in 1958 purchased the air-conditioned, Pullman-built *Mount Vernon* from the Chicago & Eastern Illinois. Here it is shown renamed and as second *Moultrie* on one of the most stylish short lines in the record.

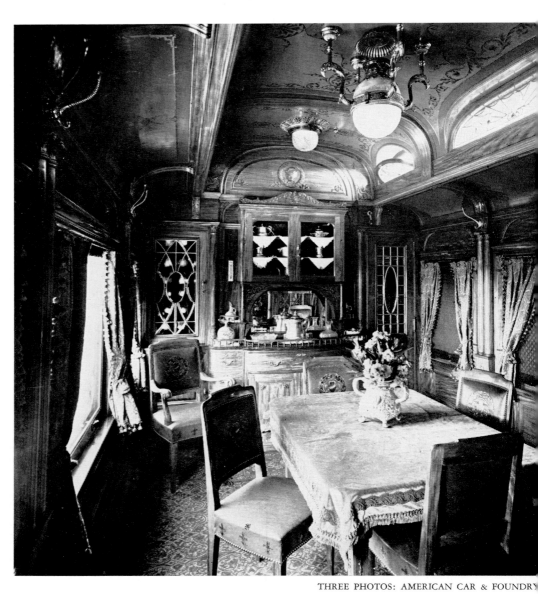

THREE PHOTOS: AMERICAN CAR & FOUNDRY

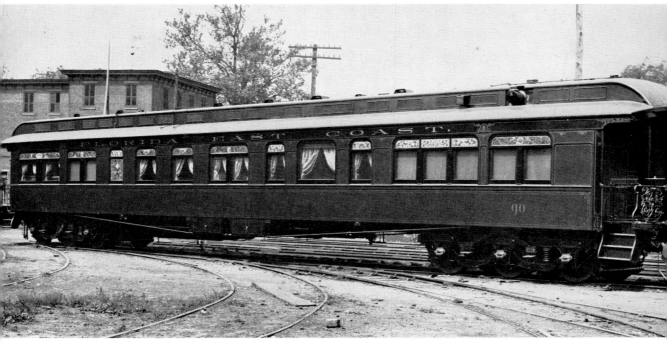

As a partner of John D. and William Rockefeller in Standard Oil and with a resulting fortune of $200,000,000, Henry M. Flagler could afford to be, and was a perfectionist. At St. Augustine he built the Ponce de Leon to be the finest hotel in the world. Thinking to improve on perfection, he then built the sensational Royal Poinciana at Palm Beach and as an afterthought he built the city of West Palm Beach "for my help." To serve his hotels he then built the Florida East Coast Railway and to ride his railroad in style he had American Car & Foundry build for his personal use the F.E.C.'s Car No. 90, later known as *Alicia*. As shown on this and the opposite page, No. 90 eschewed the mahogany paneling and velvet draperies characteristic of most private cars of the time in favor of satinwood appointments and colorful linen window curtains appropriate to the tropical climate of Florida. It provided a nice ride for an aging millionaire en route from one feudal domain to the next and owning almost everything in sight between them.

On the page opposite is perhaps the rarest of all photographs depicting a group of charter members of the private car club with an entire private train in the background against a setting that was to become inseparably associated with the private car way of life as the years passed. It was taken March 14, 1896 when the first train on Henry M. Flagler's Florida East Coast Railway arrived at Palm Beach over the Flagler Bridge and came to rest on the private car track of the spanking new Royal Poinciana Hotel. Society's outriders in derby hats and three inch stiff collars included, from left to right, Colonel Philip Lydig, Helen Morton (veiled in mourning), Gladys Vanderbilt, holding a pineapple, Amy Townsend, Captain A. T. Rose, Mrs. Cornelius Vanderbilt, Edith Bishop, Mabel Gerry, Thomas Cushing, Edward Livingston, Dudley Winthrop, Lispenard Stewart, Harry Payne Whitney, Sybil Sherman and Cornelius Vanderbilt II.

Henry M. Flagler, the creator of Palm Beach, slept soundly in the nicely paneled satin-wood master stateroom of the Florida East Coast No. 90 built for the Standard Oil archmillionaire by American Car & Foundry.

West coast of Florida counterpart of the East Coast's Flagler was Henry Bradley Plant whose railroad system serving Tampa and the Gulf Ports was represented in the field of private varnish by the two handsome cars each Pullman-built and each No. 100 shown on the page opposite. Plant was jealous of Flagler's aloof social connections and the exalted patronage he achieved for his East Coast resorts. Meeting Flagler one day emerging from Delmonico's in New York, Plant asked: "Friend Flagler, just where is this place I've heard about called Palm Beach?" "Friend Plant," replied the Rockefeller partner with a smile, "just follow the crowd." On this page is the interior of the Suwanee River's No. 100 showing a business-like approach combined with comfort and utility.

Another of the many business and private cars to which, as a collector of railroads, Jay Gould had access was the Missouri Pacific's fine official transport *St. Louis*, built by Pullman in 1889 when the Mopac was one of Gould's most resounding properties. Rich, solid and business-like in its appointments, *St. Louis* still managed to suggest that the affairs conducted aboard it were those of a railroad of wealth and importance that could afford the best of everything for its executives and made a practice of doing just that.

PULLMAN STANDARD

Following the example of the younger James Gordon Bennett, who found it convenient on his frequent trans-Atlantic trips between Paris and New York to keep a milch cow on the foredeck of his yacht *Lysistrata,* Jay Gould maintained a traveling cow in the baggage car of his private train whenever he was far from home. A dyspeptic whose diet was largely limited to fresh milk, French champagne and ladyfingers, the last of these prepared fresh daily by a pastry chef in the galley of his private car, the man of money found a cow whose butterfat content agreed with him and kept her close at hand. Gould's not inconsiderable entourage included chefs, a private physician and a multiplicity of secretaries each of whom were familiar with the affairs of certain Gould railroads, and two of these are shown awaiting the master's will aboard one of his several business cars in the below photograph, rare because it shows personalities in a private car of the nineties.

ROBERT RICHARDS

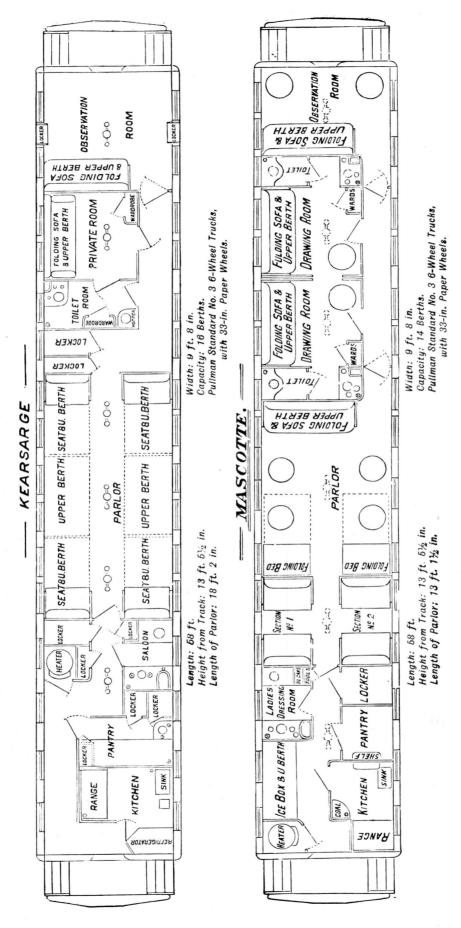

— KEARSARGE —

OBSERVATION
ROOM

FOLDING SOFA & UPPER BERTH

FOLDING SOFA & UPPER BERTH

PRIVATE ROOM

WARDROBE

TOILET
ROOM

WARDROBE

HOPPER

LOCKER

LOCKER

LOCKER

SEAT & U. BERTH

UPPER BERTH

SEAT & U. BERTH

PARLOR

SEAT & U. BERTH

UPPER BERTH

SEAT & U. BERTH

LOCKER

LOCKER

SALOON

HEATER

LOCKER

LOCKER

PANTRY

LOCKER

RANGE

KITCHEN

SINK

REFRIGERATOR

Width: 9 ft. 8 in.
Capacity: 16 Berths.
Pullman Standard No. 3 6-Wheel Trucks,
with 33-in. Paper Wheels.

Length: 68 ft.
Height from Track: 13 ft. 6½ in.
Length of Parlor: 18 ft. 2 in.

— MASCOTTE. —

OBSERVATION
ROOM

FOLDING SOFA & UPPER BERTH

TOILET

WARDS

FOLDING SOFA & UPPER BERTH

DRAWING ROOM

FOLDING SOFA & UPPER BERTH

DRAWING ROOM

WARDS

TOILET

FOLDING SOFA & UPPER BERTH

PARLOR

FOLDING BED

SECTION N° 1

FOLDING BED

SECTION N° 2

LADIES
DRESSING
ROOM

TOOLS

SHELF

PANTRY

LOCKER

ICE BOX & U BERTH

COAL

KITCHEN

SINK

HEATER

RANGE

Width: 9 ft. 8 in.
Capacity: 14 Berths.
Pullman Standard No. 3 6-Wheel Trucks,
with 33-in. Paper Wheels.

Length: 68 ft.
Height from Track: 13 ft. 6½ in.
Length of Parlor: 13 ft. 1½ in.

In the thirty years between 1869 when he organized the New York Central Sleeping-Car Company, and 1899 when all Wagner enterprises were taken over by Pullman, Webster Wagner, a one-time carriage builder from Palatine Bridge, New York placed in circulation some of the most ornate sleepers and private cars ever to roll over the expanding main lines of American railroads. Below is a rare photograph of a Wagner interior fit for occupancy by the most exacting voluptuary. Elaborate carvings, the handiwork of German master woodcarvers ornamented the upper berths. Massive chandeliers of bronze and crystal housed the Pintsch lighting fixtures. An oval doorway, also intricately carved, gave onto a corridor of carved wood screens. The ceilings were painted with colorful arabesques and the transom supported by miniature columns of turned onyx with Corinthian pediments, a rich decorative material much in vogue at the period as witness the onyx lobby, standing to this day, of the Brown Palace Hotel in Denver. Wagner's cars were designed to ennoble their occupants with rich surroundings and for many years gave Pullman a run for his money in the elegance sweepstakes. Contemporary with Wagner's most splendid creations were the Pullman private cars *Kearsarge* and *Mascotte* of the early eighties. They were listed as "Excursion Cars" available to dramatic troupes, hunting parties and similar occasions and ran in direct competition to the hunting cars of Jerome Marble's car company at Worcester, Massachusetts.

AMERICAN CAR & FOUNDRY

In the winter of 1902 the private car track of the Florida East Coast Railway under the windows of the Royal Poinciana Hotel at Palm Beach saw the arrival and departure over the Flagler Trestle to West Palm Beach of many private cars. Aboard them were names that made news in Fifth Avenue and Wall Street, in Rittenhouse Square and Bellevue Avenue. Like yachts coming to anchor in a secure harbor, the season saw the arrival aboard his car *Oceanic* of T. B. Wannamaker, of H. McK. Twombly aboard the New York Central's Business Car No. 499, of Frederick William Vanderbilt aboard the same august carrier's Car No. 493, and of C. W. Armour of Chicago, an influential shipper of steaks, amidst the comforts of Business Car No. 222 of the Milwaukee Road. It was an age when the difference between privately owned Pullmans and Wagners and the business cars of the carriers themselves was purely academic. Both were at the disposal of railroad directors, stockholders, important shippers and influential politicians. Many of these chose to winter at the Florida East Coast's new and very selective resort among the Florida palms. Here, convenient alike to the gaming tables of Colonel E. R. Bradley's Beach Club and suites at the Poinciana, Howard Fogg has depicted some of the p.v. that came that year to Palm Beach. At the left is William C. Whitney's fine new Pullman *Wanderer*, successor to his earlier Wagner-built *Pilgrim*. In the center is August Belmont's *Oriental* in the blue and gold livery of the Louisville & Nashville of which he is chairman of the board, and next is *Rambler*, outshopped by American Car & Foundry for Henry M. Flagler, discoverer of Florida, partner in Standard Oil of John D. Rockefeller, and proprietor or co-owner of everything in sight. At the extreme right being nosed to its berth, is the Pennsylvania Railroad's Business Car No. 501, assigned to Lenore F. Loree, General Manager of Lines West of Pittsburgh. It is occupied by pleasure-loving William Rockefeller, brother of austere John D., and also a Standard Oil nabob to whose vast enterprises the Pennsylvania is glad to grant handsome rebates and other favors within the gift of the management. Other and later years might see more private cars bound for Palm Beach, but none with names more conspicuously perfumed with wealthy ways and worldly importance.

Private Car "Mariquita"

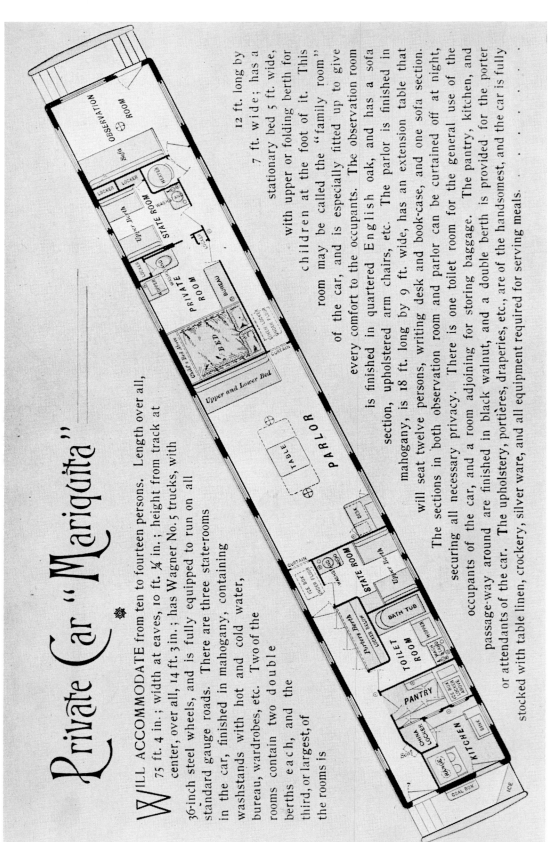

WILL ACCOMMODATE from ten to fourteen persons. Length over all, 75 ft. 4 in.; width at eaves, 10 ft. ¾ in.; height from track at center, over all, 14 ft. 3 in.; has Wagner No. 5 trucks, with 36-inch steel wheels, and is fully equipped to run on all standard gauge roads. There are three state-rooms in the car, finished in mahogany, containing bureau, wardrobes, etc. Two of the rooms contain two double berths each, and the third, or largest, of the rooms is 12 ft. long by 7 ft. wide; has a stationary bed 5 ft. wide, with upper or folding berth for children at the foot of it. This room may be called the "family room" of the car, and is especially fitted up to give every comfort to the occupants. The observation room is finished in quartered English oak, and has a sofa section, upholstered arm chairs, etc. The parlor is finished in mahogany, is 18 ft. long by 9 ft. wide, has an extension table that will seat twelve persons, writing desk and book-case, and one sofa section. The sections in both observation room and parlor can be curtained off at night, securing all necessary privacy. There is one toilet room for the general use of the occupants of the car, and a room adjoining for storing baggage. The pantry, kitchen, and passage-way around are finished in black walnut, and a double berth is provided for the porter or attendants of the car. The upholstery, portières, draperies, etc., are of the handsomest, and the car is fully stocked with table linen, crockery, silver ware, and all equipment required for serving meals.

An example of the ornate craftsmanship and luxurious detail of
Wagner construction are the
Wagner brake gear, a patent
later absorbed by Pullman, and
a side finish plan for a private
car evolved by Wagner drafts-
men. On the page opposite is a
prospectus of the Wagner rental
p.v. *Mariquita* showing dining
salon and observation compartment separated by a spacious
master suite.

TWO PHOTOS: PULLMAN STANDARD

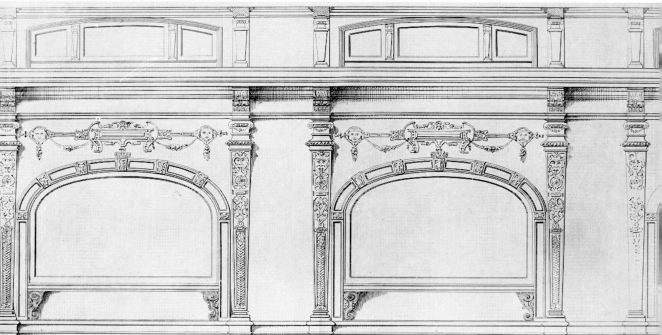

Just as, in the golden years of American travel, the private railroad car was the supreme symbol of social and financial assurance, so it was the ultimate hallmark of professional success in the theater. Many stage favorites who were also the head of their own company as were Lawrence Barrett and Edwin Booth owned their private cars outright or maintained them on longtime lease from Wagner, Mann or Pullman. Others in the employ of managers or producers stipulated in their contracts that a private car was to be provided when the show was on the road. The private car was as important in the matter of professional recognition and prestige as top billing on programs and foursheets and players of the caliber of John McCullough, John Drew or the elder Barrymore were accorded private cars in the same way they were assigned the star's dressing room backstage. In these exalted brackets the occupancy of private varnish was as much a matter of prestige as it was of comfort and convenience, but in the lower echelons of the theater, Tom shows, minstrels and dog and pony shows a private car often housed the entire company and its properties and was an article of expediency rather than grandeur. Here Alice Nielson, a stage favorite of the time, is photographed aboard a Wagner sleeper chartered for her company leaving Grand Central Depot at New York for Toronto in September 1898.

AMERICAN CAR & FOUNDRY

"The modern luxury of railway travel is nowhere more clearly exemplified than in the private palace car of the 'star' actress of today," wrote a reporter under the title "A Palace On Wheels" in *Metropolitan Magazine* for June 1898. "Mme. Anna Held is the proud and happy owner of the one-time car of Mrs. (Lillie) Langtry. Instead of undergoing the discomforts of one night stands in the conventional railroad hostelry, the fortunate owner of a palace car may summon comfort and repose suggestive of the luxury of the Waldorf Astoria . . . In cost such a property is in the neighborhood of $22,000. Few of our multi-millionaires boast of private palace cars but, with the true democratic spirit, share with others the ordinary comforts of Pullman and Wagner service. Of course Mme. Held's long tour of America has wedded her to the comforts of our railway conveniences. . . . France is in a primitive state as far as palace cars are concerned." The interior here shown is believed to be Mrs. Langtry's first p.v. *The City of Worcester.*

Private Car "Wanderer"

HAS A CAPACITY of 12 berths, and will accommodate fourteen persons comfortably. Length over all, 71 ft. 8 in.; width at eaves, 10 ft. 3½ in.; height from track at center, over all, 14 ft. Has Wagner No. 5 trucks, with 36-inch steel wheels, and is fully equipped for service on any standard gauge road. The car is handsomely finished in selected mahogany.

There are four adjoining state-rooms, with a section, or upper and lower berth in each room, washstands with hot and cold water, closets, etc. There is also a sofa section each in the parlor and observation room, which can be curtained off to secure privacy when occupied at night. The parlor is 15 ft. 4½ in. long, is supplied with a writing desk, and an extension table that will seat from 10 to 14 persons. There is a toilet room for the general use of occupants, in addition to the toilet facilities in the state-rooms.

The kitchen is fully supplied with tableware, linen, and everything required for serving meals to the full capacity of the car. The upholstery throughout the car is of blue frieze plush, with portières, draperies, curtains, etc., to correspond.

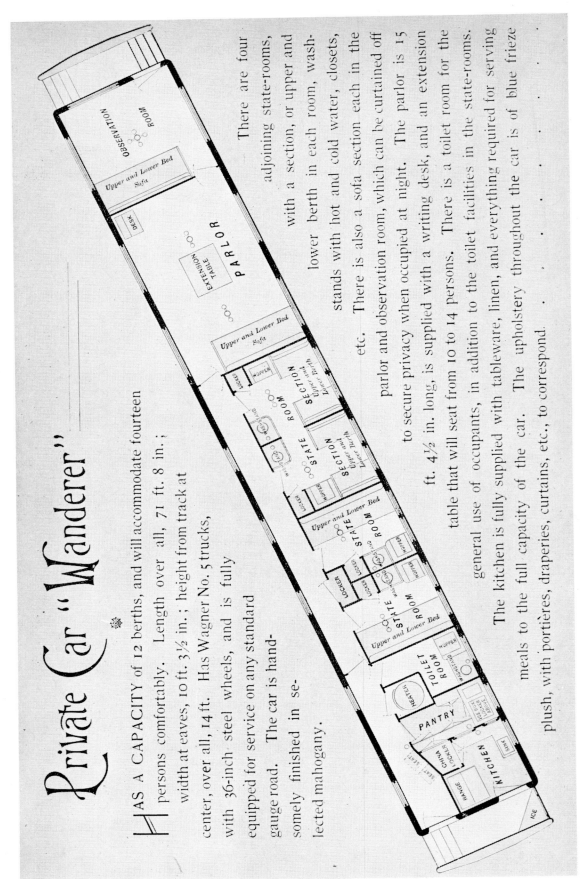

The Wagner-built private car *Edgemere*, built in the eighties as a companion car to *Ellsmere, Wanderer, Mariquita* and others assigned to the Wagner rental pool, was acquired by Pullman in 1899 among other assets of the Wagner Palace Car Company and was absorbed by the Pullman pool of charter cars for the duration of its usefulness. Over the years the Pullman Company absorbed many of the patents, properties and corporate structures of rivals including Wagner, the Haskell & Barker's Car Company at Michigan City and the Standard Steel Car Company which had been founded in 1902 by John M. Hansen and James B. (Diamond Jim) Brady. *Edgemere*, as shown below, was of chaste and austere design but well suited to the tastes of the conservative men of wealth who were its occupants. On the page opposite is the prospectus of the Wagner *Wanderer* (not to be confused with the Pullman-built car of the same name purchased by William C. Whitney in 1901) showing an interesting floor plan in which the principal salon and observation room, although separate apartments, were located contiguously at the rear end of the car.

PULLMAN STANDARD

HOWARD FOGG

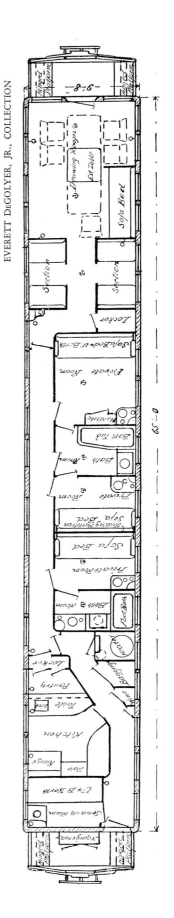

General William Jackson Palmer's second *Nomad,* shown on these pages, was standard gauge to conform with the Rio Grande's program in 1892 of broad gauging its mainline wherever practicable. It was built at the St. Charles shops of American Car & Foundry and was the second of the name in the general's service, the first and narrow gauge *Nomad* having been "the nice house car" he and Mrs. Palmer had occupied during construction days. In March, 1894, second *Nomad* turned up as far from home as Palm Beach, where it was spotted longside such ranking members of the private car club as A. A. McLeod aboard *Alexander II* and H. S. David occupying the West Virginia Central & Pittsburgh p.v. *West Virginia.* The drawing reproduced here from a contemporary source suggests that General Palmer still renounced all suggestions of the voluptuary in his private cars. Originally assigned to the Rio Grande Western, *Nomad* was acquired in 1903 by the Denver & Rio Grande, where it was extensively rebuilt and added to that carrier's roster as *Denver.*

THREE PICTURES: PULLMAN STANDARD

PULLMAN STANDARD

In the days before air lines supplied pressure to raise water from tanks beneath the cars private varnish was serviced by gravity, as shown on the page opposite, and toilet facilities were simple. On the same page the agreeably styled dining salon of a private car for the Mexico, Cuernavaca & Pacifico built by Pullman in 1896 indicates a high degree of sophisticated comfort south of the Rio Grande. Six years earlier when Pullman had outshopped car No. 1 for the Norfolk & Western, kerosene lighting fixtures were still standard practice and French plate glass mirrors lent eclat to private varnish in the up and coming coal haul trade.

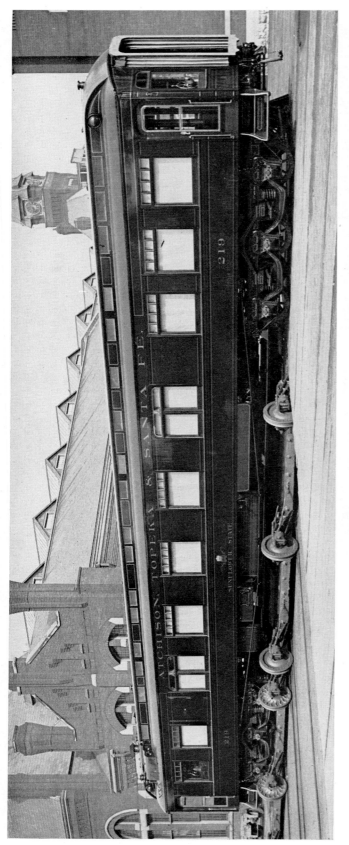

Exceptions to the rule which decreed that most p.v. in every decade should have an open observation platform were the Santa Fe's *Sunflower State* and the Baltimore & Ohio South Western's *Virginia* shown on the opposite page. Built with enclosed vestibules at either end, these opulent private varnish cars could be carried at the head-end of crack passenger consists without cutting off the view of cash passengers from observation cars that were regular schedule equipment. On this page the dining salon of *Virginia* with overstuffed armchairs, inlaid sideboard and ball and fringe portières testify to the character of a rich and haughty mainline carrier which connected St. Louis and the Southwest Gateway with Washington and Philadelphia via its associated Baltimore & Ohio.

In an age of coal smoke and no air conditioning, the white watered silk sofa with fringes and a quilted headpiece aboard John McLean's fine car *Ohio* may not have been altogether practical but it suggested opulence and the grand manner of the owner. Aboard *Ohio* McLean directed a newspaper empire so profitable that when his son Edward B. McLean married Evalyn Walsh of Hope Diamond fame the alliance was hailed as uniting two of the greatest American fortunes ever to have been joined in gilt-edged bonds of matrimony.

— 186 —

This is how Pullman's general service private car *Campania* looked before it became No. 100 of the Kansas City, Pittsburgh & Gulf occupied by the eccentric Arthur E. Stillwell. Pintsch lighting fixtures (LEFT) at the time of *Campania's* outshopping supplemented the not infallible Mazda electric light, just as a few years earlier coal oil lamps had supplemented Pintsch illumination aboard the cars.

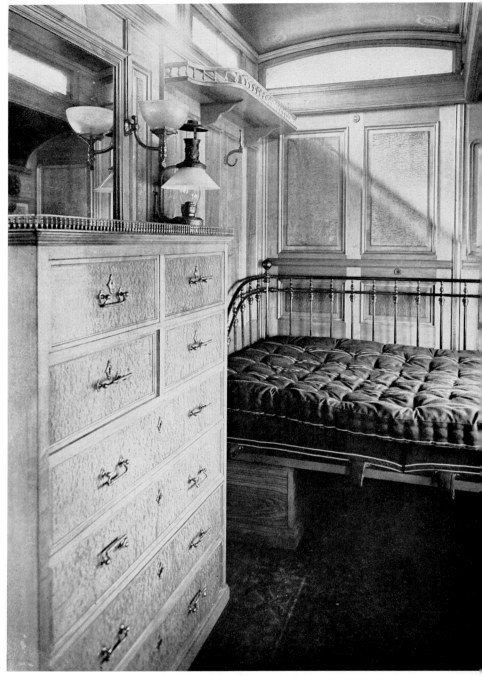

Edgemere, whose master stateroom is shown here, was one of the several Wagner private varnish cars taken over by Pullman when the latter company absorbed the affairs of the Wagner Palace Car Company into its own economy in 1899. The Pintsch gas mantle with a reliable old fashioned coal oil lamp in reserve are an indication of the date of its building, probably in the late eighties.

Such as a King Should Build

THE CHARACTER OF THE PRIVATE RAILWAY CAR in the accepted sense of a complete living apartment within the economy of a single coach of conventional dimensions evolved gradually from the car-building practices of the decades between 1830 and 1880, at which latter date compartment and sleeping cars of various designs and patents were in fairly universal use and elements of them combined to make the Wagner or Pullman car for private ownership and occupancy.

Before the advent of compartment and sleeping cars, specially assigned rolling stock had occasionally been designated private cars, but it was for daytime occupancy only and made no pretentions to being a complete and self-contained living unit.

Throughout the fifties and early sixties a number of patents had variously been issued to inventive carbuilders such as Webster Wagner, Edward Collins Knight and the brothers T. T. and Jonah Woodruff, who incorporated in 1871 as the Woodruff Sleeping & Palace Car Company. Most of these patents covered devices for adapting cars built primarily for daytime travel into sleepers through the conversion of seats into berths and the recessing of other berths into ceilings and wall panels. There were rivals to these dominant companies, notably Asa Hapgood who maintained sleeping car service on the Boston-New York run via Springfield between 1861 and 1868, the Flowers Sleeping Car Company organized at Bangor, Maine, and the Silver Palace Cars built to the order of the Central Pacific Railroad after 1869 but not seen in service in the East.

Foremost of all sleeping car designs and the one destined to absorb and outlast all its competitors was, of course, the vehicle first put into service by George Mortimer Pullman for night runs on the Chicago & Alton Railroad in 1865. The suggestion of a ship's interior was latent in this primeval Pullman car which delighted its occupants with carpeted floors, seats upholstered in expensive plush, black walnut paneling embellished with marquetry and a profusion of bevel-edge French mirrors of opulent proportions. All that was lacking to take a complete page from ship's design was compartmentation or cabins, and this was shortly forthcoming.

The sleeping cars in service on the Hudson River Railroad in 1853 had already been divided into compartments for sleeping purposes only, and when in 1865 Pullman evolved a carriage which was to combine daytime parlors and compartmented sleeping rooms in the same car, the idea of the private hotel apartment car was born. The design received further impetus from the patents issued Colonel William d'Alton Mann in 1872 for a sleeping car whose partitions extended the full width of the car and whose staterooms were entered from side doors giving onto a conductor's footboard as was the English and Continental practice of the time. The first Mann Boudoir Car found no favor in the United States and six years later the inventor revised it in favor of an all-room sleeping car whose cabins were available from an enclosed corridor along one side of the car, the whole resembling closely in its basic design the all-room Pullman corridor car of the present time. Mann's patents even covered the inclusion of individual toilet and washbowl facilities in each "boudoir" and enclosed vestibule platforms at either end of the car, and the Colonel, whatever his other shortcomings, was well ahead of his day and age in matters of both privacy and convenience in motion.

From Pullman's combination sleeping-compartment-parlor car on the Hudson River Line and the basic idea of the hotel-sleeping car which had its own kitchen, dining facilities and individually assigned conductor serving in the joint capacity of chef, waiter and porter, it was no giant step to the concept of a self-contained apartment car for the exclusive occupancy of important personages, such for instance as railroad presidents, general managers, superintendents and majority stockholders.

If railroaders and carbuilders had not until now fully appreciated the avenues of travel opened by Pullman's first hotel cars, the ecstatic press these fine conveyances received soon alerted them.

The City of Boston is one of six similar cars to be placed upon the Chicago, Burlington & Quincy line by Mr. George M. Pullman of Chicago, declared the *Daily Quincy Herald* for September 4, 1867. Four of them are already built, named *The City of Aurora, Plymouth Rock, Western World* and *The City of New York.* . . . The furniture is of solid black walnut, handsomely carved and ornamented and upholstered with royal purple velvet plush imported from England expressly for this purpose. The finest Axminster carpets cover the floor. The night curtains for the berths are of the heaviest silk and worsted; splendid chandeliers are pendant overhead; elegant mirrors grace the walls. Luxurious beds invite repose by night, and when made up for the day the cars betray no trace of the eating or sleeping uses to which they can be put. The total cost of this car was $30,000, a fact which itself speaks of its unrivalled magnificence and commodiousness.

The Chicago Times was agreeable to lifting its voice in the general exclamation of delight which greeted the innovation.

The Western World as a car is something more than a novelty, it said. Elaborately ornamented on the exterior by frescoed pictures of good taste and appropriateness, it is replete on the inside with all the conveniences of a modern American Hotel . . . heated by a large furnace in cold weather and cooled by a large ventilator in warm. It contains first, four spacious drawing rooms, each separated from the other and from the main body of the car with a passage way running around it. . . . In each of the sections of the car there is a bell which leads to the kitchen and waiting room where a regular bell register marks the room from which the call originates. Then there is a kitchen? Yes, with a perfect miniature range which has all the necessary compartments for cooking, making tea, warming plates, etc. The excursion of yesterday consisted of some of the most prominent citizens who were made fully aware of the fact from the choice beefsteaks, fried oysters and other viands that were served to them hot with iced champagne.

That individuals of means and groups of congenial travellers could now traverse the ever growing continental network of rails in comparative privacy and available to the luxuries of the time under a single roof immediately suggested to Pullman's fertile imagination the possibilities inherent in cars to be privately owned or chartered for the sole occupancy of well placed individuals and their families.

The first class of voyagers to avail itself of such opportunities alike for creature comfort and social distinction were railroad men whose easy access to transport and special services made private cars an obvious ostentation and convenience. Railroaders in those uninhibited times exploited their private conveyances as advertisements for their carriers, and still in the unforeseen future was the generation of operators who were to cringe from the words private car as from a fatal contagion.

Lacking evidence to the contrary, it seems likely that the idea of a self-contained car assigned to the special use of ranking railroad executives bore fruit in the years immediately following the close of the Civil War. In 1868 when he assumed a directorate in Erie and at the same time an almost fatal authority in that doomed carrier, Jay Gould was photographed on the rear platform of his all-white Erie Railroad Car No. 200, allocated on the company roster to his private and directoral necessities. In the same year the yellowing files of the Union Pacific at Omaha revealed photographic evidence, reproduced elsewhere in this volume, of the existence of official business cars used by railroad engineers in laying the transcontinental mainline toward Promontory Point. At the ceremonies at Promontory itself the following year both President Leland Stanford on the Central Pacific and Thomas C. Durant of the Union Pacific arrived by private car and it is probable that a similar conveyance assigned to General Grenville M. Dodge, chief of Union Pacific construction, was already on the scene in Utah.

In 1869, too, we find Commodore Cornelius Vanderbilt still admiring fast horses and minded to take a new wife in his seventy-fifth year. He was also riding in satisfactory grandeur over the Vanderbilt lines and connections between New York City and the Springs at Saratoga aboard his Wagner-built private car, *Vanderbilt*. By the last year of the seventh decade of the nineteenth century, the private railway car was already an accomplished fact and well on the way to becoming the peerless hallmark of American distinction and success, a status symbol of glittering dimensions.

Great is the pity that today no single specimen or paradigm of the primeval private railroad car exists anywhere and that its factual likeness cannot be encountered by amateurs of departed grandeurs either at the Baltimore & Ohio's Railroad Museum or amongst the treasured artifacts of the several other transportation collections in the land. Nor were its internal resources of rare woods and marquetry, French mirrors, champagne cellars and spacious master staterooms available to the photographers of the age, at least with any very satisfactory results for posterity.

Thus it will be in the mind's eye that the twentieth century student of Victorian properties must travel, and vicariously, along the summer Hudson in panoplied splendor with Cornelius Vanderbilt or across the Great Plains with Grenville Dodge to a rendezvous with destiny on the windy uplands of Utah. But that he will so travel in well upholstered resources of Turkey carpets and wide picture windows is assured.

Antedating these cars placed at the disposal of railroad men and occupying a somewhat anomalous position in this chronicle was the armor plated state car built for President Abraham Lincoln by the United States Military Car Shops at Alexandria, Virginia, and delivered for his occupancy in 1865. The car was designed by B. P. Lamason and was perhaps the first to have an underframe comprising a single massive steel girder running the entire length of the car instead of the conventional wooden sills. The car was painted chocolate brown trimmed with gold leaf and was so heavy that it rode on four separate trucks of four wheels each. It had four large sofas, one of extra length for Lincoln's extended frame, but no kitchen or commissary arrangements. It was delivered just in time to carry the martyred President to his burial.

The car was cumbersome in the extreme and was purchased in 1866 by the Union Pacific which soon thereafter returned it to the government without thanks. It then passed into the hands of the Colorado Central for use on the standard gauge portion of its trackage between Denver and Golden and in 1905 it was purchased by Thomas Lowry, President of the Minneapolis, St. Paul & Sault Ste. Marie Railroad who contemplated giving it to the public park system of the city of Minneapolis, but before any final disposition could be made of the homeless relic it was destroyed in a brush fire which swept the carrier's yards at Mendota and disappeared from the scene. Some of its furnishings, however, were in storage at the time and today the Union Pacific's railroad museum at Omaha still shows its solid silver table service and outsize sofa of horsehair and mahogany.

The first private car embodying the general floor plan and other features that came shortly into more or less universal use was Car No. 120, outshopped in 1871 by the Pennsylvania Railroad at its company shops at Altoona for the use of president of the railroad, Tom Scott. It had two six-wheel trucks and was by far the heaviest car on the carrier's roster of the time. A drawing-observation room was separated by a master stateroom and guest bedrooms from a dining salon seating eight. There was a galley and crews' quarters and iceboxes containing "comestibles sufficient for the most exacting palate for a full week." No. 120 contained what was believed to have been the first bathtub on rails. "The drawing-room of the car resembles the cozy cabin of a yacht designed for Asian sailing," marvelled the *Railroad Gazette* of that year. What most impressed the reporter, even more than the car's gold plush divans, mahogany with gold relief and fine-lining and marvels of plumbing convenience, was "a small French clock atop the bookcase which ticks sharply even when the car is idle."

Just what other behavior might be expected in a well conducted French clock, the *Gazette* neglected to state.

In two aspects Scott's elaborate varnish differed from later convention. Contrasting with the company's Tuscan red livery, it was the great man's whim to have bright green wheels and the observation end of the car was designed to run at its head end next to the train line instead of at the back. Sensitive to cooking odors, Scott felt that they might be obviated or at least abated by having the kitchen at the rear.

No. 120 achieved a wide and favorable celebrity in the railroad world of its time. Scott was well ahead of his age in an awareness of the uses of publicity and promotion and saw to it that his car was at the disposal of names that made news when they patronized the Pennsylvania. When the Grand Duke Alexis of Russia visited the United States in 1872, he went west aboard No. 120. President Garfield used it on his inaugural trip to Washington and ex-President Hayes went home to Ohio aboard it after quitting the White House in 1880. Railroaders everywhere knew its noble dimensions and green wheels as the great of the world passed on their lawful occasions, and the Pennsylvania's prestige gained accordingly.

Curiously enough George M. Pullman, for all he was to be the supreme genius of luxury varnish in general and private cars in particular, didn't turn up a p.v. of his own until 1877 when the technique of their building and use was fairly well established. When he did, however, his car which was initially known simply as P.P.C. was to establish all sorts of records for durability, grandeur and concentration of celebrities who gloried and drank deep in its rococo interior. The car was completed at a cost estimated at $50,000 at the company's Detroit shops where fifteen skilled woodcarvers had labored for a period of months turning out its satinwood and vermillion interior. It contained a seven foot observation room, a seven foot bedroom where the great man slept either on a berth or an extension couch, a dining salon with room for a table eight feet long, two open sections, a toilet apartment with a diminutive tub and the usual kitchen offices and storerooms. A small organ was a feature of the dining salon which doubled for lounge and its decor was heavy with tasseled and fringed draperies, velvet portières and heavy wall-to-wall carpets specially woven for the purpose.

In 1892 the overall length was extended to better than sixty-six feet and after Pullman's death in 1897, it was rechristened by Mrs. Pullman as *Monitor,* which had been the builder's cable code name, and remained in service until 1921 when it was scrapped at Calumet.

Few cars were occupied by such perfumed names as P.P.C. (understood to have meant President's Private Car) in Pullman's lifetime, for he was well aware of the uses of publicity to encourage the sale of his product. Among the great who knew it were the Duke of Sutherland, Arthur Balfour, Princess Eulalie of Spain and, reputedly, every President of the United States from Grant (for whose convenience Pullman sent it to San Francisco when he returned from his round the world trip in 1880) to McKinley.

The car was a spectacular advertisement both for the magnificence and for the safety of the Pullman product and railroad men from coast to coast expressed no surprise when it rolled into the yards at Kansas City, Portland, Atlanta or Bangor with its silk hatted owner aboard eager to show its advantages to purchasing agents and vice-presidents. Aboard it, Pullman's daughter Florence and her husband, Frank O. Lowden, later Governor of Illinois, spent their wedding trip, incidentally spreading the gospel of Pullman wherever they went. In the eighties, when officials of the Central Pacific were hesitant to send their heavy Silver Palace sleepers to Virginia City, Nevada, over the high trestle at Gold Hill of the Virginia & Truckee Railroad, P.P.C. was routed up to the Comstock on the night train and immediately thereafter sleeper service to San Francisco was inaugurated.

It was largely on the strength of the celebrity of P.P.C. that the name Pullman became generic in the language, but until the consolidation of the two companies in 1899 the products of the Wagner Palace Car Company gave Pullman a run for his money and news accounts and the records of car movements of the eighties and nineties refer to the presence of "Wagners and Pullmans" to show that competition existed and Pullman was by no means a monopoly.

Not only were private cars of fearful and wonderful aspect coming from the drawing boards and shops of Eastern carbuilders, the Far West, too, was sufficient to itself in such elevated matters. We have seen elsewhere how a business car constructed at the vast granite shops in Carson City of the Virginia & Truckee for its general superintendent, Henry Yerington, was borrowed by John Mackay for an extensive tour before even its owner could assay its comforts and conveniences. Unhappily, no record of the car's basic construction has survived, but it was obviously of sufficiently conforming dimensions and equipment for hauling over the Central and Union Pacific Railroads and connecting carriers in the trans-Mississippi East.

The Kimball Car Company of San Francisco in 1877 built to the order of Peter Donahue, a railroad magnate of California's Northern Counties, a private palace car of such splendor that it, too, went East and for a while was on display beside the lordly Pullmans and Wagners at the Philadelphia Centennial. *The Marin County Journal* for January 25, 1877, remarked in its news columns: "Colonel Donahue went East recently to arrange for iron for the Sonoma & Marin Railroad and made all his rounds in a palace car built specially for his own use. A few years ago he worked in a blacksmith shop on Front Street in San Francisco." Donahue's car not only appealed to the envious imagination of the Western beholder, but also to his patriotic sensibilities: it was built throughout of California materials.

Encouraged by these successes by local craftsmen, private cars for railroad nabobs, directors and executives rolled by the score from the car shops of individual carriers everywhere in the land and flourished without a tip of the hat to Webster Wagner or George M. Pullman.

Eventually the inconvenience and often enough factual danger of hauling these homegrown products over mainline carriers where the standard of safety and constructural fitting was established by Wagner, Pullman and one or two other large scale carbuilders became so manifest that big time railroads, particularly in the East, began to consider steps to abate what was becoming a nuisance of the first chop. Link and pin couplings, hand activated brakes, inaccurately calibrated wheels and irregularities of draft gear had no place in the comparatively high speed operations and long train consists of important carriers, and the letter reproduced on the following page from the old files of the Florida East Coast Railway in the year 1894 shows how the revolt was taking shape amongst superintendents and general managers along the Atlantic seaboard.*

In a few years now the automatic coupler and Westinghouse brake were to become mandatory by Federal law and superintendents like Mr. Goff everywhere slept better of nights.

For the purposes of this essay concerning the private and/or business car on American railroads, four firms of carbuilders achieved dominance either temporary or permanent in the field of private car construction: Pull-

*The railroads mentioned in Superintendent Goff's letter were railroads connecting with the Florida East Coast, some of them parts of the Plant System which later became the Atlantic Coast Line. They were, in 1891, as follows:

A C L	Atlantic Coast Line
S F & W	Savannah, Florida & Western Railway
B & W	Brunswick & Western Railroad
C & S	Charleston & Savannah Railway
J T & K W	Jacksonville, Tampa & Key West Railway
S F	South Florida Railroad

Florida East Coast Railway
Jacksonville, Florida

Mr.H.S.Haines,   September 8,1894

   V.P.Plant System,

      12 West 23rd St. NYC

Dear Sir,

     During one of your visits to St.Augustine last winter,you will remember that in conversation with Mr. Flagler in regard to the hauling of **Private Cars**, it was thought best there should be issued a joint circular by the A.C.L C.&S S.F. & W. B.&W. J.T. & K.W. S.F. and this line, That no cars would be hauled in regular passenger trains on the above roads, unless equiped with Janney Coupler and Westinghouse air signal and brake.

     If you are yet of the same opinion, will you kindly start the "ball rolling."

                       Yours respectfully,

                                Sup't.

man's Palace Car Company, the Mann Boudoir-Car Company, the Wagner Palace-Car Company and American Car & Foundry. Other less memorable firms such as the Worcester Excursion Car Company, T. T. Woodruff & Company and the Union Palace-Car Company did indeed build private and/or business cars in modest numbers, but comparatively speaking, their ventures were inconsequential. Pullman survived them all and experienced competition to the end of the private car era only from American Car & Foundry and the car shops of individual carriers.

The success of Webster Wagner, who was born at Palatine Bridge, New York, in 1817 and died, ironically enough, in a train wreck not very far from there years later, was due largely to the hold he secured at an early date on the patronage of Commodore Cornelius Vanderbilt and the New York Central he owned. In 1858, financed by the Commodore, he built four sleepers for the Central and from that time until the company closed its books in 1899, Wagner and New York Central were synonymous in terms of sleeping cars and private varnish of all sorts. A Vanderbilt in-law, Dr. W. Seward Webb, became president of the Wagner concern and it flourished in the patronage of the Vanderbilt lines until it was overwhelmed with suits for patent infringements by Pullman and eventually merged with the Pullman interests.

George Mortimer Pullman, approximately a contemporary of Wagner, was an ingenious mechanic and pioneer in innovations that eventually proved immensely profitable to him. He reportedly conceived the idea of the folding upper berth while trying his luck as a gold prospector at Central City in Colorado's Gregory Diggings where the miners made a practice of sleeping in tiers, and his patents on the Pullman berth, the Pullman car vestibule and other useful properties at length made it possible for him to eliminate all competition from rivals in his lifetime, and die rich, respected, and a name in the lexicon of two continents.

Less conspicuously austere a capitalist was the shady Colonel William D'Alton Mann who made his first fortune selling various items of military equipment to the Federal government during the Civil War. In 1872, he received a patent for a transverse partition type sleeping car and spent the following decade merchandising it in Continental Europe where vestigial traces of it survive to this day. The Mann patents, less vulnerable to theft than others which were appropriated by Wagner, became properties of the Mann Boudoir-Car Company which in turn was absorbed by the Union Palace-Car Company and, eventually and like all the others, became part of the financial economy of the Pullman Company. Colonel Mann went on to gaudier, if less reputable triumphs as publisher of the notorious *Town Topics* and secured an immortality of sorts as an eminently successful blackmailer of the socially imprudent.

Considered in terms of internal decor it would be invidious to award the palm to one of the four major car companies. The taste of the eighties and nineties was refreshingly frank in its admiration of a wealth of detail and would have held in contempt the almost complete absence of decoration that has come to characterize the styles today known as "contemporary" and "moderne." It rejoiced in rich fabrics, elaborately inlaid woods, a profusion of crystal, ormolu, marquetry and rare boisseries, fine linen and heavy service of silver and gold at table and, where possible, ostentations of marble and gold-washed plumbing in its bathing appointments.

These preferences were naturally reflected in the cars built by Wagner and Pullman for public occupancy and, if the written descriptions of the reporters and diarists of the time are to be credited, were carried over into the private varnish of people of importance. Of the two major car companies it seems probable that Wagner leaned in the direction of ostentation and opulence, especially in the field of carpets, draperies, furniture fabric, pillows, tassels and hangings, while Pullman favored a comparatively wealthy austerity of expensive paneling and elaborate woodwork generally. Certainly from earliest times when fifteen skilled German cabinet makers had been recruited to work on the P.P.C. at Detroit, Pullman had been celebrated for its woodwork and conscientious detail of the best of everything that went into its products.

By all accounts it remained for the Mann Boudoir-Car Company, true to its corporate name to produce in the car, *Adelina Patti*, to which brief mention has before been made, a decor which would have gratified Hollywood today and which assuredly popped the eyes of a less sophisticated generation of admirers. Oscar Lewis is authority for the statement that whenever her professional occasions brought her to the Golden Gate and her car was spotted at Oakland Mole, scores of San Franciscans were in the habit of making the ferry trip across the bay just to gaze on its glossy exterior and speculate on its internal wonderments.

The car was, in fact, built on contract for the Mann Company by the Gilbert Car Manufacturing Company of Troy, New York, and delivered in December 1883. It was only fifty-five feet long, almost diminutive by twentieth century standards, with three rooms en suite and a bath with tub. The car was rented to Mme. Patti on a per diem basis and carried her name both as a tribute to the occupant and as publicity for the Mann Company. When Pullman took over Colonel Mann's company and its useful patents in 1889, the Pullman Company retained its original name and continued to rent it to the singer for her tours and it was at this time that the discovery was made that papier-mâché, used by Pullman only for car wheels, had been extensively used in its interior appointments that had hitherto been believed rare woodwork. On December 23, 1901, the *Adelina Patti,* by now shorn of the glory of that name and plainly known as *Coronet,* was sold for $3,800 to Fitzhugh & Company, who specialized in circus and carnival equipment, and it disappeared from human ken.

During one of her San Francisco visits, Mme. Patti permitted the car's interior to be described by a reporter for the *Call* as follows:

> The hammered gold and silver effect of the sides and ceiling was in a design of morning glories. The parlor was lighted by plate glass windows and a gold lamp which hung from above. The windows were ornamented with designs representing the four seasons. The hand-carved piano of natural wood corresponded with the rest of the woodwork in the room. There was a couch with satin pillows ornamented with bows

and lace tidies opposite the piano. A square table covered with plush, stood in the center and all around were easy chairs of luxurious depth. Mme. Patti's bedroom was largely pink. The paneling was of satinwood, inlaid with ebony, gold and amaranth. Bevelled mirrors were abundant and the couch had a silk-plush cover of gold embroidered with trailing pink rosebuds and with the monogram "A.P." in the same delicate shade. Over the velvet carpet, beside the bed, was a leopard skin. A stand was mounted with silver and a small bathtub was concealed from view by mirrored doors. There was a closet containing the table service of solid silver, china and glass—all with the diva's monogram.

Mme. Patti lived up to every implication of artistic temperament suggested by this decor and once, during the Pullman ownership of the car, complained that the faucet leaked and had ruined a number of costumes reposing in the tub at the moment. She claimed damages. She was waited upon by L. S. Hungerford, then assistant to General Superintendent C. A. Garcelon, and told unequivocally that the bathtub was no place for the singer's attire for "Traviata" and "Lycoming" and that Pullman "assumed no responsibility for bathtub wardrobes. Tubs are for ablutions." The singer shortly capitulated to logic and, according to Hungerford, "sang him a little song to make amends."

For many years the two leading car building companies, Wagner until 1899 when it was merged with Pullman, and Pullman until the time of the 1941 war maintained pools of cars available to private rental at a variety of tariffs and ranging from single sleeper or parlor cars to, in the case of Wagner, an entire seven car train with baggage, dining, lounge, barber shop and library cars, sleepers and an observation salon car of almost imperial dimensions. Pullman operated a parallel entourage of five magnificently upholstered private salon cars which was shown at the Columbian Exhibition and aroused intense interest and admiration in a railroad conscious generation.

While the entire trains available to rental were largely in the nature of show windows and advertisement for their product and services, both companies did a brisk business in the rental of private cars to parties, families and individuals who could afford to pay premium rates for privacy and perhaps the greatest public luxury of their age aside from the de luxe hotels of New York, San Francisco and such resorts as Palm Beach.

In 1888 Pullman, for example, kept a pool of twenty-five cars classed as Hotel Cars, Sleeping Cars, Hunting Cars and Private Cars with Buffet which were available at strategic points of the compass and were shifted seasonally or as demand required. They fetched from $50 a day for Hotel Cars complete with staff of two servants to Private Cars with Buffet with a single attendant for $30 plus, of course, the hauling charges of the carriers, which were eighteen full fares east of Chicago and St. Louis and fifteen fares west of the Mississippi.

In 1888 the Pullmans available to private rental included the following:

Celtic	Idler	Olivette
Del Monte	International	Pickwick
Davy Crockett	Iolanthe	President
Fairmount	Izaak Walton	Raritan
Glen Eyre	Mascotte	Raymond
Harvard	Nimrod	Rahway
Idlewild	Ocean	St. Nicholas
	Traveler	Wanderer

Five years later in 1893 Pullman had added the following, generally available at the same tariffs save in the case of Buffet Cars whose rental had been raised to $50 daily:

Capitano	Esperanza	Regulus
Casa Monica	Hazelmere	Rover
Cleopatra	Ideal	Superb
Coronet	Mayflower	Sybaris
Edgewood	Mystic	Wildwood
El Capitan	Newport	Esmeralda

Nearly half a century after this date, Pullman's pool of rental cars in 1939 had shrunk to seventeen, some with names but not the same identity that had appeared in the nineties:

Asheville	David Livingstone	Ferdinand Magellan
Boston	Davy Crockett	Henry Stanley
Ideal	Newport	Pioneer
Manhattan	New York	Roald Amundsen
Marco Polo	Palm Beach	Robert Peary
	Philadelphia	Superb

In 1893 the longest of Pullman's available private cars had been sixty-nine feet, the *St. Nicholas* and the shortest a mere forty-nine feet in the form of *Harvard*. In 1939 all were eighty-two or eighty-three foot cars provided with air conditioning, radio reception and phone plugs for use when stopped in terminal depots. No rates were quoted in the official brochure, but $175 a day was the prevailing scale.

Rental Pullmans disappeared completely in the 1941 war and were never revived.

Because of its equivocal character and widely varied bases for occupancy, the status of a given private car at a given time in the nineties was an ambiguous one at best and is often today a source of confusion even to students of private car *mores*.

As has been remarked elsewhere, the well defined estate of being either an official car owned by a railroad and occupied exclusively by railroad personnel and the private car of a well-to-do non-railroader, each carried under appropriate tariff regulations, was still in the future. Cars owned by carriers were in fact available not only to officers of the company on company occasions, but to directors and important stockholders and carried free not only over the owner railroad, but frequently in interchange over connecting lines.

Railroads themselves, as well as Pullman and other car rental agencies, made their business cars available to charter or occupancy by private individuals or to those with only the most tenuous connections with the industry. Important shippers, politicians and journalists rode free in company cars. Well heeled private citizens chartered company cars on a per diem basis. The character of the private railroad car partook of a magnificent ambiguity.

The Derby at Louisville, the midwinter season at Palm Beach and private car sidings at French Lick and Long Beach might see private cars in an almost stupefying variety of occupancy, scores of them certified to be official cars of the Boston & Maine, Southern Pacific, the Milwaukee, Northern Pacific, Baltimore & Ohio, Santa Fe or Texas Midland without a stateroom on any of them being occupied by a bona fide railroad executive.

Swifts, Leiters and Armours in Chicago seldom had need of private varnish of their own, but rode in comfort aboard business cars gladly furnished by the Chicago & North Western or the Illinois Central. Nob Hill magnificoes of San Francisco, Camerons, Fairs, de Youngs and Tevises, simply sent word to Third and Townsend and one of the Southern Pacific's numerous and commodious varnish cars, *San Emidio, Sunset, Emalita, Santa Susana* or *Del Monte* was at their disposal, for weeks or months if need be.

If Colonel Marse Henry Watterson tired of poker at the Disreputable Club and hankered for tarpon at Aranzas Pass, the Louisville & Nashville, true to its character as "The Old Reliable," was honored to supply the general manager's business car well stocked with high tension bourbon. Charles Parsons wasn't the only occupant of the beautiful presidential car of the New York & New England; it might well be en route to Florida with Abbott Lawrence or T. Jefferson Coolidge or any one of a score of State Street doges in side whiskers and ledger ruled trousers.

Until well after the turn of the century the well placed and well connected of the world had no need to travel in public railroad accommodations unless they were so minded. Almost everyone of means and consequence had access to guest privileges in the private car club.

The pattern for internal arrangements of the private and/or business car seems fairly well to have been established by President Scott's Car No. 120 on the Pennsylvania early in the game except for his whimsical insistence on locating the galley and kitchen offices at the end of the car that came into requisition elsewhere as the observation salon and hence the most aloof precincts of the conveyance.

Once the matter of the galley and source of supply was settled (and President Scott's contemporaries and successors at once reversed his scheme of things) little remained except details to evolve the floor plan of private transport as we know it to this very day. In a few early private varnish cars a single apartment, convertible at meal times, seems to have sufficed as combination drawing room and dining salon, but since this was usually located next to the observation platform for the sake of viewing the sights, it entailed a problem of kitchen logistics and the dining room soon became a fixture amidship and as a separate entity handy to the service area.

It only remained for the individual owner or occupant to determine whether he favored devoting the greater part of his available space to private sleeping apartments or to social rooms for entertainment and the foregathering of the ship's company for cocktails, bridge whist or other aspects of relaxation. When James B. Duke commissioned *Doris,* he commanded Pullman to emphasize sleeping accommodations with the result the car contained an observation room of modest dimensions — just ten feet — and sleeping accommodations for ten. When *The Virginia City* was rebuilt, its new owners preferred a twenty-two foot drawing-observation room and but two master staterooms and a guest compartment sleeping a total of but six.

Almost all dining compartments are designed to seat six at table with room to spare, eight with a little crowding. Service quarters provide berths with washroom and toilet for two servants and occasionally on the most luxurious cars, a shower.

In the economy of the private car, fireplaces, bathtubs, built-in wardrobes and marble plumbing fixtures are strictly optional. One thing is not and that is the brass-railed observation platform which from times primeval has been the hallmark and glory of the car that rode the end of the train. In the design of the earliest cars before the evolution of the Pullman enclosed vestibule for the head-end, there were two observation platforms, but the mutations of time gradually reduced this to a single stoop or piazza more or less open to the elements but partially protected by a striped sailcloth awning around the perimeter of the platform roof.

Operating regulations of all railroads provide that a continuous passage through the last car on any train, be its occupants ever so august, must be maintained at all times for the rear brakeman in pursuit of his duties. These include flagging from the rear end, maintenance of rear markers, the bleeding of steam from the trainline when approaching a terminal and other assorted professional obligations. A result has occasionally been that royalty or even J. P. Morgan has been subject to the passage through their p.v. of a man in blue with flags, lanterns and track torpedoes variously about his person. Neither let nor hindrance may be offered the person of the rear shack.

Once aboard *The Virginia City* as its owners and a group of guests were riding the Colorado & Southern out of Denver bound for Texas, a brakeman, bound upon his lawful occasions toward the platform, made his way through the drawing-observation room where the lights were dimmed and chanced to stumble on Mr. T-Bone, the owners' 185-pound St. Bernard who was sleeping in front of the fireplace. Glancing down and identifying only a large furry body in the gloom, the rear shack politely raised his cap, said "Excuse me, sir," and passed on about his business. Those present were left to speculate if in his private car experience, owners of such properties had made a practice of sleeping in fur coats on the floor.

Many innovations and improvements that were later to become standard passenger practice had their beginnings in private cars where the whims of intelligent and inquiring owners could be gratified on an experimental basis.

We have seen how hot water at pressure first appeared on General Palmer's narrow gauge, *Nomad*, at least in the West, although it seems reasonable to surmise that it must have been inspired elsewhere with less resounding consequences. The first bathtub and the first safe for protection of valuables were incorporated in Tom Scott's car No. 120 on the Pennsylvania. In 1909, the first indirect lighting was incorporated in a business car built for B. F. Yoakum, chairman of the board of the St. Louis-San Francisco Railroad. *Killarney*, built at the Canadian Pacific's shops at Angus for presidents of that far-flung carrier, more nearly resembled the office car that executives like to publicize. It had built-in map racks which unfolded profiles and track plans of every mainline, branch, stub and passing track in the entire system.

When Henry Ford acquired the Detroit, Toledo & Ironton Railroad, Pullman was commissioned to lay down *Fair Lane* to the auto man's personal specifications. Ford was suspicious of railroad travel and took a dim view of the safety precautions as they then existed and the result was one of the heaviest p.v. cars ever outshopped by any builder, tipping the scales at well over 100 tons. Its structural strength would have resisted earthquakes and its deep sills and internal bracing of sidewalls and transoms would have done credit to a bridgebuilder. As a result, *Fair Lane* rode with marked rigidity and even today, as the property of the Cotton Belt, is notoriously an uncomfortable car, but safe as houses.

Air conditioning, which gave railroad passenger traffic a new lease of life when it became general in the early thirties, was actually installed for the first time in Major Max Fleischmann's well found *Edgewood*. The car, adjusted to its owner's sensitivity to noise and dust, had sidewalls stuffed with absorbent material and four layers of floor covering, two layers of wood over steel topped with soundproof cement, not to mention wall-to-wall carpeting. *Edgewood* also boasted an instrument panel in its observation compartment that allowed the major to read train speed, altitude, indoor and outdoor temperatures, air pressure in the train line and barometric indications. Mirrors permitted occupants to look forward along the train to view the engine on curves, and track lights flooded the roadbed at night. Many a division superintendent and general manager envied the technical resources of *Edgewood*, a miracle of gadgets and conveniences built by Hotchkiss, Blue & Company of Chicago.

The first known operating fireplace was built into The Pennsylvania Railroad's Car 90 in 1889 and, while never a feature of conventional Pullmans, was imitated aboard *The Gold Coast* and *The Virginia City* a few years later. The first all-butane activated galley was also built in as part of the equipment of *The Gold Coast* when acquired by its Nevada owners, and railroad executives throughout the West were quick to see its advantages. Even more so were business car crews who until then had been accustomed to rise at four and make a coal fire in monolithic ranges for the vice-president's morning shower and coffee.

Other stars of the stage and concert hall besides Adelina Patti and the Jarrett & Palmer management saw the advantages of travel by private car in the days when the road was as important to the legitimate theater as Broadway itself. When in the first decade of the twentieth century Maude Adams was playing "Peter Pan" in New York there was no after-theatre train to take her to her country place at Ronkonkoma on Long Island, so the Long Island Railroad maintained a special with a single parlor car for her convenience with departure from Long Island City at an appropriate hour after the final evening curtain. Over the same carrier Lillian Russell maintained a private special six nights a week to run her down to Far Rockaway in the midnight hours. It cost her $50 a night and she doubled this amount with her regular tips to the train crew, which was big money in 1910.

Elsewhere in this volume it has been remarked that private railway cars, at least in the available record, have only infrequently been vehicles of scandal and that in general life aboard the mansions on rails of the affluent has been a shining example of the moral proprieties.

Perhaps the most flagrant exception to this generality was the private car of the most notorious and bewitching actress known to the American stage in the eighties and nineties, given her as a present by an admirer, occupied by donor and recipient in flagrant and well publicized sin as they rolled across the land on professional occasions, and a property which later figured in a sensational attempt by the carbuilder to blackmail the celebrity for whom he designed the conveyance.

The participants in this gaudy saraband were the fabled Mrs. Lillie Langtry, her lover Freddy Gebhard, playboy, wine salesman and a low moral influence in the highest New York social circles, and the notorious Colonel William D'Alton Mann, builder of the Mann Boudoir Car and later publisher of *Town Topics*. It was the most exotic cast of characters ever to be mounted on four wheel car trucks.

In 1884 Mrs. Langtry, known to two continents as "The Jersey Lily" for her birthplace on the Isle of Jersey, toast of Edwardian society in London, mistress of the Prince of Wales himself and the most resoundingly controversial character of the theater of her time, was touring the United States in repertory and in private, or at least what passed for private living as the favorite of the Casanova of the wine bins. Gebhard, wealthy, personable and ardent, decided Mrs. Langtry needed a private car in which to tour the provinces. He was tired of the hotel accommodations in Racine and Kansas City where the reporters assiduously chronicled the proximity of his rooms to those of the Lily, and there were occasional scuffles with house detectives ignorant of his identity and privileged character.

The first private car secured by Gebhard was *The City of Worcester*, a car which had served Edwin Booth under the name *David Garrick* and which was chartered from the Worcester Car Company. Aboard it he and Mrs. Langtry were content to tour throughout the season of 1885-86 and a great deal of profitable publicity accrued not only from their illicit though entirely public romance, but from the car itself.

"A dainty decorative touch to Mrs. Langtry's private car is the introduction of tropical plants that add the freshness of nature," wrote a swooning reporter for the London *Decorator & Furnisher* of December 1884 when the actress was on tour in the United States. "Listen! The sounding motion of the train is lost in the exquisite symphonies of Liszt, the compositions of Verdi or the melodious canzonettas of Rubini. All this whilst flying through space at forty miles the hour!"

Mrs. Langtry's car may be presumed, from the foregoing rhapsodies to have contained a piano. It later passed into the use of another actress in the person of Anna Held.

"A variation to the scene is the production of a table," continued the correspondent, "for which ample space is afforded with viands served on silver plate and decorated ceramic ware. Presto! It disappears and leaves the space for motion on a carpet with light, elastic tread! Such is the luxury of railway travel in this year of grace. The Worcester Car Company varies its interiors: in this instance it has brought together home comforts and elegancies while answering the purpose in view, which is to while away the time of travel as pleasantly as possible."

More earthy accents characterized other newspaper impressions of Mrs. Langtry's progress aboard the *City of Worcester*.

"Her private train consists of the engine *U. S. Grant,* a baggage-ladies car, a smoking car, a coach and Mrs. Langtry's private palace car," wrote a reporter in the *Atlanta Constitution*, January 25, 1883. "The train at times achieved a speed of better than fifty miles an hour and the *City of Worcester* lunged like a ship in a storm without visibly diminishing the appetite of its famous occupant. For luncheon Mrs. Langtry consumed broiled quails, tenderloin steak, French peas, potatoes, cheese, coffee, bananas and grapes."

By the time the Langtry company was ready for its road tour in 1887, however, both the professional status of the actress and the incandescent quality of her romance with Gebhard were so exalted that her admirer felt she required something better than a mere rented hotel car and he arranged with the Mann Boudoir Car Company for something extra-special. It was to be known as *Lalee*, East Indian for flirt, and Colonel Mann himself hastened to submit blueprints and evolve innovations that might promote the safety and comfort of its occupants. Seventy-five feet long and painted a bright Jersey blue with white roof, it had bas-reliefs in gold of lilies twined around the *Lalee* of its nameboards and in luxury, according to Pierre Sichel, Mrs. Langtry's biographer, compared favorably with J. P. Morgan's steam yacht *Corsair*.

As progressive in mechanical detail as he was in the latest techniques of blackmail, Mann caused both roof and the floors separating the car interior from its sills to be built in multiple layers of shock resistant materials, cork, rubber, teak and metal, thirteen in the flooring and eleven ceilings. Sharp corners of furniture, dressing tables and projecting edges of all sorts were padded with silk and leather, the forerunners of crash pads on the dashboards of modern motor cars, with the result that *Lalee* was so heavy it had to be specially routed in transit to encounter only the strongest bridges and trestles.

The bathroom fixtures were solid silver, Mrs. Langtry's bedroom was hung in green silk brocade, the observation salon was done with rose colored silk curtains trimmed with bunched Brussels lace and there was cream and gold brocade from Lyons, France, in abundance wherever the eye might rest. There was also a piano, overstuffed furniture, bookcases, a maid's room with a sewing machine, two guest rooms, a galley and sleeping space for the staff. Beneath the car rode an ice compartment "big enough to house a whole stag" and at either end were open observation platforms of teak imported specially from India for the purpose.

"*Lalee*," records Sichel, "even to Lillie was on the gaudy side and lacked only purple sails to make it look like Cleopatra's barge."

The entire entourage, which in a single year covered 17,000 miles between playhouses from Boston to Los Angeles, was administered by Beverly, a butler of almost unearthly perfection, who wore a silk top hat and cutaway coat into the howling wildernesses of Cheyenne and Denver with the same aplomb that characterized his promenades in London's West End. Beverly saw to it there were Scotch grouse and Perrier Jouet champagne in limitless requisition and the cooking was done by the Lily's French chef, Mézirand, who turned out midnight suppers and Sunday dinners for unexpected guests on a minimum of notice with an *expertise* that dazzled outlanders wherever the party paused.

Happily *Lalee* never was called upon to withstand the shocks and concussions against which Colonel Mann had provided. It became a legend in the theater and a property of perfumed and sinful romance in the newspapers long after the romance between Gebhard and Mrs. Langtry had been shattered by the inopportune arrival of the Romeo of the magnums at the actress' London townhouse just as the Prince of Wales was emerging from her private apartments. *Lalee* perished in the grand manner of private cars by fire in the years which intervened between the Lily's American tours.

But even though Gebhard and *Lalee* were out of her life, Mrs. Langtry was not quit of Colonel Mann who, in the course of building the car itself and doing business with the devoted Freddy had picked up some fascinating details of the actress' private life with which, a year or two later, he attempted to blackmail her to the tune of $200,000. His practice was to submit a biographical sketch of a prospective victim which he had prepared for the pages of *Town Topics* complete with ruinous details of matters better left unsaid and which could be withdrawn from publication on payment of a suitable fee.

Confronted with a truly rollicking account of her dalliance with the Prince of Wales and other members of the Marlborough House Set which the Colonel had thoughtfully scheduled for an early issue of his magazine, Mrs. Langtry sought out little Abe Hummel, of the famous law firm of Howe & Hummel who, in turn, had an ample dossier on the slippery Colonel William D'Alton Mann. Hummel suggested that the Colonel meet him at the office of the District Attorney for New York County for a conference to include what jail Mann would prefer to occupy for the next several years and the *Town Topics* article was prudently dropped.

The Colonel never forgave Mrs. Langtry for not being a paying customer at his blackmail store and did her much mischief within the limits of the law in his columns as long as she was in professional circulation.

Another player whose private railroad transport aroused the admiration of the press was Richard Mansfield whose private car from Pullman's rental pool achieved remark in *The Theater Magazine* for July 1906.

"Mr. Mansfield's railroad car is a marvel of compactness and simple elegance," wrote an interviewer. "It consists of four living rooms and a kitchen. At one end is a large and comfortable dining room ornamented with Mr. Mansfield's own silver service. Then comes the kitchen and off that is Mr. Mansfield's bedroom, while at the end of the car is a splendid library of 200 or 300 volumes."

The advertising sections of *The Theater* in those golden years of the American road company fairly bristle with the display insertions of carriers, the New Jersey Central, Michigan Central, Queen & Crescent, Southern, Pere Marquette, Southern Pacific, the Milwaukee and the Alton, all eager for the patronage of ranking troupers in their private varnish or less august players occupying sleepers between one night stands.

It was during this golden age both of the speaking stage and the railroads themselves that a reporter for *Metropolitan Magazine* in its issue of June 1898 took occasion while describing Anna Held's private car to remark editorially that "Few of our multi-millionaires boast of private palace cars but, with the true democratic spirit, share with others the ordinary comforts of Pullman and Wagner service." Since the late nineties were a time when almost no man of wealth or achievement could do without the private railroad car that was the ultimate hallmark of financial success and social aloofness, it just goes to show that reporters, then as now, were fallible.

Paderewski on the occasion of his first concert tour of America shuddered at the thought of provincial hotels and restaurants even as close to New York as Poughkeepsie. He would not sleep in one or dine in the other and the p.v. *General Stanley* was finally rented from the Pullman Company for his accommodation. Nor was the great pianist favorably impressed with the conventional Negro cook and waiter that came with the car, so two certified French chefs and an accomplished French waiter were procured from the Fifth Avenue Hotel. Paderewski received $1,000 a concert, a truly princely sum at the time, and spent an estimated half of this amount for traveling expenses whenever he visited an outland city.

Grand opera troupes have always traveled by special private train of Pullmans and the Metropolitan still does. It keeps the company together and under reasonable control of the management, accelerates departure after one night stands and eliminates hotel expenses en route.

For many years and as long as the road itself survived, there was a brisk traffic in slightly used private varnish which was sold by dealers in second-hand railroad equipment to minstrel troupes, Uncle Tom companies and dog and pony shows. Many a once-haughty Pullman and Wagner that had housed tycoons of commerce and finance on their errant occasions toward the end carried the All-Afro Imperial Minstrels or Otto Floto's animal acts to the far places of the continent. A car that had once been the private conveyance of Tom Mix in his barnstorming days was available only a few years ago from a Chicago broker in such matters, but wooden undersills discouraged purchasers and it was last heard of figuring in a deal with a Greek restaurateur in Fall River, Massachusetts.

The early days of the films saw a number of p.v. rented from Pullman for promotional tours by such players as Douglas Fairbanks, Sr., Mary Pickford, Mary Miles Minter and William S. Hart, but Hollywood, whose capacity for the wrong thing is boundless, quickly cottoned to the airplane on the specious theory that an actor's time was valuable and the private car era for theater folk ended approximately with Julia Marlowe and William Gillette. Not a few film folk including the ill-fated Mike Todd and Grace Moore came to bad ends in planes when they might have lived, and comfortably too, in private railroad cars.

Newspapermen of means, however, favored private cars to the very end. Whitelaw Reid inevitably made the trip from his Madison Avenue mansion in New York to his wife's ancestral home at Millbrae, California, aboard *Ellsmere* or another private car from the Pullman rental pool. When John Russell Young, the famous editor of *The New York Herald* under the younger James Gordon Bennett, visited California to be a guest at Belmont, Senator Sharon's palatial country home south of San Francisco, he arrived in the Golden State aboard Charles Crocker's p.v. *Mishawaka,* named for the Indiana town where he had started life as a forge worker. Arthur Brisbane, for many years chief editorialist for the Hearst newspaper empire, once feuded bitterly with the New York Central Railroad because that carrier would not carry a borrowed private car in the consist of *The Twentieth Century Limited* and wouldn't even stop the *Century*, if he consented to ride in a drawing room, at his home town of Poughkeepsie. Cissie Patterson, publisher of the Washington *Times-Herald*, purchased *Ranger* from Pullman Standard in 1928 when she was Mrs. Elmer Schlesinger and maintained it after her husband's death until her own demise in 1948. John McLean, publisher of the *Cincinnati Enquirer* and later the *Washington Post*, was owner of *Ohio;* and Clarence Barron, owner of the *Wall Street Journal* and *Boston News Bureau*, was forever borrowing Franklyn Hutton's *Curlyhut* or Josh Cosden's *Roamer* to run down to Palm Beach for the weekend.

Toward the end of the private car era, Charles Clegg and the author of this volume, proprietors of *The Territorial Enterprise* at Virginia City, maintained the p.v. *The Virginia City* for their private occasions. Paul Block, the New York publisher, liked a nice train ride aboard his own Pullman-built *Friendship*.

In the early twenties of the present century there were still enough private cars in the hands of non-railroaders and of railroad executives with socially ambitious wives to make their proposed inclusion bothersome to officials charged with the Royal Train on which Queen Marie of Rumania toured the country. The conduct of the entourage was in the hands of a State Department representative, Colonel John Carroll who remarked to Gene Fowler, who covered the tour for the *New York American* that "there isn't enough motive power in the entire United States to haul all the private cars whose owners wanted them attached to us." Colonel Carroll, an old-time railroader of stately mien who was accustomed to shout "Captain, stay the cars" at the conductor when some reporter or other visitor was carried away from a terminal, spent a ponderable part of his time rejecting, with gestures, the importunities of wealthy admirers of royalty who wanted their cars hitched to Her Majesty's.

It was on this tour, too, that the irreverent Fowler, his feet snared in the unaccustomed depths of a carpet in the Queen's personal car, stumbled and fell flat on his face in front of Marie. "I abase myself, your Majesty," explained the author of "Timberline," "but not in humility!"

A private car celebrated at the turn of the century was *El Fleda*, property of a character the newspapers of the day were pleased to call "The Millionaire Brakeman," which, in fact, he was. Johnny Bunting had been employed by the Southern Pacific tying them down on the cartops on the San Joaquin Valley into Bakersfield and his great dream in life was one day to ride, perhaps even to possess a private car like those he saw reeling off the California miles filled with gentlemen in wing collars smoking four bit cigars and reading the stock quotations. California oil was not in 1898 the bonanza it was to become shortly afterwards and Johnny's friends shook their heads when he insisted on putting his savings into real estate on the outskirts of Bakersfield and started drilling.

Well, in a word, Johnny struck it rich and the first evidence of his wealth was when he walked into the office of J. A. Fillmore, the exalted general manager of the Southern Pacific, and announced that he wanted to buy himself a nice private varnish. Mr. Fillmore, a man of the world, batted no eyelash when yesterday's humble brakeman laid an impressive sum in banknotes on the desk and sold him a car that had belonged to a recently deceased director of the line. The hand-me-down served as a stopgap or interim car for Brakeman Johnny but it wasn't what he had in mind. The Bakersfield oil continued to flow and in 1901 Pullman outshopped for the personal use of J. A. Bunting Order No. 2722, *El Fleda*. *El Fleda* became a celebrated railroad property, both for the happy disposition of its owner and the variety of mechanical improvements he incorporated in its design, innovations whose identity have, unhappily, been lost over the years.

"Nearly everyone who goes in for private railroad cars does so with the general notion that nobody heretofore has had any adequate notion of what that sort of vehicle should be," said Judson T. Welliver of the Pullman Company in connection with the personal whims of customers. "He is going to produce something different, something better, something to impress the world. A car meeting all these grandiose requirements would have to be a completely appointed hotel, including a moving picture palace, ballroom, swimming pool, state dining room, sun parlor, bathrooms, nine hole golf course and conservatory." As a matter of fact, many of the requirements listed by Mr. Welliver as captious were eventually realized. The ultimate in private car designing was nothing less than a complete hotel in mobile form. Dancing to Cuban rumba orchestras for a time was featured aboard special equipment for the Florida seasonal trade on the Seaboard Air Line. Private cars with enlarged dining salons seating up to fourteen were built for special customers including the Mexican Presidential Train. The major domo in charge of operations aboard *Ranger* when it was owned by Cissie Patterson, Washington newspaper publisher, mindful of his mistress' exotic taste in blooms, wired ahead elaborate orders for fresh flowers to be put aboard when the car was moving and first run motion pictures were often shown in the spacious salon of the same car. One of Mrs. Patterson's intimates and a frequent guest was Evalyn Walsh McLean, owner of the Hope Diamond, who was a film addict.

Beginning early with Commodore Vanderbilt, there was a tradition of multiple private car units for the convenience of truly towering tycoons of their age. George Pullman himself who, like many successful men of his time, was proud of his stables often journeyed abroad with a specially constructed Pullman Horse & Carriage Car with accommodations for grooms and coachmen along with his matched bays and the broughams and landaus, victorias and demi-daumonts they drew. Collis P. Huntington soon found *Oneonta* insufficient for his requirements when away from San Francisco and had *Oneonta II* built along more modest lines by Pullman to accommodate the overflow. Jay Gould, a dyspeptic who travelled with his own staff of physicians and a chef trained in dietary practice, when making safari to the Far West took along a special cow whose butterfat content was precisely suited to his needs and the cow rode in a private converted baggage car at the head end of the train. Gould attributed the device to James Gordon Bennett whose oceangoing yacht, whenever he crossed the Atlantic carried a milch cow on the foredeck.

Unique, so far as the record shows, was St. Paul, Minneapolis & Manitoba Private Car No. 22 built at the company shops at St. Paul in 1905 for Louis W. Hill, son of the Empire Builder, which contained an eighteen foot automobile compartment complete with upper and lower berths for mechanic and chauffeur and an auto-door and ramp to facilitate the unloading of the owner's early Rolls-Royces and Renaults of which he was an avid collector. Almost as rare, although not entirely unique, were private varnish with such cultural facilities as libraries. Dr. Seward Webb's Wagner car *Ellsmere,* which later appeared in the Pullman rental pool, possessed an ample gentleman's library.

No swimming baths are in the record although shower baths and marble tubs became more or less commonplace on private and business varnish as well as some of the extra-fare transcontinental luxury trains, and the owners of *The Virginia City* combined its shower space with a steam bath working off the train steam line that was found to be restorative after strenuous nights-before.

Over the decades the private railroad car received an almost unexceptionally fair press in the newspapers of the United States and if the style of reporting abated somewhat the florid raptures of Victorian prose in favor of a more jocund approach, the city desk of 1958 still knew a good feature when it saw one and by-line writers had fun with occupants less stuffy than General Palmer had been about *Nomad*. Witness an account by Herb Caen, ranking columnist of the Pacific Coast, in the *San Francisco Chronicle* after a visit to *The Virginia City.*

GILDED CAGE DEPT.: Fellow peasant, let me tell you how the rich people are living. (I won't keep you in suspense. They're living real good.)

Tuesday noon, for lack of something worse to do, I ferried across the Bay to Oakland Mole for a first hand view of the talk of the railroad industry—the private railway coach of the Messrs. Lucius Beebe and Charles Clegg, the toast of Virginia City and the pride of Nevada. Let me tell you this, that Oakland has never seen the like of *this* before. It made the East Bay metropolis look positively shabby.

The coach, named of course *The Virginia City,* is an all-steel job by Pullman, painted a wild yellow and red on the outside and decorated on the inside (by Los Angeles' Robert Hanley) to the extent of "more than $100,000," unquote. Mr. Clegg refused to talk price. Vulgar.

The Virginia City is the only really private railway car in the country . . . "It's for pleasure only," says Mr. Clegg and to prove it mixed Martinis in the drawing room bar and we then walked into the dining room for lunch prepared by Wallace, the chef, and served by Clarence, the steward, (both hired from the Southern Pacific.) Nice little lunch. A creole fish soup with rice, Southern fried chicken, ham and beans, hot cornbread, pumpkin pie, a fine dry Bollinger champagne. "Wallace always prepares a light lunch," said Mr. Beebe. "You should stay for dinner. He's cooking a cow."

Parked next to *The Virginia City* was the private coach of John P. Kiley, President of the Chicago, Milwaukee & St. Paul Railway (most railway bosses have private cars but they don't count as "pleasure" cars.) "Frankly, Mr. Kiley's car isn't much on the inside," said Mr. Clegg. "Mrs. Kiley dropped in for a look at ours and was positively bug-eyed. I don't think Mr. Kiley will hear the end of it."

A member of Kiley's staff went through *The Virginia City* while I was there and observed in a thin, small voice: "Very nice!" He peered into the service area, looked at the ice container and crowed: "WE have a deep freeze!" "WE have a Turkish bath," retorted Mr. Beebe. "Oh," said the Kiley man, leaving. Be that as it may, I think private railway cars are the nicest thing. Everybody should have one.

Even though railroad executives cringe or bristle, as their temperament inclines, at the words private car, newspaper reporters obstinately refuse to take seriously their determination to speak of railroad property as business cars. In the winter of 1958, a convocation of highranking railroaders converged on Washington for a meeting with President Eisenhower, and Phil Casey, ace reporter for the Washington *Post Times-Herald*, wrote: "They're called office cars, which is a good enough name, except they don't have any offices. A railroad man told the reporter, 'I've never seen any office cars with real offices.' The work area, it turns out, is a loungey thing of coffee tables, divans, chairs and lamps."

In the golden age of American railroading, however, the designation of palace cars for special occupancy as either private cars or business cars was purely academic. Commodore Vanderbilt, James J. Hill, Jay Gould or E. H. Harriman owned the railroad or even the system of railroads over which their varnish rolled. They had few stockholders to placate and were not intimidated by the good way of life. It made little difference to Charles Crocker if his fine car *Mishawaka* with the Southern Pacific insigne on its nameboards was called private or an office car. He owned a controlling interest in the railroad and, one way or another, it was his car.

It was an age when giants were abroad in the land and many of them rode in brass bound state aboard dark green cars with the word Private on the door. Which was as it should be.

PULLMAN STANDARD

Porfirian Magnificence Below The Rio Grande

At once the Big Rock Candy Mountain and the boneyard of private railway cars, Old Mexico is believed by such authorities as Everett DeGolyer and Gerald Best to have a greater density of private cars than either the United States or Canada. For Mexican magnificoes some of the most sumptuous varnish in the history of carbuilding was outshopped at St. Charles and Pullman, and dictators and military adventurers have commanded transport of almost unearthly splendor. Here, too, gravitated the once haughty private cars of Yankee wealth and fashion overwhelmed with the ruin of years to find final service with lonely mining companies in distant provinces. Beneath the tarnished insigne of the Sonora Railway on an obscure siding at Guaymas the diligent archivist can detect the lineaments of a car that once rolled on the occasions of Whitneys or Berwinds. A track gang's shelter along the three-foot rails of the Mexican Southern at Oaxaca once knew the presence of David Moffat or Charlie Boettcher on the narrow gauges of the Shining Mountains. Business cars of American mining companies in Chihuahua, now cluttered with engineer's reports and smelter assays, in other years knew other properties, the evening studs of Joseph Widener en route to Palm Beach, the high-tension Bourbon and fancy tales cigars with which Thomas Fortune Ryan regaled his guests. The seedy grandeur of observation platforms diminishing in the tropic night south of Eagle Pass once rolled to greater destinies at Del Monte or in the autumn Adirondacks. For every Mexican minister of state the Republic provides a private car. For presidents an entire presidential train. Railroad officials in the almost numberless multiplicity of bureaucracy south of the border each have their official car of greater or less vintage and panache. What must have been the rococo grandeurs of private varnish in Mexico in the seventies and eighties when Boston financiers and British milords were building the Central Mexicana, the Ferrocarril Interoceanio, the Ferrocarril Mexicano del Sur and the National de Tehuantepec under the benevolent regard of Don Porfirio can best be left to the imagination. No vestigial trace of their being has survived to attest the florid corruption of generals and governors, the stupendous thirsts and taste for ornate transport of military chieftans and the proud hidalgoes of the great ranches. English-built directors' cars and Wagner palace cars alike have faded into the mists of antiquity. The mists are golden as befits the dreams alike of Francisco Vasquez de Coronado and Collis Huntington who built the Mexican International.

Eagles In The Dust

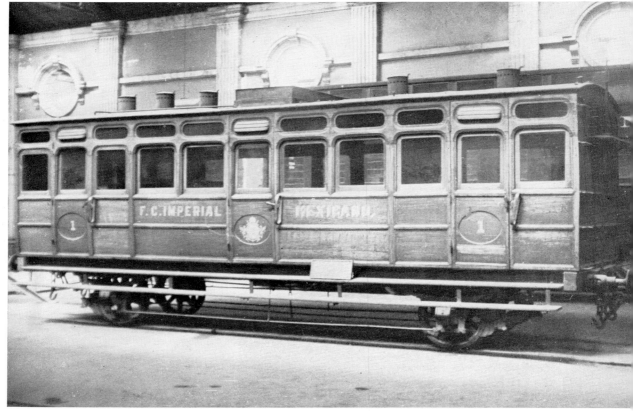

Tragic destinies rode aboard this primeval private car of the Imperial Mexican Railways when the Archduke Maximillian of Austria was set up as Emperor of Mexico in 1864 in an attempt on the part of Napoleon III to establish a French colonial empire there. Destined a few years later to become part of the Ferrocarril Mexicano reaching from Mexico City to Vera Cruz, the first tracks were laid from Vera Cruz to Paso del Macho, at the foot of the mountains, a distance of fifty miles, and over these Maximillian and his Empress Carlotta rode in state on his way to assume his brief-lived rule in Mexico City. Built with English capital, the carrier's imperial car suggests the English car-building practice of the time, and it was for many years on exhibition in the Mexican Railway depot in Mexico City until it was destroyed in a careless switching accident in 1949.

In contrast to the primal simplicities of the imperial carriage depicted on the page opposite is the sumptuous interior of one of the staterooms aboard the private train of Don Porfirio Diaz built by Pullman in 1898 for the Mexican dictator. Rare woodwork, rich damask hangings, ornate ceiling design and a profusion of French mirrors testify to the voluptuary tastes of an era of great magnificence below the Rio Grande.

PULLMAN STANDARD

In 1899 Pullman outshopped to the order of the Mexican government two presidential cars to be occupied en suite by Don Porfirio Diaz. The exterior of the observation drawing room car is shown on the page opposite and on this page the magnificently appointed details of one of its private apartments. Everywhere the eye encountered plush, velvet and brocaded silk, luxurious sleeping accommodations and stately reception salons, and over all the emblematic eagles of the Republic and the interlocking R-M that was the cypher of the Mexican state.

The noble apartments depicted in mahogany and marquetry magnificence on these two pages present the master rooms on the car built in 1897 by Pullman for the personal use of Don Porfirio Diaz, Dictator of Mexico and a man who, knowing how little of this commodity the world affords, wanted nothing but the best of everything. To this day the word Porfirian in the lexicon of Old Mexico is synonymous with splendor and excellence in the grand manner of a vanished regime.

TWO PHOTOS: PULLMAN STANDARD

The nineties saw railroad building at its peak south of the Rio Grande and carriers in Old Mexico no less than their counterparts in the United States were ordering private cars of individuality and voluptuousness of decor. On the page opposite are the Pullman-built exteriors of the narrow gauge Interoceanic's *Carmen* and No. 96 of the Mexico, Cuernavaca y Pacifico while below on this page its narrow gauge reality is belied by the spacious look of the three-foot Interoceanic's gem-like directors' car *Isabel*.

THREE PHOTOS:
PULLMAN STANDARD

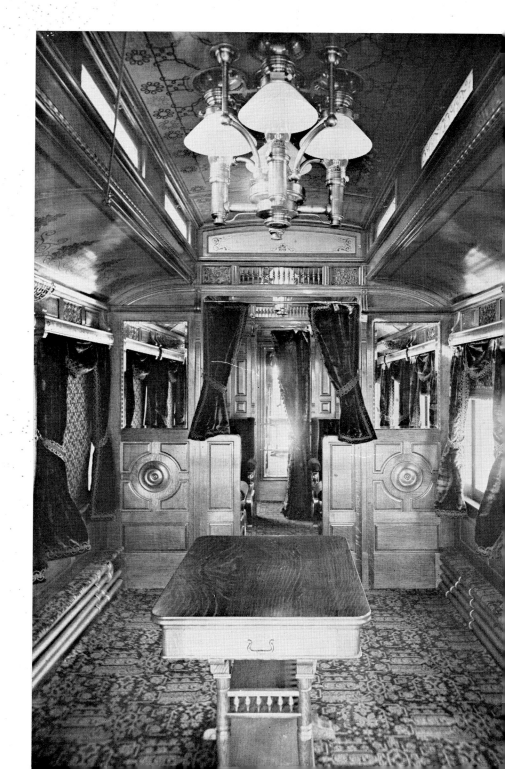

Some of the most ornate and stately private varnish outshopped by Pullman in the wealthy nineties was for service in Old Mexico. The photographs on the page opposite depict the beautifully frescoed ceiling and richly tooled leather chairs of *Carmen,* ordered in 1896 for the chief operating officer of the Central Mexicano, and the drawing salon of Mexico, Cuernavaca y Pacifico's No. 96. Above is one of the state apartments of the private train of Don Porfirio Diaz.

PULLMAN STANDARD

The imperial dimensions that Mexico refused to acknowledge in the unfortunate Maximillian were realized by Don Porfirio Diaz whose Presidential Train, built by Pullman, bespoke luxury in loud, emphatic tones through the agency of satinwood paneling, intricate marquetry, fixtures of Carrara marble and silk brocade portières in stately vistas of compartmented comfort.

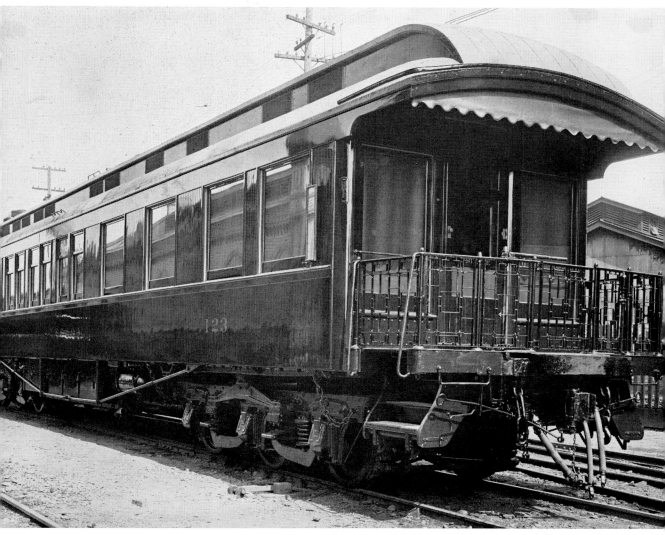

The venerable Southern Pacific car No. 123, shown here as *Tucson*, was one of the atmospheric properties of Western railroading, having originally been the historic *Stanford* in which the first President of the Central Pacific and later his widow rode thousands of miles in the eighties and nineties. Built in the Sacramento shops at a cost of $25,000 in 1882 by Master Carbuilder Benjamin Welch, it was sold shortly after 1900 to a now forgotten private owner who rechristened it *Sunland*. In 1911 it was repurchased by the Espee for the use of the carrier's by now legendary General Manager Joseph Dyer and renamed, for the third time, as *Tucson*. It came to a spectacular end when Dyer's son and heir, Joseph, Jr., accidentally fired it with a secret store of patriotic fireworks hoarded against the Fourth of July at Yuma, June 27, 1911.

The Chicago & Eastern Illinois official car No. 501 (PAGE OPPOSITE) was built by Pullman in 1891 and reflects nicely the degree of luxury suited to an unpretentious but still profitably conducted mid-Western carrier. On this page the working fireplace on a Pennsylvania business car built a decade later suggests that its occupants were minded to keep warm even when the car was set out on sidings not available to train line steam.

PULLMAN STANDARD

At much the same time that J. Ross Clark was running surveys of his railroads in the Amargosa Desert as depicted on the page opposite, the directors of the Tidewater Railroad, among them the late Junius Beebe of Boston, father of the author, might take their ease and view the passing countryside from the observation platform of the company car *Dixie*. Handsomely polished mahogany with gold fine-lining, exposed steam radiators and pointed electric light bulbs with hairpin filaments were signs of the times in 1906 when *Dixie* was built by Pullman. Junius Beebe entered the Tidewater scene when his railroad, the Piney River & Paint Creek merged with the Virginian which shortly absorbed the Tidewater as well. The P.R. & P.C. owned valuable coal producing properties in the area and was coveted by the larger and to this day prosperous Virginian.

TWO PHOTOS: JOHN B. WORDEN

Although less publicized than his spectacularly acquisitive brother, Senator William A. Clark, J. Ross Clark was very much a mover and shaker in the fields of Western mining and railroads at the turn of the century. His best known creation was the San Pedro, Los Angeles & Salt Lake Railroad between Southern California and the mainline connections at Salt Lake and Ogden that is today the Los Angeles Division of the Union Pacific. J. Ross Clark also had mining interests in Rhyolite, Greenwater and other Death Valley properties and projected the Las Vegas & Tonopah Railroad to achieve them. These two photos of a private special train ordered on the S.P.L.A. & S.L. to inspect its right of way by Clark in 1903 provides an interesting study in bowler hats and boiled shirts and shows that friends of the family came along, too.

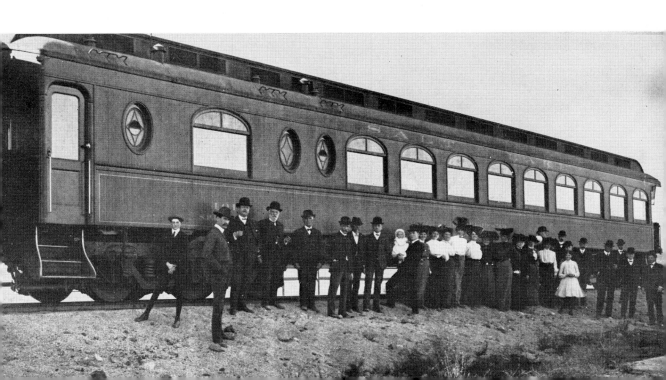

Eloquent expressions of Pullman craftsmanship are the Lehigh Valley's private parlor car *Seneca* and *Veritas,* an observation-compartment sleeping car built in 1898 and placed in the rental pool for private occupancy. The exterior appearance of *Veritas,* whose silver and maroon marked it as a departure from the general practice of solid color liveries on other Pullman p.v., was complemented by its handsome interior shown on this page. Here Mazda electric bulbs shone upon magnificently inlaid woodwork from the pullman "marquetry room," tête-a-tête love seats and the potted palms and fringes dear to the age of William McKinley. *Veritas* was designed without dining facilities, presumably for the accommodation of parties and individuals agreeable to eating in the dining car up forward.

Not all the private varnish of the golden age was designed for prolonged occupancy or fitted with complete hotel facilities; some was for groups on holiday of modest dimensions requiring privacy only between dawn and dusk. Here elegant daytime comfort is represented by a truly magnificent parlor car built soon after the turn of the century by American Car & Foundry for the Boston & Maine Railroad at a time when such conveyances were in great request to achieve resorts of fashion or popular acceptance within daylight run of Boston's North Station. Aboard it Saltonstalls and Hallowells were able in congenial privacy to make summer pilgrimages to the innumerable Down East spas served by the Yankee carrier. Going to Prout's or Seal Harbor over the B & M in early June was part of Boston's ordained routine, one with Commencement at Harvard and opening night at Mary Garden's Boston Opera Company.

AMERICAN CAR & FOUNDRY

The cafe observation car *Seneca* was delivered by Pullman to the Lehigh Valley Railroad in 1901 for daytime charter as private varnish and, as occasion demanded, in regularly scheduled train service out of Jersey City on the run through Eastern Pennsylvania. Comfortably appointed and meticulously built, it was a good example of the special equipment which even secondary carriers could afford to have assigned to them until the coming of the automobile age.

THREE PHOTOS: PULLMAN STANDARD

The Colorado Midland's gleaming car No. 100, which was also known as *Cascade* was eventually to be occupied by Cripple Creek millionaire A. E. Carlton and was delivered to the road's Colorado Springs terminal in 1898. At once business-like and luxurious it was well suited for the entertainment among the towering Rockies of notables including Theodore Roosevelt, President Taft, David Moffat and the ubiquitous and urbane Count James Pourtales, lord of nine Silesian villages and an adventurer in a green velvet frock coat who almost but not quite unloaded his glittering Colorado Springs gambling casino on George M. Pullman. On the page opposite newspaper publisher John McLean's *Ohio* built by Pullman in 1894 and the Hocking Valley's *Hocking* of a decade later illustrate the transition from private varnish with open platforms at either end to the enclosed forward platform of later practice.

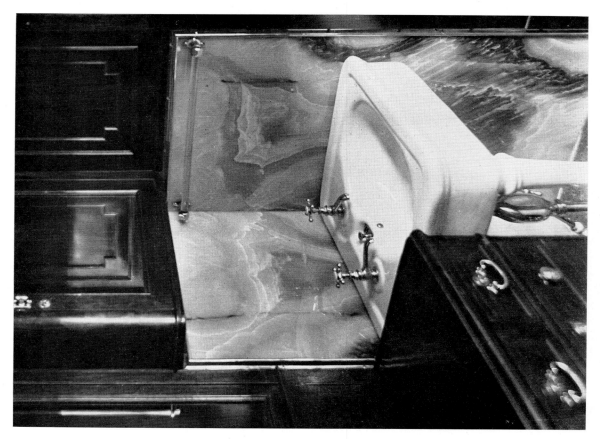

Varying the conventional arrangement of a single double bed in the master stateroom of private cars, the principal sleeping apartment aboard *Ohio*, built in 1894 for John McLean, publisher of the *Cincinnati Enquirer* contained narrow twin brass beds. A frequent figure aboard *Ohio* was McLean's daughter-in-law, Evalyn Walsh McLean, owner of the Hope Diamond and most celebrated Washington hostess of all time.

THREE PHOTOS: PULLMAN STANDARD

An early private car bathtub, although by no means the first, was the wood-sheathed fixture of 1888 vintage shown on the page opposite that was part of the luxury equipment of the Pullman-built *Golden Gate*, designed for the Central Pacific Railroad in California. Shown next to it is the hand bowl enclosed in polished onyx panels aboard *Idlehour* built seventeen years later for the New York Central and the private occasions of William K. Vanderbilt.

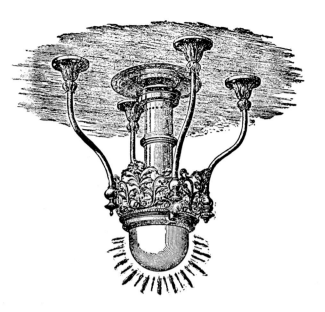

The Pintsch Patent illuminating gas system made its appearance on American railroad cars early in the seventies and continued in use as an auxiliary illumination long after the coming of electricity on business and private cars alike. Electricity was regarded as at best unreliable and private varnish was in some cases equipped with gas as late as 1910. Day coaches and suburban cars were lit by gas well into the twenties for reasons of economy and practicability. While gas was for decades regarded as a standby against electrical failure, it will be noted from the pictures on these pages that *Atlas* was equipped with coal oil lamps as a precautionary standby against failure of the Pintsch lamps.

Shown on this and the page opposite, the Central Railroad of New Jersey's official car *Atlas*, built by Pullman in 1896 may be taken as the archetype of solid, comfortable and above all utilitarian business car of the closing decades of the last century. The below photograph indicates that the carrier took no stock in the "business car" delusion of a later age and boldly engrossed its property with the legend "Private Car."

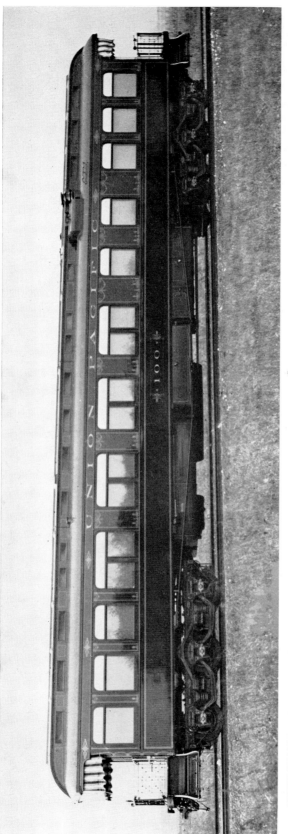

THREE PHOTOS: PULLMAN STANDARD

Two of the most advertised private cars of the Far West were James Ben Ali Haggin's *Salvator* and the Union Pacific No. 100 whose exteriors are shown on the page opposite while an interior prospect of No. 100 appears here. This uncommonly handsome car with the unique elegance of a gaily striped awning over both front and rear platform was used upon his personal and executive occasions by the great Julius Kruttschnitt. One of the glittering names of railroad operation of all time, Kruttschnitt had been a former chief operating officer of the Southern Pacific and, under the Harriman consolidation, became "Director of Maintenance & Operations" of the combined Union Pacific, Southern Pacific, the Oregon Short Line and the Oregon Railroad & Navigation Company. The Harriman-Kruttschnitt alliance is celebrated in legend for Harriman's remark to his lieutenant when he earmarked $18,000,000 for on-line improvements of the Espee: "Spend it in a week if you can." Haggin's selection of the Northern Pacific as home railroad for *Salvator* at this remove remains a mystery, but it might well have been indicated by the San Francisco millionaire's close business association with Senator George Hearst in mining properties in South Dakota.

One of the most celebrated private cars in the golden age of rail transport is shown on the opposite page. *Wanderer* was outshopped in 1901 for William Collins Whitney, a towering mogul of society and finance, Cleveland's Secretary of the Navy and founder of a dynastic succession in which Vanderbilts, ambassadors and ownership of private cars were commonplace. *Wanderer* replaced Whitney's earlier Wagner-built *Pilgrim* and when it was photographed that now distant day at Pullman had not even been christened, since its nameboards were bare. It was assigned as its home railroad to the New York Central and, at Whitney's death some years later, passed to his son Harry Payne Whitney and was in service as late as 1930. On this page, the interior of Santa Fe's *Sunflower State* built for occupancy by the road's directors in 1890 was inviting without being sumptuous. Most Santa Fe directors were Bostonians who enjoyed comfort without ostentation.

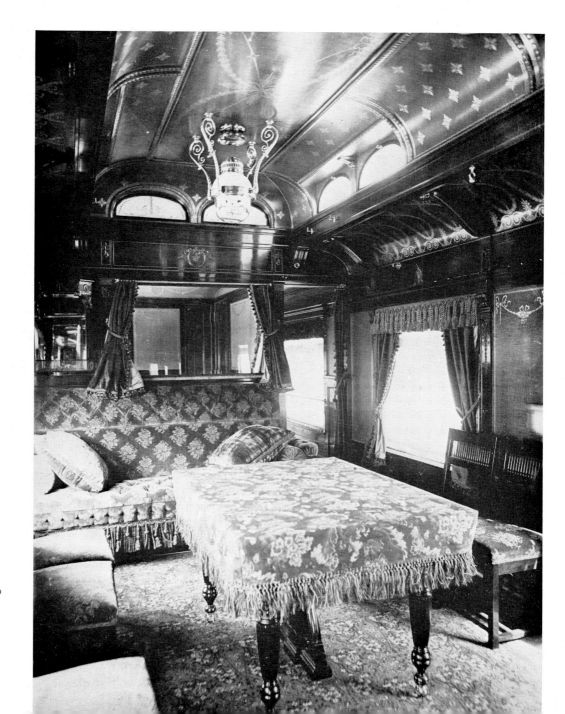

TWO PHOTOS: PULLMAN STANDARD

Superb examples of pure and unequivocal business cars for carriers of major dimensions are the mahogany sheathed No. 37 of the Pennsylvania on the page opposite built by Pullman in 1890 for the general manager of Lines West Lenore F. Loree, later famed as President of the Delaware & Hudson, and the classic-lined No. 100 ordered for the President of the Southern in 1905. On this page is the Burlington's venerable *Texland*, assigned to the remote and picturesque Fort Worth & Denver run from Pueblo south through the Texas Panhandle. *Texland* was photographed in the spring of 1959 while being serviced at the Colorado & Southern depot at Trinidad, Colorado, itself the scene of so many railroad excitements in the glory years of the transcontinentals.

LUCIUS BEEBE

Over the years the Baker Patent Car Heater was generally accepted as the solution for heating private cars when main train line steam heat was not available or the car was spotted on a siding and occupied. Although its eccentricities induced frustration in generations of trainmen and servants it worked after a fashion and, as is suggested by the elaborate metal sheathing in this photograph, seldom induced conflagration in the event of wreck or other accident. The Espee's *Houston* (BELOW) set what may be an all-time high in car numbering.

PULLMAN STANDARD

SOUTHERN PACIFIC

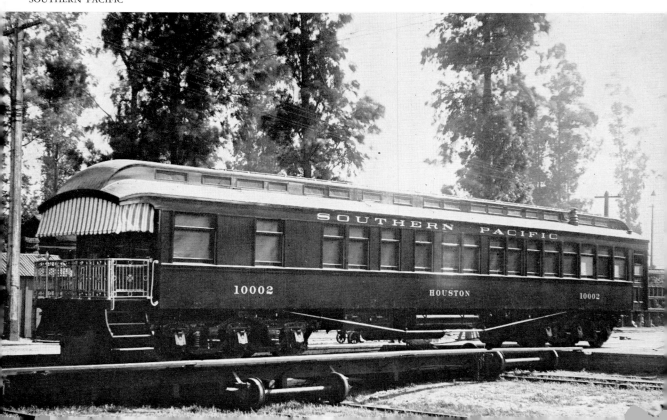

In the vanished age of steam, the Southern Pacific maintained the great tradition of immaculate varnish in such stately cars as *Del Monte* (LEFT) and even in division superintendents' cars such as *Portland*, shown below. No railroad boasted such a spectacular variety of private and business cars deriving from many and often distant sources, but with the passing of time the Espee allowed the designation "Private Car" to lapse and made a gesture toward austerity with the legend "Business Car" or "Official."

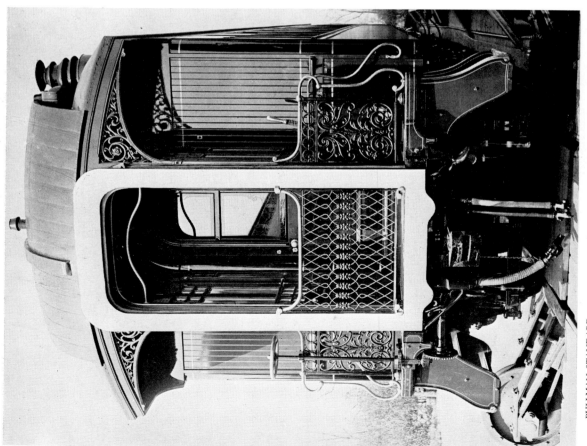

Amidst a splendid profusion of wing collars, Ascot ties and four button suits, Ignatz Jan Paderewski is surrounded by his professional entourage on the platform of his car, *General Stanley*, hired on a rental basis from Pullman's general service pool of private cars. The year is 1906 and of the $1,000 fee for his every performance, it was estimated that the pianist paid out $500 for travel expenses and the maintenance of his suite of concert master, publicist, personal physician and valets, porters and chefs beyond counting. The grand manner was an integral element of his calling and Paderewski was very much the master of personal grandeur.

On the page opposite, the front platforms of Pullman-built *Electric* (LEFT) and *Iolanthe* illustrate the classic lines and painstaking detail that were invested in the building of private varnish in the golden age of car-building in the late eighties.

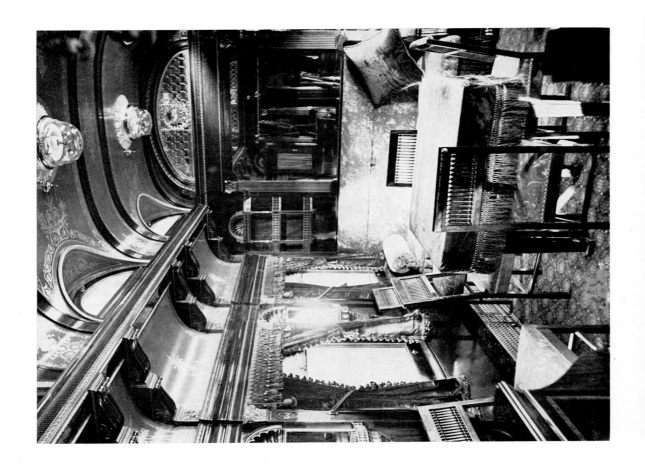

Examples of the painstaking craftsmanship invested in Pullman private cars as the finest flower of the carbuilder's and decorator's *expertise* are the interiors of the Savannah, Florida & Western's No. 100 (LEFT) and the *Lucania* from the Pullman Company's general service pool depicted on the page opposite. The Suwanee River Route was part of the system of railroads built by Henry B. Plant on the Florida West Coast to rival the glittering resorts strung along Henry Flagler's Florida East Coast Railroad, while *Lucania*, built by Pullman in 1897, was the twin of *Campania*, a private car which achieved even greater celebrity as Arthur E. Stillwell's car No. 100 on the Kansas City, Pittsburgh & Gulf. On this page the observation platform of *Tryphena* is a superb example of the metalworker's craft in the nineties surmounting the latest draft gear of the period and the laminated paper car wheels which were one of Pullman's most sensational patents.

Perhaps the finest flowering of the private railroad car as built by Pullman dated from the opening years of the twentieth century when wide observation platforms, arched windows with colored transoms and a prudent amount of gold finelining still characterized exteriors and Eastlake influence had not entirely disappeared from interior decors. *Eudoxus* and *Sunset*, the latter the first of this name, on the page opposite exemplify the great style and feeling for grandeur of the period. On this page is the dining salon of *Zamora*, outshopped by Pullman in 1901 to the order of H. C. Pierce at a time when ornate light fixtures were still in vogue and finely matched cabinet work was still the pride of Pullman's world-famous "marquetry room." Henry Clay Pierce was Chairman of the New York Board of the National Railways of Mexico and President of the Tennessee Central, and it was to the former that *Zamora* was assigned as its home railroad. Aboard it, the lordly Pierce was accustomed to attend to his affairs in Old Mexico while, in leisure moments, shuttling between his country estates at Pride's Crossing, Massachusetts, and Brule River, Wisconsin, and his town residences at St. Louis and New York City.

TWO PHOTOS: PULLMAN STANDARD

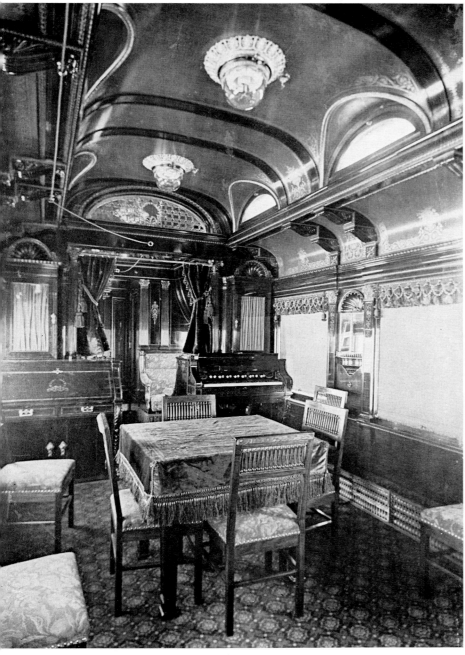

Two classics from the golden age of Pullman p.v. on the page opposite were the Minneapolis, St. Paul & Sault Ste. Marie's No. 999 and the famed *Iolanthe* built for the general service pool of private rental cars at Chicago. On this page is the interior of Arthur E. Stillwell's Car No. 100 of the Kansas City, Pittsburgh & Gulf with its parlor organ around which, by Stillwell's command, train crews gathered for observance of the Sabbath. In No. 100's master stateroom, too Stillwell received ghostly messages at night on the basis of which he guided the affairs of the railroad. The car later passed into ownership of Bet-a-Million Gates and was characterized thereafter by a less austere atmosphere. It was aboard No. 100, the former *Campania*, that Gates was reported to have wagered a cool $1,000,000 with James Keene, the stock manipulator, on a race between two raindrops down a car window, with the resulting identification as "Bet-A-Million."

KANSAS CITY MEXICO & ORIENT 100

ORIENTAL

TWO PHOTOS: PULLMAN STANDARD

On the page opposite are depicted the Pullman-built business car No. 100 of the Kansas City, Mexico & Orient acquired by President Arthur E. Stillwell after he had relinquished management of the Kansas City, Pittsburgh & Gulf and showing the twined flags of the two countries it was planned to serve. Also depicted is the exterior of the Pullman-built *Oriental* at the time it was delivered to the Louisville & Nashville in 1898. On this page is the dining salon of *Oriental*, much of whose fine woodwork and ornamentation was produced in the famous Pullman "marquetry room" at Calumet.

Wayfarer, shown on the page opposite, was built in 1905 by Pullman for Alfred G. Vanderbilt and in 1908 achieved the shady distinction of being named in divorce proceedings instituted by Mrs. Vanderbilt as the scene of infidelities on the part of her husband with Mrs. Agnes O'Brien Ruiz, wife of the Cuban attaché at Washington. It was one of the few private cars in the record to which an atmosphere of scandal specifically attached. No. 100 of the Colorado Midland, later named *Cascade,* was also the private conveyance of a man of secure wealth in the person of Bert Carlton, Cripple Creek millionaire and associate in many profitable ventures with Colorado's legendary Spencer Penrose and Colonel Daniel C. Jackling. Built at Pullman in 1898, No. 100 on the Midland was one of the last of the long and handsome succession of private cars with two open platforms. By the time *Wayfarer* was commissioned seven years later the enclosed service platform was almost universal, providing as it did not only shelter from the elements but additional service area. On this page the master stateroom on *Imperial* reflects the solid comforts of private car travel in the well-upholstered nineties, as represented by deep beds, ample drawer space and gas-mantle illumination.

When the elder J. P. Morgan was in process of forming the giant United States Steel Company with Charles M. Schwab as its head, he sent a genial Irishman named H. W. Oliver out as a land-looker for ore deposits and fuel resources within practicable distance of Pittsburgh. Aboard *Tyrone*, shown on this page and the page opposite, named by the sentimental Oliver for the county of his birth, Morgan's agent discovered the vast Messabi deposits of iron ore upon whose seemingly inexhaustible lode U. S. Steel was predicated. Of approximately the same vintage as *Tyrone* was August Belmont's *Mineola*, built for the New York capitalist and magnifico who was American representative for the House of Rothschild by Pullman in 1905 and also depicted on the opposite page.

On the page opposite is shown *El Fleda* the day it was outshopped by Pullman to the order of J. A. Bunting, the Southern Pacific millionaire brakeman. Visible in the photograph are the patent Pullman laminated paper wheels, whose merits Mr. Pullman himself is shown demonstrating in the drawing to the left. In the below photograph *El Fleda* has passed into the ownership of the Colorado & Wyoming Railroad where it is known as *Sunrise*. A group of pilgrims are shown in the enjoyment of its resources at Glenwood Springs circa 1912. Although he abjured braking for the Southern Pacific after striking it rich in oil, Bunting remained loyal to his former employer and *El Fleda's* home railroad, as demonstrated on the upper nameboards, was the San Joaquin Valley, one of the Espee's far-flung California operations.

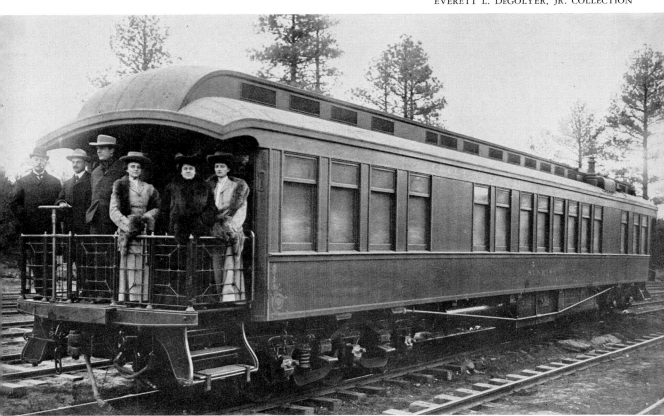

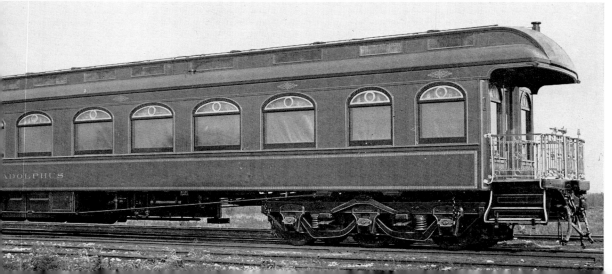

THREE PHOTOS: PULLMAN STANDARD

It may be presumed that the austerity depicted in the builder's photograph of William K. Vanderbilt's *Idlehour* as it came from the shops in 1905 was mitigated before delivery to its exalted occupant by the attentions of an interior decorator. On the page opposite *Adolphus*, ordered for the personnel of Anheuser Busch, the brewers, became something of an institution on the railroads of the land. Beer, appropriately enough, was on tap throughout the car and Rule G was generally abrogated when trainmen came aboard.

Although not in the strictest sense appropriate to this book since it was placed in public service and availability on the Pennsylvania's *Broadway Limited*, the bridal suite of the Pullman *Republic* is interesting as a nuptial couch in motion, or romance on a sixteen and a half hour schedule between New York and the Great Lakes.

Not all Pullman products were rich in velvet portières and plate glass. Taking a page from the book of Jerome Marble of Worcester, the management of the San Antonio & Aranzas Pass Railroad in deepest Texas commissioned this Pullman hunting lodge for the use of its directors and favored guests. Wide side doors gave easy access when the game was afoot, and the Aranzas Pass of its corporate name is to this day celebrated for its gigantic tarpon. Other views of this unusual car are shown elsewhere and in an earlier portion of this book.

The magnificence of overstuffed armchairs,
fringes, tassels, marquetry and stained glass
shown here is the interior of the private parlor
car *Countess* built by Pullman the year Dewey
took Manila and in service thereafter as one of
the wonders and glories of the company's pool
of rental cars.

The Last Resorts

ROM THE EARLIEST BEGINNINGS of American resorts the railroad, and close on the iron shod heels of the steamcars themselves, the private cars of the moguls were an integral part of the social scene. Among the earliest health spas to achieve national recognition was Arkansas Hot Springs in the Ozarks and there, from primeval times, the specially assigned coaches of wealthy valetudinarians arrived over the rails of the St. Louis, Iron Mountain & Southern Railroad. There is no trace of privately owned varnish in the pre-Civil War record of the Arkansas Springs but invalids are known to have arrived from New York and Washington aboard conveyances appointed for their special comfort and accommodation in an era before private varnish had yet materialized in the form of President Lincoln's armored car of state.

Eventually, however, private car tracks were to become standard fixtures at various other springs, Saratoga Springs, White Sulphur Springs, French Lick, Poland Springs and at places lacking any therapeutic pretensions at all such as Newport, Palm Beach, Tuxedo Park, Louisville and Miami. Some of the favored resorts of society have never been achieved by rail at all: Bar Harbor, Block Island and Seal Harbor among them and Hobe Sound on Jupiter Island, the last of all resorts of defensive snobbism, is only a brief pause on the Florida East Coast Railway without a private car track of its own. But as the Pullman porter remarked to a passenger who commented on the scant heed paid by the railroad to so concentrated a stronghold of privilege, "It's a small station but still some punkins."

At all the resorts of society the private railroad car encountered competition in the elegance sweepstakes from architecture and in many of them from yachts. Yachts reigned supreme in a number of places where the railroad didn't run at all and everywhere boating was available it offered far greater vistas of costliness and ostentation than were implicit in the limited dimensions of Pullman. A million dollars for a yacht came, in time, to be a fairly commonplace investment while few private or business cars in the record represented an investment of half as much. But the private railroad car managed to maintain its own cachet of ultimate desirability, especially at such advantageous spots as Palm Beach and Asheville, North Carolina, where the Southern Railroad thoughtfully established a private car track so that George Vanderbilt's magnificent estate, "Biltmore" might be available to its owner and his guests.

"On Christmas Eve, 1895, the personal Wagner palace cars of many members of the House of Vanderbilt rolled into sidings at Asheville," wrote Wayne Andrews in "The Vanderbilt Legend," "Dr. and Mrs. Seward Webb, their children and domestics, Mr. and Mrs. Cornelius Vanderbilt II, their children and domestics, Mr. William Kissam Vanderbilt I, and his domestics, then alighted and entered carriages which conveyed them to Biltmore, the domain of George Washington Vanderbilt II." This was, of course, in the time when the New York Central was a patron of the Wagner Palace Cars and the Vanderbilts majority stockholders in that company. In a few years Pullman was to enjoy the family custom of the Vanderbilts for private cars.

But though Vanderbilt patronage was to be a glittering advertisement for Newport, North Carolina and Palm Beach, the resort that basked in the reflected glory of the Vanderbilt name first and longest was Saratoga Springs. Here the old Commodore delighted to repair in his two cars *Vanderbilt* and *Duchess* en suite, while at the head end of his special train, at first over the tracks of the Harlem Railroad and then along the river on the rails of the Hudson River Railroad, the engine, *Red Devil*, was in the talented charge of Jim Wood, a consummate throttle artist regularly assigned to the Commodore who admired speed.

Already established before the Civil War as a resort favored by the planter aristocracy of the Old South, Saratoga Springs flowered as a mecca of society with the recurrent appearance there during the racing season of Commodore Vanderbilt and his private cars and after the Commodore's death successive generations of Vanderbilts and their varnish cars were a name to conjure with at the upstate spa. In the golden age of Saratoga in the Diamond Jim Brady-Lillian Russell-Richard Canfield years, the private cars of such national celebrities as Bet-a-Million Gates, Lucky Baldwin and William C. Whitney were often spotted on the private car track of the Delaware & Hudson Railroad which, as it happened, was directly below the windows of one wing of the United States Hotel. One hot August night shortly after the turn of the century De Wolfe Hopper, the comedian famed for his recitations of "Casey at the Bat," was trying to get some needed sleep as the D & H night switching crew shifted a heavy traffic in private Pullmans directly under his bedroom. Toward dawn the clatter of couplings and shouts of the crew became insufferable and Hopper picked up the bedside phone and called the front desk. "Can you tell me," he inquired sweetly of the night clerk, "what time this hotel gets to Chicago?"

It was at Saratoga while a guest aboard the New York Central's business car No. 100, then occupied by Chauncey M. Depew, that President Chester A. Arthur, a worldly and sophisticated gentleman made his one remembered contribution to the folklore of the presidency. Asked his views on alcohol as Depew was pouring him a liberal three fingers of twenty-year rye, Arthur replied, "I may be President of the United States, madam, but my private life is nobody's damned business."

Although he was one of the most loyal of Saratoga visitors and lent the spa a radiance of showmanship, conservative Saratoga cottagers felt that Diamond Jim Brady was going a bit far the year he arrived aboard a private car with silver plated trucks, draft gear and brake rigging. Other properties of his entourage that summer were twenty-seven Japanese house servants and Lillian Russell's gold-plated lady's bicycle.

Another private car arrival each season at Saratoga was Bet-a-Million Gates, the barbed wire salesman whose grossness and vulgarity were so offensive to J. P. Morgan that the banker refused to allow him to participate in the formation of the billion dollar United States Steel Corporation even though the original idea had been Gates'. Possibly the ostentatious possession of private cars by such *arivistes* as Gates strengthened Morgan's preference for yachts. "You can do business with anyone," the great man said pointedly when someone mentioned Gates and his car, "but you can only sail a boat with a gentleman."

Less cryptic was a far more specific reference to Gates made by Morgan to Judge Elbert H. Gary during the preliminaries to organizing United States Steel. "I don't think property is safe in his hands," said Morgan and promptly demonstrated what he meant by purchasing Gates' American Steel & Wire Corporation which had elevated the man of dice and barbed wire to membership, if not esteem in the private car club.

Although the fortunes of the House of Morgan were closely involved with the financing of railroads and J. P. Morgan himself served as arbiter, for a reported fee of $3,000,000, when full scale war threatened between the New York Central and the Pennsylvania in 1885, the great banker never seems to have owned the private cars his estate and wealth suggested. His taste ran to yachts, as the magnificent *Corsair* was witness, and the hierarchical affairs of the Episcopal church, so that in 1901 he chartered an entire private train between New York and San Francisco on which a select posse of church dignitaries and the financier himself attended an Episcopal convention in California. "The Morgan train is one of the most luxurious that has ever reached the Coast," declared the *Examiner*, "with six cars and three chefs who served President McKinley on his Western tour, plus the famous Louis Sherry." Morgan's selection of Sherry as his personal chef aboard the cars and while visiting William Crocker on Nob Hill wasn't altogether favorably received in San Francisco whose own chefs and restaurants were already legendary, but the press lost no opportunity to catalogue the extravagant properties of the outing whose commissary bills alone came to $200 a day as the cars flashed across Wyoming and Nevada. What most set San Francisco by the ears was Morgan's wine cellar for whose accommodation a baggage car had been equipped with racks and bins appropriate to their vintage contents. The *Examiner* informed its readers that the tycoon's favorite luncheon wine was a Rhine which his Berlin agent had picked up at auction for $35 a bottle, a sum which the reporter figured out came to just over $4.00 a glass when served to Morgan and his Episcopal companions.

The elder Morgan's preoccupation with Episcopal affairs and their conduct through the medium of private railroad cars was not limited to his spiritual safari to San Francisco with a private trainload of gaiters and aprons. As the terrible money panic of 1907 was gathering force he was in interested attendance at a convention of bishops at Richmond, Virginia. As bank after bank throughout the nation closed its doors and clouds gathered ominously in Wall Street, the banker was deluged with telegrams urging him to return to the scene of battle and stay the carnage as only the House of Morgan might. Morgan shoved the yellow messages under the tails of his frock coat and leaned closer as the Right Reverend William Lawrence, Bishop of Massachusetts, expounded aspects of the Anglican Communion. When the convention had closed its business and not before, the man of millions ordered his two private cars headed north loaded with spiritual advisers and champagne. The next morning as the train was on the home stretch between Philadelphia and Jersey City Morgan was discovered at breakfast reading the details of the emergency in *The New York Times* "sitting at table and singing lustily some tune which no one could recognize."

Arrived in New York and refreshed by his communion with holy men, Morgan at once took charge of the situation and within a few days the panic began to abate. The House of Morgan had saved the nation's economy but not until its head and the assembled bishops were good and ready.

The younger J. P. Morgan closely followed the pattern of his father's prejudices even to maintaining the great steam yacht *Corsair II* and he also preferred renting or borrowing railroad property to owning it outright.

Nevertheless, in 1924 the Pullman shops turned out for the personal use of J. P. Morgan the younger a private car which was assigned for its home railroad to the Erie where it was numbered 400 and held in readiness for the financier's convenience. The number was completely without anything that could be described as social significance since the Morgan tradition, so far as formal or upper case society was concerned, was one of complete indifference, tempered in the case of Mr. Morgan's father with disdain. The elder J. Pierpont underscored his contempt for the conventions which governed New York's fashionable circles in his own generation by openly expressed preferences for what one wag characterized as "old masters and old mistresses" and his fondness for the actress Maxine Elliott was no secret. The Morgan car was assigned to the Erie Railroad because the banking firm of which the younger Morgan was head distrusted the management of the New York Central's affairs, then firmly in the hands of heirs of Commodore Vanderbilt and so to remain until the unquiet arrival on the scene of Robert R. Young of Texas.

In the thirties Mr. Morgan had added reason for taking passage on almost any Chicago connection other than the Central.

"If we had to take space on the Vanderbilt cars," recalled Bernard Stewart, Morgan's major domo at the time, later in the employ in a similar capacity for Lloyd H. Smith of Houston, "Mr. Morgan always had the shades of his suite drawn before we passed through Ossining. As we went by Sing Sing Prison he would sigh and sigh for poor Mr. Whitney."*

The elder Morgan's preference for not owning private cars, even though the House of Morgan was actively involved in the affairs of Erie and the Central Railroad of New Jersey, extended to Morgan partners, and George F. Baker, Sr., famed for his square derby hats and mutton chop whiskers long after these had ceased to be current in banking circles, refused to own one although, like the senior Morgan, his prejudice did not extend to steam yachts.

Following the lead of the younger Morgan, in 1926 George F. Baker, Jr., commissioned Pullman to outshop for him a private car which was simply carried on the rolling stock roster of Erie as No. 99. When an acquaintance remarked it was odd for son to own so fine a property while his father had none, the crusty old banker had a ready answer. "My son can afford it," he said. "He has a rich father."

When the elder George F. Baker was at last gathered to his fathers, the funeral was the most important ever to be held at Tuxedo Park, the resort of conservative fashion of which he had been the foremost and most conservative patron. Three special trains were run between Jersey City and Tuxedo over the Erie, one for flowers and two for delegations from the First National Bank of New York, J. P. Morgan & Company, Harvard, Columbia and Cornell. To the last of these the railroad attached as its final tribute Erie Observation Car No. 901, the Tuxedo Club Car of long established tradition. A wreath marked Seat No. 7 which, since anyone connected with the railroad or its most celebrated resort could remember, had been reserved for Baker. Occupants on this historic run imagined they saw the outline of a ghostly square derby in the hat rack above.

In California the silver seventies saw the emergence of a group of men of substance and power in no way obligated to tip their hats, metaphorically speaking, in the direction of New York's Goulds, Vanderbilts and other moguls of transportation. The gold rush prosperity of the fifties and sixties had made San Francisco a city of millionaires celebrated for their princely ways and hospitality which dwarfed all in the record at least since the Medici and whose way of life called for private railroad cars as urgently as it presupposed villas at Belmont and rococo mansions on Nob Hill.

---

*Richard Whitney, one time President of the New York Exchange, convicted of financial improprieties.

Piled Peleon-like atop the vast resources of San Francisco's primal nabobs, Tevises, Haggins, Millses and the patrician Trenor Park, many of whose fortunes derived from such agencies of communications, transport and banking as Wells Fargo & Company, the Panama Railroad and the Pacific Mail Steamships, now came the even more imposing millions of the Big Four of the Central Pacific Railroad, Collis Huntington, Governor Leland Stanford, Charles Crocker and Uncle Mark Hopkins. And, as if enough wealth were not already concentrated in the vaults of the Bank of California, a seemingly illimitable flow of gold and silver cascaded into San Francisco from the deep mines of the Comstock Lode across the Washoe Hills in Nevada to elevate John Mackay, Jim Fair, James Flood and William O'Brien to the Coast's financial peerage. Gold, silver, real estate, railroads, banking and outright speculation created in San Francisco a citadel of such solvency that its memory has never been overshadowed in the American legend even by Dallas or Houston.

Private cars to name the Central and Southern Pacific as their home railroads came as naturally to Nob Hill as Pisco Punch and suites at William Ralston's incredible new Palace Hotel at the intersection of Market Street and New Montgomery. The ball was started rolling by Governor Stanford's gleaming new car *Stanford* which raised genteel envy in nabob bosoms and was shortly followed by Collis P. Huntington's *Oneonta*, Charles Crocker's *Mishawaka* and James Ben Ali Haggin's splendid *Salvator*.

A curious footnote to the social and economic destinies of the Big Four of the Central Pacific is contained in the record of a private car named *San Carlos*, outshopped by Pullman in 1889 for the C.P. and assigned to Edward T. Searles. Searles was a young decorator who married Uncle Mark Hopkins' widow to make resounding headlines throughout the nation and many Californians believed the June-and-September romance — Searles was in his twenties, Mrs. Hopkins in her seventies — was engineered by Collis Huntington to obtain voting control of Uncle Mark's quarter interest in the railroad. From the record it would seem that Huntington's favor and approval included the building and assignment of a private car to the young man, perhaps to get the Widow Hopkins out of his hair, for the ill-assorted couple shortly headed for New York and the East and never again visited California.

Another private car of the time and place to figure as a bower of Cupid was one of Charles Crocker's several such properties, the record fails to show whether it was *Mishawaka* or one of the railroad's available pool of special varnish, aboard which Prince Andre Poniatowski of Paris met and wooed Beth Sperry and so became Crocker's brother-in-law.

In an age when the private car was the outstanding hallmark of substance and conspicuous aloofness, a long series of magnificent palaces on wheels rolled westward with participants in other alliances which joined the wealth of California to titles of the Old World and with established names and fortunes from New York and Chicago. George Mortimer Pullman's own P.P.C. was pressed into service and arrived at Oakland Mole when his daughter Harriet married San Francisco attorney Francis J. Carolan and departed with the bride on board upholstered in three separate trousseaux, "one scented with sandalwood, one of heliotrope, and one of violet orris."

Other stylish weddings such as the colossal do which accompanied the nuptials of Tessie Fair and her formidable Comstock wealth to middle aged "howling swell" Herman Oelrichs of New York evoked private cars by the score. For his wedding in 1890, Oelrichs arrived in San Francisco aboard a New York Central car belonging to William K. Vanderbilt that had been renamed *Cupid* for the occasion and sported its sentimental blazon on nameboards only infrequently so frivolous.

From 1880 on to the very present here and now San Francisco society took pleasure in routing its private varnish over the Southern Pacific's Monterey branch line to be spotted on the private car track of the railroad's swaggering real estate project centering around the Hotel Del Monte. Here, as depicted photographically elsewhere in this volume, Charlie Crocker entertained President Benjamin Harrison and his party including Darius O. Mills aboard *Mishawaka*. Here every year of his life appeared William Sanders Tevis aboard the Espee's *San Emidio* named for the rancho that had been one of the original Spanish Grants in California. Another regular at Del Monte whose *Pelham* arrived each summer at the end of the *Del Monte Express* was Edward S. Harkness whose millions had revitalized Yale and aboard which Samuel F. B. Morse and other veteran Peninsular residents remembered many pleasant hours.

In 1958 another President of the United States, Dwight Eisenhower came to Monterey over the Southern Pacific's rails to play golf at the world-renowned course at Del Monte Lodge. For the occasion the Espee arranged a Presidential Special with two diners for the press and an assortment of division superintendents' business cars for the Presidential entourage and bodyguard. Mr. Eisenhower himself rode in air conditioned splendor aboard the carrier's own Presidential car, *Sunset*, the second Pullman built p.v. of this name to carry the Southern Pacific insigne on its nameboards. The first *Sunset* had been built for the use of directors of the Central Pacific before the turn of the century and had included in its comfortable economy many amenities of the good way of life. It is depicted at an appropriate place elsewhere in this book.

In less festive mood than the gay wedding parties which shuttled back and forth across the continent in the nineties was the hurried return from Paris in 1893 of Mrs. John Mackay when an assassin had attempted Mackay's life and the archmillionaire lay in his suite at the Palace, critically wounded. From Jersey City to the Oakland Mole, Mrs. Mackay and their son Willie hastened aboard the Pullman *Corsair* in what the newspapers of the day, even though Mackay's doctors had pronounced him out of danger, insisted on calling "a race of death." On her arrival in California Mrs. Mackay explained that she had ridden in democratic simplicity on the end of the *Overland Limited* from Chicago. "Regular trains hauled our car," she told reporters. "I dislike the jolting of a special engine pulling a single car."

Newport, generally speaking, was more conscious of yachts and, in later years automobiles, than it was of private railway transportation, although the dark green Pullmans of Vanderbilts and Whitneys were not unknown to the depot of the New York, New Haven & Hartford. Newport was the objective, as we have seen elsewhere of Alfred Gwynne Vanderbilt's *Wayfarer* freighted with Gladys Vanderbilt and her husband the Count Széchényi after their marriage in 1908. The widow of Cornelius Vanderbilt II, contrived to arrive at the Rhode Island resort where her summer residence, *"The Breakers"* was perhaps the most formidable of all Newport cottages in the private Pullman that had once been her husband's, and evidenced her contempt for the motor car age by maintaining a venerable Simplex that was so shabby and disreputable that her son-in-law, Harry Payne Whitney, ridiculed her into disposing of it. And, of course, Newport was the favored seat of one of the last great resort fanciers in the person of Robert R. Young who contrived to lend even his spectacular suicide in 1958 a cachet of distinction by accomplishing it at Palm Beach.

But Newport's most spectacular private car interlude was one of implications rather than the specific presence there of varnish cars themselves.

The social contretemps that shook Buzzard's Bay resort to its solid marble foundations is hinted in the entry in Pullman's private car order book of invoice No. 394 of May 1906 for a new business car No. 15 for the Illinois Central Railroad for the personal use and occupancy of the carrier's President Stuyvesant Fish.

Undisputed, at least, by any contender of consequence, queen of Newport society at the moment was Mrs. Stuyvesant Fish who, for some reason not available to archeology, took a dim view of the social aspirations of Mrs. Edward H. Harriman. At some crisis in the conduct of Newport's dinners and receptions in that summer of 1906, Mamie Fish failed to invite the Harrimans to a levee whose other guests included J. P. Morgan, Chauncey M. Depew and Lord Charles Beresford.

This was imprudent, as events almost immediately disclosed. Edward H. Harriman was at the time in sole control of the greatest system of railroad transportation America had ever known, those of Collis Huntington and Jay Gould not excepted. Tucked away in the Harriman portfolio was the Illinois Central of which Stuyvesant Fish was momentarily president and over which he was pleased to pass Mrs. Fish's social friends as guests of the company. The next morning after the Harrimans had been so conspicuously disinvited to Mrs. Fish's party, Stuyvesant Fish was no longer President of the Illinois Central. The Pullman Company's roster of private rolling stock served as a sort of *Court Circular* for the recording of the

Bellevue Avenue Trafalgar. It read: "Illinois Central No. 15, Fish, Sold to U.P.RR. as No. 99."

Perhaps the only electrically operated private car to become associated with a resort of major fashion and one ranking in general celebrity among electric cars with Henry E. Huntington's *San Marino,* was the *Mineola* of August P. Belmont who was a traction magnate, perfectionist and upper case socialite all rolled in one.

Note has been made elsewhere of Belmont's resoundingly patrician father, the first August and of Belmont's more conventional private car *Oriental* which came to him as, among other directorates, chairman of the board of the Louisville & Nashville.

August P. Belmont's interests were many and varied and none of them more complex than the Manhattan Elevated Railway which he purchased from its original operators and the Belmont-financed Interborough Rapid Transit with which he eventually combined New York's first elevated carrier. Another of his properties was the well-remembered Belmont Hotel located in Forty-second Street directly across from Grand Central Depot. The Belmont was for many years one of New York's complex of hotels in the Grand Central area, famed for its peculiar architecture which decreed that it should be built like a barrel so as to be a foot or so thicker at the tenth story than at its top or bottom, for its lavish profusion of beautiful red marble in its broadstaired lobby and its magnificent circular bar in the basement. The Belmont was a great favorite with Bostonians from State Street who could board the New Haven's *Merchants Limited* or *Yankee Clipper* almost directly from their apartments via an underground passageway, and so remained until it was torn down late in the thirties to make way, ironically, for an air lines terminal.

Still another of Belmont's varied interests was horseracing and when he built New York's most socially acceptable race track at Belmont Park near Mineola on Long Island, he forethoughtfully arranged with the Long Island Railroad to lay a private spur track right to the clubhouse.

To achieve Belmont Park over Belmont-controlled carriers from the Belmont Hotel through the agency of a Belmont private car was a whim that appealed mightily to August P. Belmont, and to this end *Mineola* was commissioned in 1905 as one of the few electric p.v. ever built. Henry E. Huntington's *San Marino* was another.

A private elevator in the Belmont Hotel led to a private siding in the Interborough's underground station at Grand Central. On it he maintained the car *Mineola,* staffed with servants, stocked with appropriate vintages and ready to roll on race days with select parties of the owner's guests. To achieve Belmont Park the gleaming green car followed the trackage of the Interborough the length of Manhattan Island to South Ferry where it passed under the East River at the South Ferry Tunnel to emerge at the carrier's

Flatbush-Atlantic Avenue terminal. Here a switch passed the Belmont entourage to the tracks of the electrified Long Island Railroad and the *Mineola* was, quite literally, off to the races.

There was a large drawing room compartment at either end of *Mineola,* connected by a corridor and separated by a galley where the steward was able to mix drinks from an opulently supplied service bar and prepare light collations in the electrically activated kitchen. In the drawing rooms the arched Empire ceiling was tinted a delicate apple green with gold trim, there were ample banquettes, settees and arm chairs for the convenience of guests and, somewhat incongruously, Belmont had a roll-topped mahogany desk placed against the bulkhead in one of them. It gave him an opportunity to refer to the arrangement as his business car. Broad picture windows supplemented the view of the track ahead which appeared past the motorman's compartment. A perfectionist in all things, Belmont sent the motormen assigned to his car for their uniforms to Wetzel, New York's foremost and easily most expensive gentleman's tailor.

In the golden noontide of its fortunes, the *Mineola* carried many names that made news, Lillian Russell, Diamond Jim Brady, Evander Berry Wall, king of the dudes, Richard A. Canfield, the socially correct gambler from Saratoga Springs and the conventional clutch of Vanderbilts. Mrs. August Belmont, however, found the company recruited for trips aboard the *Mineola* a little Bohemian for her taste. Times were changing, she was the first to admit, and if the New York correspondent of the Rothschilds wanted to drink champagne and bet on horses with play actresses and railroad equipment salesmen, her husband was his own master. For herself she preferred the famous Belmont *demi-daumont,* a carriage of French importation drawn by four horses with no driver but guided by postilions riding the near horses and attired in shell jackets, white cord breeches and jockey caps.

With the years the Belmont glories faded, although Belmont Park is a proud name in sporting circles to this day. August Belmont was gathered to his fathers, the Belmont Hotel was razed and the car *Mineola* was withdrawn from service and stored on the Interborough's tracks at 149th Street. When last heard of, negotiations were under way for its acquisition by the Branford Electric Railway, a trolley museum near New Haven. In any event the *Mineola* had ridden with the best of them far away and long ago.

Perhaps the greatest gathering spot of all, next to the Louisville yards of the Louisville & Nashville Railroad at Derby time, was Palm Beach in the opulent twenties when as many as twelve or fifteen private cars could be discovered at a time spotted on the private car track beside the Poinciana Hotel of fragrant memory. Here Harry Payne Whitney's *Adios,* Joshua Cosden's *Roamer* on board which he had entertained the then Prince of Wales for a nation-wide tour a few years earlier, Harry F. Sinclair's *Sinco,* Franklyn Hutton's *Curlyhut* and J. Leonard Replogle's *Westmount* were sometimes parked drawbar to drawbar under the palm trees provided by a thoughtful management while white coated servants threaded the well tended lawn with invitations to cocktails or dinner from one of the lords of creation to another. Aboard the cars of these tycoons of their time were held poker games that became legendary and whose participants for one reason or another shunned the limelight that beat upon less reticent players in Colonel Edward Riley Bradley's casino just down the road.

Some notion of the stakes involved may be suggested by the circumstance that one evening on W. F. Kenny's *St. Nicholas,* George Loft, the New York candy baron, asked if he might sit in on a game. To prove his solvency he flourished a thick sheaf of crisp new $10,000 banknotes. John Studebaker, the motor manufacturer, handed him one white chip.

The protocol and language of private cars at this period briefly was a subject of controversy in the society department of the *New York Herald Tribune* whose society editor, Howard White, was daily put to it to print Palm Beach dispatches covering the arrival and departure of names that made news. Was Paul Block *aboard* or *on* board *Friendship?* Higher authority in the form of Ogden Reid, publisher of the paper and a member of the Navy League and the New York Yacht Club, was invoked. Reid, a stickler for such matters, ruled that since the *Herald Tribune's* style book decreed a person to be *in* board a ship, yacht or other vessel, he should also be *in* board a private car. The next printing of the style book contained a note to this effect.

Palm Beach in those days was connected with the mainland at West Palm Beach by a single motor road and the trestle across Lake Worth for private cars of the Florida East Coast Railway, an arrangement which made screening by the resort's private police of all arrivals a simple matter. Most northbound private cars were taken from the Poinciana track to be coupled to the end of an F E C train which departed at the socially inconvenient hour of 3:30 a.m. Colonel Bradley made one exception to his usually inviolate rule requiring evening dress at his casino. Patrons going away on the 3:30 could play roulette and chemin-de-fer until the last moment in business attire.

The Flagler Trestle across Lake Worth in the nearly four decades of its operation before it was destroyed in the hurricane of 1932 (which also destroyed another monument to the memory of Florida's greatest promoter, the railroad viaduct to Key West), probably accommodated a greater density of personages than any comparable span in the world. Its beginnings were auspicious when on March 14, 1896 the first train, composed wholly of private equipment and bearing no fewer than four Vanderbilts, crossed and was spotted under the luxurious lane of palms that made the Poinciana house track one of the most harmonious of all settings for leisured opulence. Among its seventeen hand-picked guests were Gladys Vanderbilt, later the Countess Laszlo Széchényi, Gertrude Vanderbilt, who became Mrs. Harry Payne Whitney, Mr. and Mrs. Cornelius Vanderbilt, Harry Payne Whitney,

Lispendard Stewart, celebrated as society's most pretentious bore, Edith Bishop, Mabel Gerry and Colonel Philip Lydig. They posed for an historic photograph that today represents the flower of New York's nineteenth century society with the Florida East Coast's eight wheeler and the Royal Poinciana itself framed in palms in the background. In an age before the evolution of sports attire, or indeed almost any informal dress for gentlemen, Thomas Cushing and Stewart wore hard bowler hats and Cornelius Vanderbilt gloves.

The consist of the train itself is difficult of precise identification.

"It was like a houseparty," wrote the Countess Széchényi in later years. "We had a sleeper for the men and a sleeper for the women, a sitting room car and a dining room car and even a car for our luggage. On the way back we stopped at Aiken."

"That's in South Carolina," she added by way of explanation.

A commentary on the society to which private cars were an accepted property and convenience might be discerned in this junket, all of its members recruited from the inner circles of New York's Four Hundred to promote the Flagler interests at Palm Beach, and a parallel gesture of publicization some four decades later to promote the fortunes of the Chesapeake & Ohio Railroad's resort hotel, the Greenbrier at White Sulphur Springs. In 1948 Robert R. Young, owner of the Greenbrier and himself a business car fancier of exacting tastes, took 400 guests on one of the most elaborate free rides in modern history for a four day houseparty to reopen the Greenbrier after the 1941 war. The list included the Duke and Duchess of Windsor, Elsa Maxwell, Sam Goldwyn and Bob Hope. "I was frightened cruelly by my maid," deposed Bing Crosby later. "She used a lorgnette to look under the bed."

From the beginning the private car clientele of Palm Beach was above criticism from the viewpoint of either society or finance. Barbed wire salesmen of deplorable antecedents like Bet-a-Million Gates or railroad equipment vendors like Diamond Jim Brady who openly traveled with his mistress who was also a play actress, might skirmish successfully with the proprieties at Saratoga Springs. Brewers, Montana copper kings and meat packers from Chicago might be hail fellow at Louisville when Derby came 'round, but Palm Beach was effectively restricted to the accepted Wideners and Wanamakers, Whitneys, Vanderbilts, Stotesburys and Huttons.

Now and then, to be sure, there were present aboard Harry Bingham's *Pawnee* or Franklyn Hutton's *Curleyhut* (a peculiar name even among the private cars of the mighty and stemming from his daughter Barbara's nickname of Curley) guests so ingenuous as to be impressed by working fireplaces and gold service for the table. It was aboard Mrs. Donahue's almost mythical *Japauldon*, named for her husband James Paul Donahue, that Palm Beach veterans still tell of a visitor who went on a self-conducted tour of the car while his companions tarried with their hostess in the observation room. Returning from his safari forward, the bug-eyed explorer button-holed a companion while Mrs. Donahue was out of hearing and announced in a stage whisper: "You ought to come out and see the dining room; all the silver's gold!"

At one time during the spendthrift twenties, a Florida lady reporter who had obviously not been entertained upon *Japauldon* reported to her fascinated readers that the car was possessed of a working fireplace fuelled exclusively with cedar logs from the Donahue shooting preserve in the Adirondacks whose scent, when burning, reminded Mrs. Donahue, a homey soul, of a simpler way of life. Alas for this contribution to the mythology of private car life, the ground plans of *Japauldon* reveal no fireplace at all and it may be doubted if Mrs. Donahue, who has never been credited with over-acute perceptions in any field, would have known cedar from stink-weed.

A clue to the prevailing philosophy of private car owners and users in the nineties is contained in the form of two letters reproduced in this volume. One of them indicates that the carriage of private varnish for free when occupied by persons of social and financial importance was taken for granted and that Edward T. Stotesbury, soon to be a Morgan partner and at that time an important member of the banking firm, wasn't above throwing his weight around to procure transportation to Palm Beach on the cuff. Just in case the august name of the House of Morgan were not of sufficient weight, the general manager of the Florida Central & Peninsular mentions Stotesbury's connection with Morgan's correspondents in Philadelphia, the firm of Drexel & Co., but it is probable that the Morgan association would have done the trick.

Thirty years later Mrs. Stotesbury was undisputed queen of Palm Beach and Stotesbury himself was a figure of such dimensions that on his own personal cognizance and without recourse to other references he might well have asked for free passage over the Florida East Coast. But time, alas, had caught up with the free-loaders even though they might be multi-million-aires, and he would have had to pay the eighteen full first class fares decreed by the I.C.C. even if he had managed to borrow p.v. from an available Whitney.

Stotesbury was a non-railroad man although the concern of the house he represented for the carriers was well established. The letter from the management of the Florida East Coast to General Torrence, reproduced elsewhere, indicates that other railroad executives were assiduous in promoting free transportation to Florida in the same period, and it was eventually the abuse of the courtesy of interchange by directors and executives of small time railroads in obscure outlands that resulted in the scrapping of the practice altogether. That General Torrence was a regular at the free lunch counter is suggested by the closing paragraph of Mr. Goff's letter.* According to the Florida East Coast's record he had visited Palm

*Please see page 292.

JACKSONVILLE, FLA. March 5th, 1896.

Movement Southern Railway private car "Frances."

REFERENCE
Number...... 6324.

Mr. J. R. Parrott,

    Vice-President, F.E.C.R'y,

        C i t y.

Dear Sir;-

    Mr. Duval has a letter from President Spencer of the
Southern Railway in regard to the *free* movement of private car
"Frances" to Palm Beach and return, occupied by **Mr. E. T. Stotes-**
bury, a member of the firm of J. P. Morgan & Co. of New York, and
Messers Drexel & Company of Philadelphia, and party. The car
will reach Jacksonville on our train No. 31 Saturday evening.
Mr. Duval asks if you will move it through to St. Augustine that
evening, allowing the party to remain there over Sunday, thence
to Palm Beach Monday, returning the car to us at Jacksonville
at such time as Mr. Stotesbury may desire. Please let me know
by bearer if it will be agreeable to you to do this for our account, and greatly oblige.

        Yours truly,

        D. E. Maxwell

        General Manager.
        DH

Beach the year before aboard the Atchison, Topeka & Santa Fe Business Car No. 220. He played all the angles.

Apparently a good deal of correspondence was involved in routing a private car across the continent on a free-loading basis, as permission had to be obtained from the management of each carrier of interchange, but with perseverance it could be accomplished and no doubt many executives well able to afford the tariff required of ordinary p.v. riders made it a point of pride rather than actual economy to travel on the cuff.

As instructive, perhaps, as anything in the conduct and protocol of private car travel to a resort of fashion and relaxation in a day before the blighting hand of the Interstate Commerce Commission will be found in the record of private car movements over the main line of the Florida East Coast Railway during the season of 1901-02 reproduced in this volume.

Here is a fairly representative cross section of the traffic in private cars and special train movements ranging from the exalted presence of such names as Frederick W. Vanderbilt and William Rockefeller to the New Orleans Minstrels and a party of Raymond Whitcomb clients, then in the golden noontide of the guided tour.

A careful chief clerk in that now distant day has scrupulously marked with an asterisk the movement of business cars of connecting railroads entitled by reciprocal courtesy to be carried on a different tariff schedule from other special varnish cars. The New York Central & Hudson River Lines Car No. 493 was occupied on January 17 by Frederick William Vanderbilt, a son of William Henry Vanderbilt and a director of the Vanderbilt Lines. Carried at the identical tariff between Jacksonville and Palm Beach and return aboard another New York Central Car No. 499 a few weeks later was Harrison McKown Twombly, a Vanderbilt in-law and also a New York Central director who enjoyed using the company cars and company courtesies.

William Rockefeller although an occupant of an "N.Y.C. Priv. Car," was not a railroad director but high on the list of approved shippers over the Vanderbilt lines whose South Improvement Company, predecessor to Standard Oil had long enjoyed rebates on his extensive shipments of petroleum products.

William Collins Whitney arrived aboard his own venerable Wagner *Pilgrim* without recourse to his Vanderbilt connections even though, five years previously, his son Harry Payne Whitney had married Gertrude Vanderbilt, a daughter of Cornelius II. The Whitney family were themselves in ample funds to afford private cars, almost literally by the score and had no need to travel on the prestige of the New York Central. William C. Whitney was to take delivery on his second car, the Pullman-built *Wanderer*, later in the same year that he visited Florida in *Pilgrim*.

C. W. Armour, whose family in Chicago were immense shippers of beef and bacon, apparently had borrowed a business car, at this age indis-

STATEMENT OF REVENUE RECEIVED

f r o m

MOVEMENT OF PRIVATE CARS

Date	Route	Owner	Car	Amount
Nov.12/01	Jacksonville to Daytona	J.Morse	Day Coach	$ 20.00
Nov.16/01	Jacksonville to St. Lucie & Return	Hon.W.W. Durham	"Grassmere"	191.00
Nov.16/01	Palatka to Daytona		"Endres"	79.20
Dec/9/01	Jacksonville to St.Lucie	M.S.Quay	"Olivette"	171.00
Jan.3/02	St.Augustine to Jacksonville		*Lehigh Valley #353	27.00
Jan.4/02	Jacksonville to Palm Beach & Ret.	T.B.Wannamaker	"Oceanic"	342.00
Jan.14/02	Jacksonville to Palm Beach & Ret.	M.Crocker	"Emilita"	342.00
Jan.17/02	Jacksonville to Palm Beach & Ret.	F.W.Vanderbilt	*N.Y.C. #493	342.00
Jan.19/02	St.Augustine to Palatka	Cincinnati Carnival Co.	P.S. Coach	89.00
Jan.31/02	Jacksonville to Palm Beach & Ret.	B.F.Jones	"Hazelemere"	342.00
Jan.31/02	Jacksonville to Miami & Ret.	H.W.Oliver	"Tyrone"	395.10
Feb.3/02	Jacksonville to Palm Beach & Ret.	H.Darlington	*Pa. Private Car	342.00
Feb.12/02	Jacksonville to Palm Beach	C.J.Coulter	F.E.C. Sleeper	270.50
Feb.13/02	Jacksonville to Palm Beach & Ret.	W.A.Patton	"Olympia"	342.00
Feb.14/02	Jacksonville to Palm Beach & Ret. to Palatka	R.Weinachte	Two Pullman Cars	644.00

--- 2 ---

Date	Route	Party	Car	Amount
Feb.15/02	Palatka to St.Aug., Daytona to Palatka	New Orleans Minstrel Co.		156.20
Feb.19/02	Jacksonville to Palm Beach & Ret.	W.C.Whitney,	"Pilgrim"	342.00
Feb.20/02	Jacksonville to Plam Beach & Ret.	S.H. Ashbridge	"Cleopatra"	342.00
Feb.21/02	Jacksonville to Miami & Ret.	J.P. McNichol	"Edgemere"	395.10
Feb.22/02	Jacksonville to Ormond	Dillingham Party	Special Train	140.00
Feb.25/02	Jacksonville to Miami & Ret.	T.DeWitt Cuyler	"Idler"	395.10
Feb.26/02	Jacksonville to Palm Beach	Judge Williamson	"Concho"	220.50
Feb.27/02	Palm Beach to Jacksonville	O.G.Murray	*B & O Car #903	220.50
Feb.28/02	Jacksonville to St.Augustine	Mr.Deering	C & N W Priv. Car	27.00
Mar.1/02	Jacksonville to Palm Beach & Ret.	H.McK.Twombly	*N.Y.C.Car #499	342.00
Mar.6/02	Jacksonville to Palatka	T.B.Harrison	"Mishawaka"	47.70
Mar.4/02	Jacksonville to Miami & Ret.	C.W.Armour	C.M.& St.P. Car #222	527.40
Mar.14/02	Sanford to Miami to Jacksonville	Raymond & Whitcomb Party	"Elysian"	456.10
Mar.14/02	Palm Beach to Jacksonville	Wm.Rockefeller	N.Y.C. Priv.Car	220.50
Mar.15/02	Miami to Jacksonville	T.C.Platt	"Idler"	263.70
Mar.15/02	Palm Beach to Jacksonville	D.G.Reid	"Columbia"	220.50
				$8256.40

* = Railway lines.

tinguishable from privately owned varnish by anything except the initials on its nameboard and not always then, from the Chicago, Milwaukee & St. Paul and made the grand tour all the way to Miami, then not a such-a-much resort steaming in the Everglades at the end of the Flagler system. It is notable that during the entire private car season of 1901-02 only four car movements were routed as far south as Miami.

Sandwiched in between the exclusive and glittering excursions of the lords of creation on the East Coast's trainmaster's sheets were less august comings and goings: the New Orleans Minstrels whose conveyance is unidentified, the Cincinnati Carnival Company en route to rejoice Palatka, and the anonymous but by no means negligible tourists recruited by Raymond & Whitcomb. There was also Mr. J. Morse who, on November 1, 1901, was minded to take a nice train ride and covered the 120 miles from Jacksonville to Daytona in solitary grandeur (the record makes no mention of the usual "and Party") for a modest $20 aboard a private day coach.

This was the happy age when anyone with currency in hand could step up to the ticket window and ask for a coach for single occupancy to be attached to the next train to yonder and the railroad was glad to accommodate his whim. A similar but somewhat more expensive urge was evidently gratified on February 12, 1902 by C. J. Coulter who was in a hurry to get to Palm Beach when no lowers were available and ordered an entire sleeper made up for his convenience. That it was a home line movement without origin elsewhere or at more distant remove, is suggested by the fact that it was a Florida East Coast sleeper that he got.

The spacious days of private cars in Palm Beach when Drexels, Stotesburys and Whitneys occupied the private car track at the Royal Poinciana in winter, were recalled for the author of this book by Schuyler Livingston Parsons, a Palm Beach veteran since the time when there was no Everglades Club, which is practically Early Ordovician, socially speaking.

"The car furnished in the best taste to my recollection," writes the bearded Parsons, a perennial bachelor and authority on the mores of Newport and Florida, "was Harry Payne Bingham's *Pawnee*. Later on Jessie Donahue's *Japauldon* was supposed to have solid gold plumbing, although I never saw it personally. Harrison Williams' *Warrior* was the most comfortable and in my youth Alfred Vanderbilt seemed to be always with us. I made several trips as a young man to Sagamore in the Adirondacks, arriving by special Vanderbilt train at Raquette Lake station in the early, freezing dawn.

"On one occasion Tony Biddle wired me at Charleston to meet him at Columbia, South Carolina, aboard his car to visit at Palm Beach for a week for the opening of Ziegfeld's 'Frolics'! The girls were on another car. I got on late at night to find the car full and had to sleep on a sofa in the observation room. It was Mary Duke Biddle's father's car. I nearly froze to death for the heating seemed to be defective. Anyway, it was the start of the Big

Freeze which killed the Florida boom and the 'Frolics' was a costly failure. It turned out Biddle was interested in unloading Olympia Island, now Hobe Sound, but none of the group could see anything in the 'Frozen South' and showed no interest. Later Joseph Verner Reed bought the island for a song and made a fortune. What fools we were!"

Parsons' most endearing recollection of the private car club was when he was living in Charleston and running what old-timers recall as the most exquisite and expensive antique shop ever to stock Hepplewhite south of the Mason-Dixon Line. Mrs. Harrison Williams, later celebrated as the world's best dressed woman, was coming through on her husband's car and wired ahead that if Parsons had anything specially choice, to have it on the depot platform at North Charleston when the train pulled in.

"I hired a truck," recollects Parsons. "Business had been slow and I took practically the entire shop and arranged it in a nice display, if I do say so myself, along the side of the Atlantic Coast Line track. The result was that everything down to the last spinning wheel was sold, if not to the Williams, then to the other passengers. There was a twenty minute wait for water for the engine and in that time I made my banner haul of the year. Everybody seemed to think it the most natural thing in the world for an antique shop to be doing business there."

On still another occasion Parsons encountered what amounted to a private car shortage during the Kentucky Derby week.

"It was in my palmy days in 1927," he says. "I went to Europe in February to return in early May and had asked fifteen people to go to Louisville with me aboard a car I had chartered and paid for from the Pullman Company. We were to leave New York on Thursday and when my boat docked on Wednesday I was met at the pier by my butler with the dire intelligence that, through some error, a car with no kitchen or dining room had been assigned to me and it was too late to get it changed. We were all right for staterooms but no food.

"Just to show you what servants were in those days, the faithful Walters assured me I had nothing to worry about; he had arranged everything. The first meal had been ordered from the Brook Club in New York. That was dinner. Breakfast the next morning was coffee and champagne and he could look out for that himself. Lunch was put on at Cincinnati and we would have dinner Friday night at Brown's Hotel in Louisville. It worked without a flaw and I don't think people ever had a better time or better food."

Parsons recalls that at America's other fabled resort of formal wealth, Newport, a handful of elderly dowagers still arrived for the season over the rails of the New Haven long after regular train service had disappeared from the pages of the *Official Guide*. Among them were Mrs. Watts Sherman, the durable Miss Julia Berwind of anthracite millions and the Grand Duchess of Buzzard's Bay herself, Mrs. Hamilton McKown Twombley.

"The upper servants and main household staff would accompany them," says the chronicler of Bellevue Avenue.

In the case of Mrs. Twombley, the last surviving grandchild of Commodore Cornelius Vanderbilt, this constituted a formidable array of domestics including chauffeurs, footmen and butlers in the traditional Vanderbilt maroon livery and, most formidable of all, M. Josef Donon, the Twombley *chef de cuisine*. M. Donon, who received a salary of $25,000 annually and had a Newport cottage of his own, somehow made do in a Pullman galley and produced *caneton a l'orange* and *asperges Argenteuil au beurre* on order.

Also of antiquarian interest is the frequent appearance of the beach resort of Palatka, a retreat of the well-to-do at the turn of the century sharing favor with Palm Beach and located sixty-one miles south of Jacksonville. Today it has vanished from the Florida East Coast map in the *Official Guide* although it is still listed as a stop for the once a day mail train in each direction.

At the turn of the century with which this record deals, it must be remembered that Florida was little more than the feudal domain of Henry Morrison Flagler, a partner of John D. Rockefeller in Standard Oil who had seen his first orange tree when he came south for his health in 1874. Flagler was delighted with everything about Florida. He had resources of something better than $100,000,000 which, as Cleveland Amory has remarked, "was evidence that in those days it was almost impossible to dispense with a Standard Oil fortune." As adjuncts of his Florida East Coast Railway, Flagler started building a series of enormous resort hotels, the first the Ponce de Leon at St. Augustine, and in 1896 the incredible Royal Poinciana at Palm Beach.

But five years later Palm Beach was relatively unknown save as a resort of upper case fashion impervious to the multitudes who today pass through it every winter. Undreamed and far in the future were Paris Singer and Addison Mizner, the Josh Cosdens, Horace Dodges and Atwater Kents whose names were to be synonymous with Palm Beach a quarter of a century later. Palm Beach in the nineties and at the turn of the century was a private preserve of Standard Oil and Morgan partners.

In 1901 private equipment was still partly the product of Wagner and partly Pullman, although the merger of the two car builders had been effected two years earlier. The New York Central had favored Wagner with its patronage from earliest times when the Commodore had commanded his *Commodore Vanderbilt* and *Duchess* from the firm. Dr. Seward Webb, a Vanderbilt in-law, was President of the Wagner Palace Car Company and such cars on the East Coast's list for 1901-02 as *Grassmere, Edgemere* and *Pilgrim* were all Wagner products while it is entirely probable that some of the Central lines business cars listed were the same. Within a few years, however, the name of Wagner was to disappear from the builder's plates on private and sleeping cars entirely and Pullman to assume a complete monopoly of its patents.

In all, the Florida East Coast listed thirty-one private or special car movements for that year. During the Palm Beach season of 1926-27 Floyd B. May of the F.E.C. passenger department supervised no fewer than eighty-five private car movements across the Flagler trestle to Palm Beach alone. In 1957 the railroad carried three varnish cars owned by private or non-railroad travelers, Daniel E. Taylor's *Sea Level*, Bruce Dodson's *Helma II*, and *The Virginia City* of Charles Clegg and the author.

A notable figure of Palm Beach's great days who visited diligently among the private cars on the Poinciana track, although he himself maintained no such ostentatious conveyance, was Clarence W. Barron, bearded like Moses, shrewd as a tinker and owner and publisher of the *Wall Street Journal* and its State Street counterpart, the *Boston News Bureau*. Barron, although abstemious where spirits were concerned, was a mighty doer among the fleshpots of food and wine. He considered the food at Colonel Bradley's Beach Club the best in America and spent the season at Palm Beach ostensibly to enjoy its menu which connoisseurs compared favorably to that of Maxim's and the Cafe de Paris in Paris. Actually Barron was one of the smartest reporters of his generation. Trusted by the financiers who flocked to Florida in the winter months, his integrity was legendary and he never violated a professional confidence, but his dispatches to his papers had a profound impact on the money marts of the world. Otto Kahn, Andrew Mellon and Atwater Kent talked freely of their affairs in his presence, certain that their confidence would be respected in matters involving billions. Barron wove well manicured fingers through his brown beard, said little, printed what was proper and knew all there was to know of American finance in the 1920's.

It was aboard his wife's personal private car *Adios* one Palm Beach evening that Harry Payne Whitney remarked: "If Barron ever talks in his sleep, they'll have to build a private car track at Atlanta."

By the end of the Florida season the ace financial reporter of them all had eaten himself out of his most capacious dinner suit of which he had a dozen or more in progressive dimensions, and a kind friend like Harry Sinclair would send him aboard *Sinco* to Battle Creek to take the waters and reduce his girth.

Almost forgotten by a later generation of wealth and fashion which went further afield from New York to achieve privacy and repose was Lakewood, New Jersey, a resort on the Central Railroad of New Jersey which once attracted members of the private car club in impressive numbers. In its golden noontide of favor, Lakewood was the setting for George Gould's "Georgian Court," a rustic cottage whose premises included, among other conveniences, a private gaming casino with sleeping accommodations for eighty guests and a race track the size of Madison Square Garden. Naturally the private cars of the heirs of Jay Gould who had died in 1892 flocked like homing birds over the Central's seven mile branch line from Farmingdale where it connected with the Pennsylvania and *Atalanta, Stranrear, Dixie* and other Gould cars on the siding at Lakewood indicated that the family was at home among the sixty servants that regularly staffed the establishment.

John Hays Hammond had a summer home at Lakewood and every fall a reliable sign of changing seasons was the departure of his car *Kya Zami* for Georgia with the great mining engineer and his family aboard. W. W. Willock, Pittsburgh steel magnate of Jones & Laughlin, made an annual appearance, usually aboard a charter Pullman as did James J. Hill who arrived on a Great Northern business car but was satisfied to commute to downtown New York several times a week aboard the regular commuter coaches of the C of N J. William C. Whitney, in the days before Whitneys had migrated to Newport and Long Island, was a regular aboard his Pullman *Wanderer* and Lakewood was for some forgotten reason greatly favored by Rock Island executives whose business cars were sometimes three deep on the private car siding.

Long after Lakewood's social cachet had departed, there were seasonal echoes of the solvent past when the aging John D. Rockefeller took off there for his winter sojourn at Ormond Beach, Florida. E. T. M. Carr, one-time Central of New Jersey traffic manager now living in retirement at Long Branch, well recalls these annual arrivals and departures and the precautions taken to shroud the nonagenarian moneybags' movements from the press.

"His routine was to leave Lakewood each fall for Florida on a special train movement that we originated consisting of a ballast coach and a single private charter Pullman," Mr. Carr recalls. "We turned the train over to the Pennsylvania at Farmingdale and from there it ran special to Trenton or Philadelphia to be attached to a through train for the South. When the old gentleman returned in the spring his train was usually stopped about two miles out of town at a station called Larrabee where he boarded an automobile for his Lakewood home.

"On his last trip, the year he died, quite a number of photographers and reporters were on hand at Lakewood to cover his departure, but the old man asked us to hold his special while he got aboard at Lakehurst, eight miles south of Lakewood, and when the special stopped at Lakewood for the luggage he was already in his stateroom with the blinds drawn. He had very few people in his private party, a few doctors I believe and bodyguards and I understand the car carried oxygen equipment and other hospital gear as well as his special food and medicines."

When Rockefeller died and the last remembered glory departed the C of N J, Lakewood had long since been no more than a boarded depot on a freight only branch line.

Possibly to be regarded as symbolic of the passing of the private car generation was the death at Palm Beach early in 1958 of Robert R. Young, the bantam-weight Texan whose dream had been of a railroad empire to rival those of Gould and Harriman reaching from coast to coast as a single operation in the portfolio of the Allegheny Corporation which he had inherited and reassembled after the collapse of the Van Sweringen dynasty in the mid-thirties.

Young took his own life at his Florida mansion after his boasted reorganization of his prime property, the New York Central, had failed to bring about an upswing in that road's affairs. His body was taken north for burial at Newport aboard the New York Central business car No. 28 which Young had caused to be decorated by Dorothy Draper in happier years, and a saddened group of friends who watched its departure from the Florida East Coast depot at West Palm Beach might well have reflected that, as the markers diminished down the tangent, the longest night of all was claiming at once a notable aficionado of the private car way of life and one of the last of the truly flamboyant business cars as well.

Other observers remarked that on his last of all railroad journeys while it traversed the Florida East Coast, the Atlantic Coast Line, the Richmond, Fredericksburg & Potomac, the Pennsylvania and the New York, New Haven & Hartford, at no time did the funeral cortege roll over iron either owned or controlled by the dead man. And, if a crowning irony were needed when the funeral train paused in New York for brief memorial services, it was at the Pennsylvania Station, and Al Perlman, Tom Deegan and other associates in the New York Central were obliged to pay their last respects in the presence of the greatest vested competition of the Littlest Texan of them all.

The Lighting System

The Celebrated Pintsch Compressed
◎ *Oil Gas Method ∴*
◎ *In use on over 40,000 Cars in*
◎ *Europe and America ∴*
◎ *The Best, Most Economical and*
◎ *Only Safe Light for Railroad Purposes ∴*
◎ *In Brilliancy and Cleanliness Unsurpassed ∴*
THIS SYSTEM HAS BEEN ADOPTED BY THE U. S.
LIGHT-HOUSE BOARD FOR LIGHTING BUOYS ∴

GRAHAME HARDY COLLECTION

Florida East Coast Railway
Jacksonville, Florida

Feb.12,1895.

Dear General:-

Your favor of the 4th inst. received. We will
be more than glad to haul your car over our line, and will take
it from connecting lines either at Jacksonville,Palatka,Orange
City Junction or Titusville, whichever point you find it most
convenient to come to us.

The road for which Mr.Hindekooper was Receiver was
Richmond & Danville,which is now operated by the Southern Railway;
and if you will write to Mr.W.H.Green, General Manager Southern Ry.,
Washington, D.C., he will, I am sure, take pleasure in hauling your
car over his line.

For transportation over the Plant System from Montgomery
south to Tampa, you had better apply to Mr.H.B.Plant, President, or
Mr.H.S.Haines, Vice-president, No.12 West Twenty-third Street, New
York, and I am sure they will also take pleasure in giving you transportation for you and your party.

It will give us great pleasure to have you with us again,
and I trust you will arrange to make your stay with us as long as
possible.

Yours truly,

Sup't.

To Jos.T.Torrence, Esq.,
        Pres't Chicago Elevated Terminal Co.
                Chicago, Ill.

PULLMAN STANDARD

Archetypal and characteristic property of the private railroad car on American
steam carriers was the brass enclosed open observation platform from which its
occupants take the air and view the sights. The earliest private and/or business
cars often had an open platform at each end, but the practice was modified in
time to enclose the forward entrance with its purely utilitarian implications and
leave only the back platform with its ornate rails of tradition and gaily striped
awning such as is shown here on the beautiful p.v. *Illinois*, built in 1905 for the
Alton. As high speeds which sucked grit and ballast up from the roadbed gradually eliminated open platforms from club and lounge cars, enclosed solariums
appeared in the design of a few private cars, notably Franklyn Hutton's ACF-
built *Curleyhut* and the business car of Benjamin F. Fairless, chief executive officer
of the United States Steel Corporation. But even in an age of Diesel power, elec-
tronic train control and other questionable devisings of what passes for progress,
the tradition of an open platform on the car that rides the end of the train has
been maintained as an integral part of cars outshopped in the fifties for such
important railroads as the Southern Pacific, Great Northern, Missouri Pacific and
Illinois Central.

In 1906 the affairs of the Buffalo, Rochester & Pittsburgh Railroad were sufficiently flourishing to permit ordering from Pullman the fine p.v. *Virginia* for the use of company officials and influential friends and its likeness appears on this page as well as the page opposite. The private car of Herbert Coppell, *Manana* was also out-shopped by Pullman five years later and presents an interesting profile of picture windows and leaded lunettes indicating a compartmentation to suit the whim of a well-to-do individualist.

THREE PHOTOS: PULLMAN STANDARD

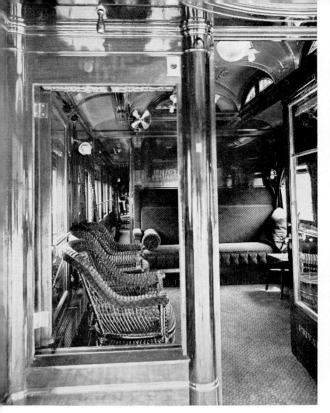 

Brakeman Johnny Bunting's *El Fleda,* three views of which are shown on this page, once one of the most widely advertised of private cars, finally came to rest as a diner near Peoria, Illinois.

Shippers, important friends and the official hierarchy of the Buffalo, Rochester & Pittsburgh Railroad could watch the countryside roll by while having a highball or nourishing Martini in the well-upholstered observation compartment of the company car *Virginia*. Pintsch lamps or electricity were available when the shadows fell and a speedometer and air pressure gauge told experienced railroaders all they needed to know about the progress of the train.

Framed in polished mahogany panels with inlaid marquetry, the dining salon of Henry Clay Pierce's *Zamora* is an example of what $40,000 could purchase in the way of private cars from Pullman in 1901.

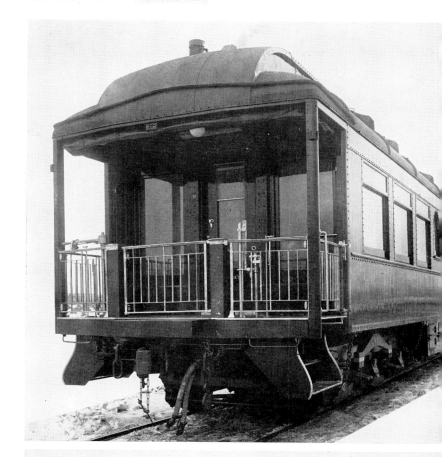

Structural strength was incorporated in the plans for James Cox Brady's *Adventurer*, when it was built by Pullman in 1914 at the expense of esthetics when steel columns ran from roof to underframe at the corners of the observation platform.

As beautifully proportioned as any private car toward the close of the era of wooden sidewalls reinforced by steel sheathing was the rear end of A. K. Macomber's *Seminole* built for the wealthy sportsman by Pullman in 1916 with the brass railed observation platform of hallowed tradition.

No American family was ever more addicted to private car travel than the Goulds whose immense fortune stemmed from Jay Gould's rape of Erie, his corner of gold and other financial maneuvers which excited the dim view of the ethical. Helen Gould, George Gould and Edwin Gould each had private cars of varying splendor and George upon occasion liked to hire Pullman's entire private train for $500 a day. On the page opposite is the Pullman-built *Dixie* which Edwin acquired in 1901. On this page is the interior, modest for such a colossal fortune as it represented, of *Wanderer*, built the same year for William C. Whitney, sometime Secretary of the Navy, Vanderbilt in-law and grandfather of the American Ambassador to the Court of St. James's. Both William C.'s sons, Payne Whitney and Harry Payne Whitney were members of the private car club in their turn.

By 1918 when Pullman Standard built *Lynnewood* for Joseph E. Widener of Philadelphia, its guest staterooms, except for the fine woods used for paneling, were indistinguishable from those sleeping cars in general service available to the traveling public.

Although 1906 was not a vintage year for interiors, the Southern Pacific's No. 120, the *Ashland* was luxurious in keeping with its occupancy by the president of one of the greatest of all carriers.

Half a century later the Espee's No. 150, the *Sunset,* built for the use of President Donald Russell, represented every improvement to be incorporated in private car technique and was used by dignitaries visiting the West including President Eisenhower when he went to Del Monte to play golf.

Depicted on the page opposite are two interiors of Charles M. Schwab's Pullman-built *Loretto II* at the time it was outshopped to the specifications of the ironmaster. In Mrs. Schwab's personal stateroom (LEFT) the occupant had a choice of seven bells with mother-of-pearl pushbuttons to summon the services of her staff aboard one of the most widely celebrated private cars of its time. On this page *Loretto II* is depicted in its ownership by Colonel Elliott White Springs, heir to vast cotton mills and owner of the Lancaster & Chester Railroad in South Carolina. In the photograph Colonel Springs, flanked by his secretary Lunsford McFadden and other guests, orders the best of everything from Steward Willie Patterson.

PULLMAN STANDARD

GERALD M. BEST

PULLMAN STANDARD

That business cars with open platforms at either end didn't altogether disappear with the advent of the more conventional enclosed forward end in the nineties is evidenced on the page opposite by the Tidewater Company's stunning official car *Dixie* and the Southern Pacific's Maintenance of Way No. 5, a narrow gauge veteran in service on the Owens Valley three-foot branch that is a survival of the legendary Carson & Colorado. *Dixie* was built at Pullman in 1906 and the Espee car, whose origins are shrouded in the mists of antiquity, was in service as late as 1940 when this photograph was taken by Gerald Best at Owenyo. Equally as stunning as *Dixie* is the interior (ABOVE) of the private car built by Pullman in 1889 for the Duluth & Iron Range Railroad. It was a period in car design when every inch counted and the dining apartment had four upper berths of superbly polished oak.

Hallmark and property of executive dignity in the golden age of private cars, the outsize brass bed was found in all the best master staterooms from the Maine Central to the El Paso & South Western. On the page opposite it appears in two versions: at the right in the Missouri-Kansas-Texas presidential car No. 110 and at the left aboard *Adolphus* of cheerful and beery fame. On this page the interior of *Ideal*, added to the general service rental pool by Pullman in 1911, suggests a departure from the somber mahogany and massive decor of earlier private cars in favor of more relaxed colors and simpler fixtures.

THREE PHOTOS:
PULLMAN STANDARD

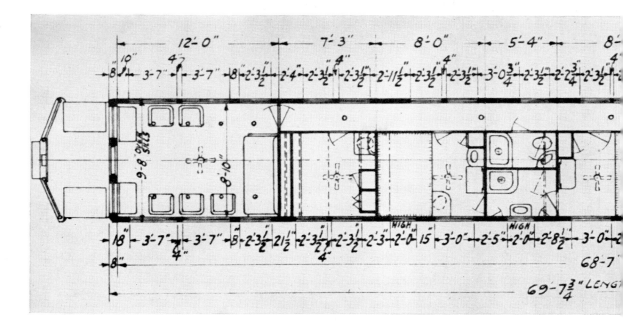

On the page opposite at the top is the comely rear platform of the Tidewater Company's official car *Dixie,* one of the last p.v. to be built with open platforms at either end. Below it is the noble profile of Colonel Daniel C. Jackling's first *Cyprus* built by Pullman in 1909 and later to pass into the hands of Julius Fleishman as *Hopedale,* a name it carried with it when it was finally acquired as a business car by the Pittsburgh & West Virginia Railroad in 1925.

For a thirty-eight mile short line with twenty-four miles of branches, the Munising Railway running between Munising, Michigan, and Little Lake, had fancy ideas. The business car shown above with its fine quilted leather banquette and oil lamp was assigned to President William C. Mather, and the secret of such profligacy lay in the circumstance that the Munising was part of a rich little industrial enclave that included the Cleveland-Cliffs Iron Mines, the Marquette & Southern Railroad and the Lake Superior & Ishpeming Railroad. In 1924 all three carriers were consolidated as part of the last named.

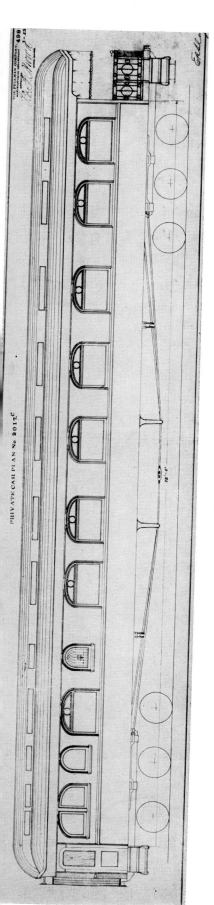

When, in 1904 the El Paso & South Western ordered a fine car from Pullman, the business car neurosis which was later to afflict the railroad world was unknown and the order went on the books for a "Private Car No. 2017 C." Named *Arizona*, it passed to the Southern Pacific and ended its days as the p.v. of G. Allan Hancock who bought it for $6,000 for his Santa Maria Valley Railroad in Southern California.

TWO PHOTOS: PULLMAN STANDARD

Coeval with *Arizona* and shown with it on the page opposite was the strikingly handsome Pullman p.v. *Hidalgo* of the Nacional de Mexico. On this page elaborate fretwork decorations characterize the ceiling of the principal salon of the p.v. *Cornwall,* maintained by the Canadian Pacific for the Governor General of Canada on his travels.

PULLMAN STANDARD

SOUTHERN PACIFIC

Two of the most celebrated cars in the Old West are depicted on the page oppo-site in the Southern Pacific's *Del Monte*, endeared in retrospect to San Francisco's first families as one of the familiar properties of travel among the well-to-do at the turn of the century, and Senator William Andrews Clark's No. 2001 on the Northern Pacific. *Del Monte* was named of course for the railroad's splendid resort hotel on Monterey Peninsula, scene of many of romances and much good cheer in other times. Senator Clark's No. 2001 was built by Pullman for the copper king in 1905, a vintage year in the golden age of private cars generally. Clark, the interior of whose rolling mansion is shown here, was the archtype of silk hatted, starched and haughty capitalist of his era, cold, acquisitive and possessed of a brilliant mind. Unseated from the United States Senate by political rivals headed by Marcus Daly, Clark joined forces with the formidable Henry H. Rogers of Standard Oil and F. A. Heintze to regain the toga. No. 2001 was a familiar fixture on private car tracks throughout the West, the visible capstone of success in a veritable tycoon in the grand, uncompromising manner. Legend holds that the only mistake of Clark's career was when he miscalculated the population of Butte at election time by adding a zero to the census and provided free whisky for a town ten times its size.

Despite the classic panache of its traditional exterior and noble brass-bound observation platform, the Rock Island's car No. 1900, built by Pullman in 1910, gathers and multiplies in its interior decor most of the appalling aspects of the taste of its period: fumed oak panels, leaded glass deadlights and illuminating fixtures, mission furniture and a pervading suggestion of Hof-Brau or Early North German Lloyd overall. Conventional Pullman with its universal mahogany and marquetry had much to recommend it; the Morris chair period had nothing.

Not all private varnish was maintained in the gleaming splendor suggested by social pretentions and massive wealth on the part of its owners. An atmosphere of slightly seedy grandeur was characteristic of Colonel D. C. Jackling's *Cyprus* as depicted below, while the crammed shelves of technical volumes testified that the owner was still a mining engineer whose way with copper had made him so rich he didn't have to care for appearances. *Cyprus* to the end carried on its nameboards the insigne of the Nevada Northern while lesser billing was given to the initials of the long since vanished Bullfrog & Goldfield and the Tonopah & Tidewater, short lines with sentimental associations for the owner. Another mining engineer member of the private car club was the great John Hays Hammond whose princely salary of $250,000 from Dan Guggenheim enabled him to maintain his car *Kya Yami*, meaning "One of My Homes" in Zulu. On the page opposite are the classic profiles of *Isabella*, the Columbian Exposition Pullman, and *Ranger* a Pullman rental pool car at the turn of the century and not to be confused with another *Ranger* built in the twenties for Cissie Patterson, the Washington lady newspaper publisher.

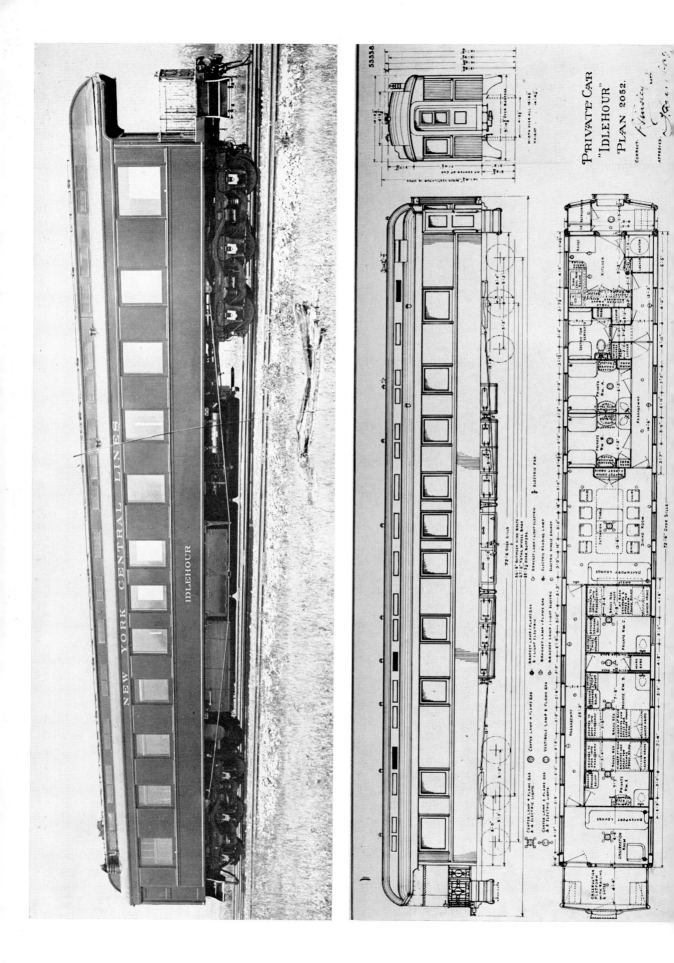

NEW YORK CENTRAL LINES

IDLEHOUR

PRIVATE CAR "IDLEHOUR" PLAN 2052.

Names perfumed by worldliness and wealth are associated with the private varnish depicted on these pages. Opposite is one of the legendary Vanderbilt cars on the family railroad, the New York Central. William K. Vanderbilt's *Idlehour* was built by Pullman in 1905 and represented a long tradition of splendid private varnish dedicated to the occasions of the mightiest railroad dynasty in the land. On this page, Peter W. Rouss's *Winchester* was outshopped by Pullman in 1917 for the well-to-do New York real estate dealer. Its simple decor and the upright telephone set nesting in the corner behind gold portières are a clue to the period that saw it in service whenever its owner was minded to take a nice train ride to Palm Beach or the races at Louisville.

In 1913 when Pullman built *Adventurer* for James Cox Brady, the private car of society and finance had so closely come to resemble the decor of a railroad business car as to be almost indistinguishable. Guests aboard *Adventurer*, however, soon sensed a difference for Brady was an amateur of fine things generally and of the pleasures of the table in particular. His chef de cuisine had been snared from New York's Metropolitan Club and the Brady cellars were famed as the repository of potables long since vanished elsewhere in the world. After his death, the Brady collection of Medford rums, venerable Madeiras and priceless cognacs brought sensational prices when auctioned in New York. The decor of *Adventurer* may have been utilitarian, but the Mousse of Sole Anglais, Sauce Cardinal, and the Grouse à la Broch from its galley were supernal.

Still in the Pintsch lamp era, *Ohio* delivered by Pullman to the Baltimore & Ohio South Western in 1894 for the use of its President Edward R. Bacon, was notably uncluttered for a private car of Victorian times and was the second p.v. to be outshopped for Mr. Bacon within two years, its predecessor having been *Virginia* in 1892. The B & O S W was a 600-mile trunk line between Belpre, Ohio, and East St. Louis which, when it was shortly absorbed by the Baltimore & Ohio, gave that carrier Western access via the St. Louis gateway. Although a presidential car every two years may have been ostentatious, it was by no means without precedent or parallel, as witness the *Alexanders* of President A. A. McLeod of the Philadelphia & Reading in almost the same years.

MAYNARD L. PARKER

After nearly half a century of service during which time it had seen much of life the length and depth of the continent, *The Gold Coast*, full of years and honors, passed by deed of gift of its owners into possession of the Pacific Coast Chapter of the Railway and Locomotive Historical Society with its decor and properties intact as shown on the opposite page. Sentimentalists to the core, its owners carried the memory of its last home railroad, the Virginia & Truckee with them when they commissioned their new Pullman *The Virginia City*. In each of its staterooms and drawing rooms, as shown above, an artist depicted a scene from the well-remembered V & T, and souvenirs of the most romantic of all short lines still rode the rails long after its own right of way had vanished from the Nevada countryside.

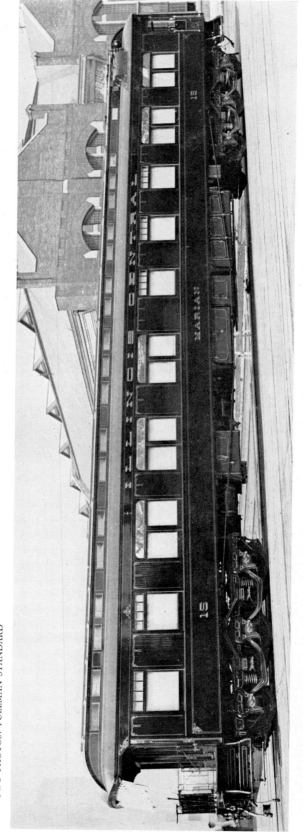

TWO PHOTOS: PULLMAN STANDARD

ILLINOIS CENTRAL

No carrier over the years was characterized by greater style or more meticulous maintenance of its private and/or business cars than the proud Illinois Central, Mainline of Mid-America, a notable repository of history and, in the regime of Stuyvesant Fish, "the railroad of society." On the page opposite are its cars No. 1 and No. 15, the *Marian*, outshopped by Pullman in 1891 and 1894 respectively, the latter for the personal occupancy of the aristocratic Mr. Fish himself. As late as 1915 when American Car & Foundry designed No. 16 whose observation platform is shown here, the I.C. scorned the designation "Office Car" and had its property engrossed in shaded letters with the proud blazon "Private Car," but the glory of Newport had departed the railroad a decade previous when Mrs. Fish made the mistake of affronting Mrs. E. H. Harriman, whose husband happened to own it at the time.

TWO PHOTOS: ARTHUR D. DUBIN COLLECTION

A spirit of cheerful eccentricity characterized the private and business cars of the Illinois Central, "Mainline of Mid-America" in the nineteenth century which saw in its employment such names of magnificent individualism as Abraham Lincoln, Mark Twain, Grenville M. Dodge, Sir Robert Van Horn, Daniel Webster, Stephen A. Douglas, Hannibal Hamlin and General George B. McClellan. In the below photograph of an I.C. official car in the late eighties is shown in a cutaway coat leaning on the drawbar no less a celebrity than General Pierre Gustave Toutant Beauregard, C.S.A., surrounded by clerical dignitaries on some now forgotten occasion. On the page opposite I.C. business cars No. 9 and No. 2 testify to the rich diversity of design on the carrier's p.v. roster. No. 2 had its origins at Pullman in 1883 and was still in useful service in the mid-thirties, its pointed windows suggestive of the Gothic influence of the still earlier director's car of the Chicago & North Western sixties.

ILLINOIS CENTRAL

Reflecting the subdued tastes of its exalted occupant was the dining salon (BELOW) of Edward H. Harriman's Pullman-built *Arden* at whose table many decisions were made affecting the destinies of the far-flung Harriman railroad empire. *Arden* carried the insigne of Union Pacific on its nameboards and the number 1900, the year of its delivery by the builder.

A handsome example of company property shortly after the turn of the century before style and distinction yielded entirely to the blight of austerity was the Milwaukee's *Como*, shown on the page opposite and available to ranking executives as well as large shippers, friendly legislators and helpful people generally.

TWO PHOTOS:
PULLMAN STANDARD

Under a California sun and in the golden age both of private cars and of the fortunes of the mighty Southern Pacific, *San Emidio* (PAGE OPPOSITE) basks at the company's shops at Sacramento in 1895, a radiant illustration of the term "varnish car." On this page is the bulkhead plan from the drawing board of a long dead architect in Pullman's "marquetry room" for the first *Sunset*.

BULKHEAD, PLAN 2001

PULLMAN STANDARD

The black and white reproduction below shows the dining salon of *The Virginia City* facing toward the galley and the car's kitchen offices. In color on the page opposite is the same apartment facing toward the rear of the car and its two owners Charles Clegg (LEFT) and Lucius Beebe dining alone.

TWO PHOTOS: MAYNARD L. PARKER

The three pictures on these pages suggest that wide range and variety of character have been part of the pattern of Southern Pacific private cars over the years. On this page is the interior of *Sunset,* built by Pullman Standard in 1956 for the President of the far-flung western carrier. In its decor there is no trace of the plush and ormolu, velvet drapes and satinwood trim that had been the hallmarks of prestige two generations previously. On the page opposite the window locations of car No. 119 suggest an interesting compartmentation while a double side door gives access for loading in the forward service area. And if the lines of *Emalita* seem familiar to students of private car folklore it is because far away and several years before it had been built by Pullman as *Alexander,* the pride of Angus A. McLeod, President of the Philadelphia & Reading in that railroad's golden noontide of prosperity and pride. In the mid-nineties, however, hard times came to the Reading. The clammy hand of bankruptcy claimed superfluous elegances among its assets and in 1896 *Alexander* turned up as *Emalita* on the Southern Pacific. McLeod had dreamed of a transport empire to dominate New England, but it transpired that, after all, the course of empire was Westward.

PULLMAN STANDARD

The Baltimore & Ohio has long been known as "The Railroad of Presidents" since every chief executive of the United States since the first Harrison and heads of other states by the score have ridden its cars out of Washington. Here we see Benjamin Harrison, the twenty-third president, aboard a private parlor car en route to New York for a political conference amidst the full beards, frock coats and pre-Gibson Girl hairdos of that eminently respectable and now, how distant age. On the page opposite Charles Clegg, Nevada editor and historian, poses at Miami aboard *The Virginia City* to point a contrast in whiskers, attire and private car decor. The fireplace is activated by bottled gas.

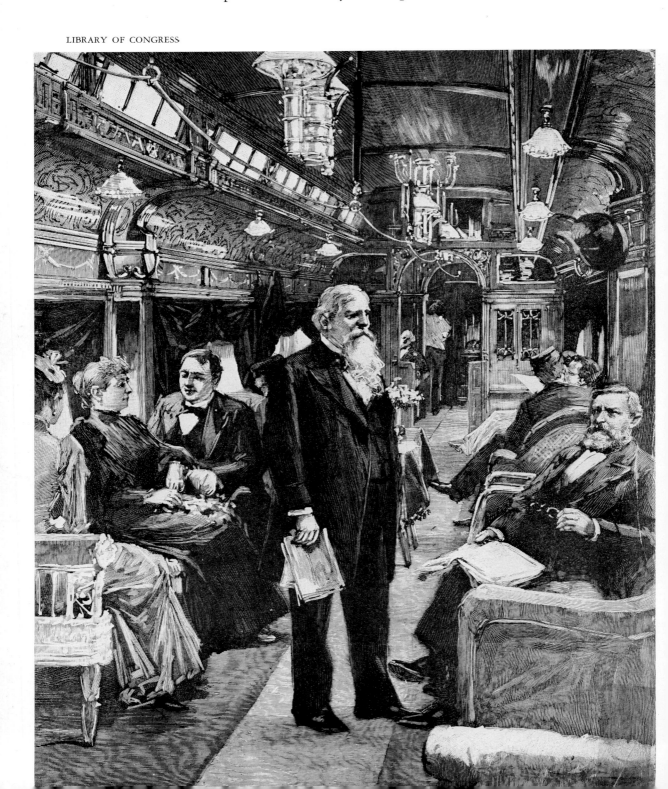

Charlie Yee in His Pantry on
The Virginia City

The Butler's Wine Cellar Aboard
The Virginia City

TWO PHOTOS: JULIAN GRAHAM

In his all-butane galley aboard *The Virginia City* Chef Hazzie Wallace from the Southern Pacific dining car pool consults about the day's menu with Mr. T-Bone Towser, the 185-pound St. Bernard who calls the car his when away from home.

Almost the last of the simon-pure private cars with no over-tones of commerce about them was *Helma,* the second car of that name owned by Bruce Dodson, a Kansas City insurance magnate. *Helma* had first been built as *Esperanza* for Harry S. Black by Pullman in 1929 and had passed into the hands of A. C. Burrage, a Boston moneybags of formidable proportions, on the death of its first owner. Mr. and Mrs. Dodson are shown aboard *Helma* below. At the right is a genial portrait in yachting attire of Clarence Barron, founder of the *Wall Street Journal* and a gifted financial reporter so privy to the affairs of members of the private car club that it was once remarked "If Barron ever talks in his sleep they will have to build a private car track at Atlanta." On the page opposite are the rear platform (LEFT) of the Tidewater Company's *Dixie* and the rear platform and interior of Herbert Coppell's Pullman-built *Manana* reflecting the best in private cars as of the year 1911.

ESTATE OF CLARENCE BARRON

THREE PHOTOS: PULLMAN STANDARD

A growing trend toward severity of decor in Pullman private varnish manifested itself as the twentieth century progressed and is suggested in Herbert Coppell's *Manana* on the page opposite and A. K. Macomber's *Seminole* shown here. *Seminole* was built in 1915 for the wealthy sportsman with a celebrated racing stable who was the acknowledged leader of the American social colony in Paris. It made an appearance on the correct private car tracks at the right season of year, at Palm Beach until Washington's birthday, at Louisville for the Derby in May, and in the California autumn at Del Monte on the Monterey Peninsula, a resort of superlative fashion with a railroad background. Del Monte had come into being in the eighties at the behest of the Pacific Improvement Company, the real estate catchall for the Southern Pacific.

Although their nameboards carried the insignes of many home line railroads which undertook their supervision, maintenance and storage, the cars on these pages were all owned by private individuals and devoted to their social or business convenience which in no case involved railroading. *Cromarty* (PAGE OPPOSITE) was built in Canada for J. K. L. Ross, a wealthy Canadian sportsman whose personal crest appears on its side. It is now the Canadian Pacific official car *Thorold*. Colonel Daniel C. Jackling's *Cyprus*, the second of that name, was built by Pullman in 1913 for the Utah mine operator and was unique in that when it was photographed, as shown here, at San Jose, California, in 1938, it bore the insignes of three railroads, the Nevada Northern on its center nameboards, and the initials at either end of the then long vanished Bullfrog & Goldfield and the Las Vegas & Tonopah. One of the last bona fide private Pullmans was *Helma*, belonging to Bruce Dodson of Kansas City and Palm Beach. It carried the initials of the Florida East Coast Railway. On this page *The Gold Coast,* first p.v. of Charles Clegg and Lucius Beebe is shown under the cottonwoods at the Carson City, Nevada, yards of the Virginia & Truckee Railroad.

LUCIUS BEEBE

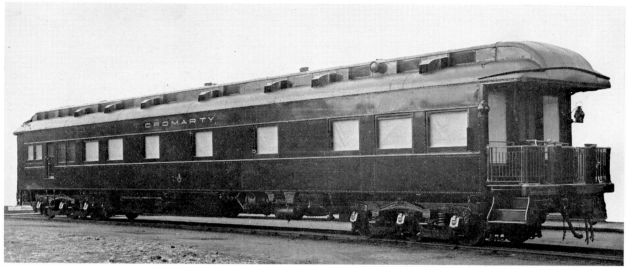

CANADIAN PACIFIC

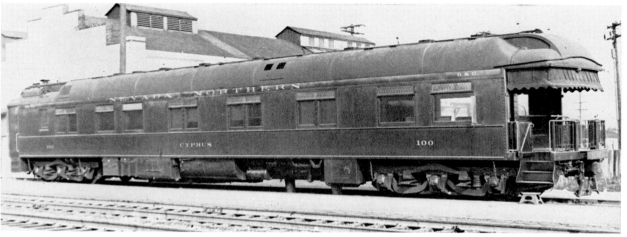

GILBERT KNEISS COLLECTION

FLORIDA EAST COAST

On these two pages are business cars of contemporary usage in the year 1959. The Burlington's General *John A. Hulen* is a converted Pullman ten section buffet lounge assigned to official use on the Fort Worth & Denver City in its joint operations in Texas with the Rock Island. The Texas & Pacific's No. 3 is a superb example of Edwardian or Early Colonel E. H. R. Green period of steel underframe wooden car, since rebuilt with plywood sheathing. Delaware & Hudson No. 300 is an older car than it looks, having been rebuilt with steel sheathing over wooden sidewalls while, on this page, the Missouri-Kansas-Tex No. 400 has also seen long and honorable service and only in recent years acquired roller bearing trucks for high speed service. Its multiplicity of track lights, markers and Mars patent beacon is unusual. Unusual, too, in the year 1959 is the steam switch engine still in service when Everett DeGolyer, Jr., took this atmospheric photograph at Dallas.

EVERETT L. DeGOLYER, JR.

TWO PHOTOS: EVERETT L. DeGOLYER, JR.

DELAWARE & HUDSON

TWO PHOTOS: AMERICAN CAR & FOUNDRY

Airflow lines, wide picture windows and great simplicity of styling all terminate in the open observation platform of tradition with a massive metallic railing in this beautiful Missouri Pacific business car built by American Car & Foundry at its St. Charles shops in 1957. Its interior is a far cry from the Eastlake decor of the nineties with ball fringe portières, Pintsch lamps and inlaid mahogany, but the Mopac's general manager riding in the contemporary comfort of the master stateroom (BELOW) had all the conveniences known to Jay Gould or James J. Hill and a few more. They include air conditioning, flourescent lighting and improved plumbing fixtures as well as ship-to-shore telephone connections and radiant heat.

AMERICAN CAR & FOUNDRY

Gone from the Southern Deserts are the glory and the gold, and the once splendid *Esmeralda,* private varnish of the narrow gauge Carson & Colorado, serves as a humble shelter for Southern Pacific track gangs at Keeler, California, beside the three-foot rails it once rode to wealthy destinies. In the days of Goldfield and Tonopah it knew the tread of nabobs and the skirted frock coats of gamblers, Key Pittman, Wyatt Earp, Tex Rickard and Tasker Oddie. Now the captains and the kings depart—Lo, all thy pomp of yesterday. . . .

GERALD M. BEST

Coachyards of Eternity

 PERUSAL OF THE LIST of private and/or business cars out-
shopped by the Pullman Company between the years 1882
and 1930 which is contained in the appendix of this volume will furnish many instructive commentaries on the
house rules and characters of the members of the private
car club. The copy of the list made available to the author
through the courtesy of Arthur D. Dubin is in bad order physically and
some of its details hopelessly illegible, but the essentials are there and
constitute an interesting footnote to the folklore and legend of the lords of
creation in the golden age of railroading.

The Pullman list is, of course, by no means the complete story of private
cars since scores of such vehicles derived from other sources of manufac-
ture, American Car & Foundry and its predecessors, Jackson & Sharp, and
the shops of numerous carriers which built their own business cars and those
of stockholders, shippers and influential friends. Henry E. Huntington, one
of the outstanding private car fanciers of all time, had five p.v. during his
well upholstered lifetime. *Oneonta I* and *Oneonta II* he inherited from his
father, Collis Huntington. Some years later Pullman built for his use over
his vast network of electric lines in California *San Marino*, an electric conveyance, and in 1916 Pullman also built him a conventional private car for
use on steam railroads with the identical name. A fifth car on the Henry
Huntington roster is reported to have been named *Pilgrim* and the Huntington Library at San Marino has a photograph to prove it. No such entry
appears anywhere on the Pullman private car list although a *Pilgrim* was
added to the general service pool in 1917 and may very well have been
purchased from there by the California millionaire.

Perhaps the outstanding private car traits suggested by the Pullman
record are those of family cohesiveness, sentimentality and continuity.
Whitneys and Vanderbilts ordered private cars as families and over periods
of several generations. Angus A. McLeod of the Reading Company ordered
not one but two successive *Alexanders* from Pullman. The same was true
of Charles M. Schwab with *Loretto*. General William Jackson Palmer at one
time was proprietor of two Rio Grande cars named *Nomad*, a narrow gauge

p.v. and a standard. A chip off the old mahogany block, Charles Clark like his father before him was a member of the club with *Errant*. Bet-a-Million Gates took over the Kansas City, Pittsburgh & Gulf's No. 100 from Arthur E. Stillwell, and his son Charles Gates had a car of his own, scandalously named *Bright Eyes*. Jay Gould had at least six private cars during his lifetime and both his daughters Helen and Anna and his sons George and Edwin were members of the club in a big way.

The age that saw the finest flowering of the private railway car was a sentimental one and the names it gave its palatial conveyances had sentimental associations for their owners: *Katharyne* for R. C. Kerens' daughter, *Mishawaka* for the birthplace of Charlie Crocker's wife, *Doris* for James B. Duke's daughter, *Mineola* for the site of another of August Belmont's properties, Belmont Park, *David Garrick* as a professional salute from its occupant Edwin Booth, Bruce Dodson's two *Helmas* for Mrs. Dodson, Henry W. Oliver's *Tyrone* for the Irish county of his birth, Anheuser Busch's *Adolphus* for the founder of the family fortunes, *Oneonta* for the Upper York State birthplace of Collis Huntington, *Stranrear* for the Scottish seat of one of Helen Gould's ancestors, the third Mrs. Flagler's *Whitehall* for the palatial Florida home her husband had built her, and *Nomads*, *Wayfarers*, *Adventurers* and *Wanderers* by the score among owners who seldom adventured or wandered, but beneath whose conventional facades there lurked a latent urge to romance. Even Mrs. J. P. Donahue, credited with being the world's richest woman and barely able to read and write, had *Japauldon* for James Paul Donahue while John Hays Hammond, hardest headed mining engineer of them all rode in *Kya Zami*, "One of My Homes."

It was also an age of classical education and tastes, as witness *Seneca, Lucania, Elysian, Thanis, Marcia, Tryphena, Sybaris, Alexander, Cleopatra, Cassius, Atalanta, Jupiter, Olympia, Parthenon, Hesperia, Hebrides, Cyprus, Veritas* and *Iolanthe*.

But most frequently the naming of private cars ran to the primal simplicities of geographic place, as the record will testify with *Wisconsin, Bay State, Ohio, Virginia, Bay Shore, St. Louis, Alamogordo, Cape Girardeau, Arizona, Rock Island, Clinchfield, Dixie, Herkimer, Baltimore, Oak Ridge, San Marino, Scranton, Winchester* and *Alamo*.

Now and then the strictly utilitarian obtruded on the private car consciousness as when E. B. McLean named his Pullman *Inquirer* after the Cincinnati newspaper that had contributed to his immense fortune or when the Delaware, Lackawanna & Western engrossed the nameboard of a business car with the title *Anthracite*, but practicality, as a general thing, ran to mere numbers such as distinguished the varnish of such captains of finance as J. P. Morgan, Senator William A. Clark and George F. Baker, Jr.

Numbers in the neighborhood of 100, conventionally 99, 100 and 101, designated the business cars of the presidents of mainline carriers, although the Norfolk & Western's ranking varnish was No. 1 and multiples of 100 up to 1900, the number of the varnish of chief executives on both the Union Pacific and the Rock Island at one time, were sometimes encountered. Now and then roads with a considerable roster of business cars numbered them for the year of their acquisition such as the Chicago Great Western's No. 1910, Union Pacific's No. 1900 (known as *Arden* during its occupancy by E. H. Harriman), the Rock Island's Nos. 1902, 1910 and 1912, and the Kansas Pacific & South Western's No. 1914. No car with the designation of No. 1000 seems to be in the record but the Southern Pacific had a 999 assigned to Thomas A. Scott as did the Minneapolis, St. Paul & Sault Ste. Marie, while 500 turns up with reasonable frequency as a mystic number on the Delaware & Hudson, the Chicago & Alton and Florida East Coast. The haughty Atchison, Topeka & Santa Fe ordered business cars in such numbers that little time was wasted on mystic combinations and the order books of Pullman's car works simply list them in sequence "Santa Fe: Cars No. 400, 401, 402, 403, 420, 427, 428 and 429."

Only infrequently in the private car roster is there a suggestion of levity such as was implicit in Charlie Gates' *Bright Eyes* and Charles Clegg's and Lucius Beebe's *The Gold Coast* and nowhere at all is there a trace, happily, of the corruption of taste and morals which induces vulgarians to devise presumably humorous names for their homes and yachts such as *Wits End, The Poore House* and *Chez Noose*. The nearest approach to such squalor is Mrs. Donahue's *Japauldon* and the Ringling car *Jomar* which may be excused if only because they didn't set a style.

Whimsy in the naming of private cars once appeared, fairly improbably, in the business car No. 100 of the Bangor & Aroostock when President Percy Todd, after inspecting the newly delivered varnish, remarked "It suits me." The next day the name *Itsuitsme* appeared in gold on its nameboards.

The names selected by the Pullman Company for its general service private cars were ever innocuous: *Mayflower, Colonial, Constitution, Pilgrim, Patriot* and *Pioneer*. But it must be remembered that the private car whether owned outright or maintained on a rental basis from the Pullman pool was not only a hallmark of wealth, it was also and of necessity an oriflamme of the most intense respectability. Wealth in the nineteenth century took itself seriously and its possessors were at pains to justify their custodianship of great fortunes by a conspicuous if not always authentic moral tone. A frivolous name on a private Pullman could give the masses the wrong impression. Members of the club were almost always circumspect.

Not all who ordered, acquired, chartered or borrowed private cars in their golden age were either headline names or moguls of towering resources, but all were solvent beyond the average and of sufficient distinction to put a premium on privacy. Some had claim to modest social elevation without being actually numbered among the godlike Whitneys, Vanderbilts and Rockefellers; all were aware of the uses of the best of everything, knowing that this commodity was in short worldly requisition.

Brief recourse to the dead files, for example, reveals that Colonel William Boyce Thompson for whom Pullman built *Alder* in 1925, at the time of his death was variously identified by the New York press as a financier, diplomat, philanthropist, a stalwart of the finances of the Republican party and a collector of precious jade. His fortune, upon his demise in 1930, was at first estimated at an impressive $150,000,000 by the *Herald Tribune,* a sum which subsequently was pared to a mere $17,000,000 by the probate court, but a clue to his private car ownership was apparent to any student of the club in that his wealth, such as it was, derived from investments in Anaconda Copper and he had been a close associate of Colonel Daniel C. Jackling, the inferential peer of A. C. Burrage and Senator William Andrews Clark.

John R. McLean, owner of *Friendship,* which was also the name of his Washington home in Wisconsin Avenue, was proprietor of the *Washington Post* and *Cincinnati Enquirer,* a close friend of William Howard Taft and father-in-law of Evalyn Walsh McLean of Hope Diamond celebrity. He easily qualified for membership in the club.

A. K. Macomber, master of *Seminole,* was characterized in his obituaries as "the undisputed head of American society in Europe," wealthy from California oil properties and allied to the ruling private car families through purchase of the racing stables of William K. Vanderbilt which included Cesarwitch and other champions.

Peter W. Rouss was no more distinguished than any other New York real estate operator, although owner of *Winchester* by Pullman in 1917, while John Palmer Gavit, for whom *Anacapa* had been outshopped, reached the pinnacle of his professional career as chief of the Associated Press bureau in Washington. He had, however, good connections as his wife was a sister of Thomas W. Lamont, a Morgan partner.

Herbert Coppell was a New York stockbroker and a coal and iron magnate without any social claims of Bellevue Avenue dimensions, but liked a nice train ride and had Pullman lay down *Manana* to accommodate his whim in 1911. Henry Clay Pierce who was so little known that his name was misspelled on the Pullman private car roster when he commissioned *Zamora* in 1901, was at least a professional. He was a director of the Baltimore & Ohio, Mexican Pacific and other Mexican carriers and an associate of Harry L. Doherty which made him eligible financially if not socially to bow to Harknesses and Ryans in passing on private car tracks at Louisville.

John Smith Cravens, owner of the Pullman *Nomad,* not to be confused with a similarly named but narrow gauge p.v. of General W. J. Palmer of the Rio Grande Railroad in Colorado, was a Kansas City banker and business man whose dossier in "The National Cyclopaedia of American Biography" reveals no railroad connections of any sort, so it must be assumed he was of the purest breed of private car *aficionados,* a wealthy and fastidious gentleman who could indulge in private varnish.

Richard C. Kerens, while not a railroad operative in the professional sense had the very best possible railroad connections in the nineteenth century. He was a vice-president of the Cotton Belt, a director of the old Iron Mountain, a director of the St. Louis & North Arkansas and of the Virginia Central & Pittsburgh. He was an associate of Mark Hanna of Cleveland and a director of Senator William Andrews Clark's Los Angeles & Salt Lake Railroad, a circumstance which immediately would suggest him for membership in the private car club and justify his maintenance of the Pullman-built car, *Katharyne,* delivered in 1894 and named for his oldest daughter. Although his name doesn't register in the general awareness in company with Webbs, Flaglers and Vanderbilts as a railroad executive, he might be taken as typical of the wealthy railroad director of the golden age of steam transportation with influence and interests in a large and catholic variety of continental carriers.

Of the same generation as Kerens was Calvin S. Brice, owner of *Marquette* (not to be confused with Thomas Fortune Ryan's *Pere Marquette*) which Pullman built to his order in 1887. Brice's railroad associations were more specifically executive, however, as he was closely connected with operations of the Nickel Plate, Hocking Valley, Richmond & Danville, Ohio Central, the Mobile & Birmingham, the Atlanta & West Point and the Chicago, Indianapolis & Louisville, as well as others whose identities have disappeared in the mergers and mutations of time. He seems to have been a cultivated and liberal gentleman of what is loosely known as "the old school," a student of music, a collector of Chinese porcelains and rare books and a patron of the fine arts, in a word the kind of princely mogul who knew the good things of life and exercised fastidious taste in their acquisition and enjoyment. It is pleasant to imagine that, in addition to the conventional resources of Bourbon and strong cigars, *Marquette* also had bookshelves filled with fine bindings, soft Bokhara carpets and Madeiras that would have had the approval of Philadelphia's Dr. S. Weir Mitchell, most knowing of all Madeira fanciers of a cultivated generation of wine lovers.

Angus Archibald McLeod, owner of two successive cars named *Alexander* was one of the railroad professionals who scorned the conventional euphuism of "business car" and engrossed the nameboards of second *Alexander* with the proud title "Private Car" in bold, gold letters. McLeod, a New Yorker of Scotch ancestry who specialized in the reorganization and economical management of faltering properties, eventually became receiver for the Reading and a power in the affairs of coal haul roads throughout Pennsylvania and Maryland. Like the legend on his cars, his biographer in the "Dictionary of American Biography" scorned the indirect approach and recorded that McLeod had "by close application, untiring industry and indomitable energy, passed rapidly through various steps of advancement in the employ of several railroads . . . he was made general manager of the

Philadelphia & Reading Railroad by men who were determined to bring this road out of the slough of despond where it had fallen."

Other biographers, to be sure, viewed the activities of A. A. McLeod with a more jaundiced regard and it is in the record that he attempted while in control of the Reading to invade New England through the agency of the New York & New England and establish there an allied empire of transport with himself in the role of a sort of road company Gould or Harriman. He briefly dominated the Boston & Maine, stealthily bought up the key Connecticut River and was laying the groundwork for a major grab to include the New Haven and the Central New England when the Reading itself, the basis for his operations, collapsed and McLeod and his dreams of empire went up the spout. Two years later his superb first *Alexander* turned up 3,000 miles away on the roster of the Southern Pacific as *Emalita* and the Massachusetts Railroad Commission had written his epitaph when it declared of the attempted rape of the B & M that "no more unconscionable transaction has occurred in the railroad history of the State."

Thomas Fortune Ryan, owner of the Pullman-built p.v. *Pere Marquette,* was a swaggering Catholic magnifico whose huge fortune derived, in part, from speculation in tobacco on an almost astral plane. His imperiousness, when his wife wanted a garden, suggested the purchase and demolition of the $1,250,000 mansion of Henry Yerkes, the traction king, adjoining his own Fifth Avenue home, and its replacement with roses. The Carrara columns of Yerkes' grand staircase he retained as an arbor. "They would have been expensive to build," he explained.

It has been remarked elsewhere in this study of the private car *Zeitgeist* that the moral tone of the private railroad car was largely an elevated one and above the reproach that sometimes extended to steam yachts and Adirondack shooting lodges. And so it was despite the boudoir connotations of Lillian Russell's gold plated bicycle on board Diamond Jim Brady's private varnish and the presence of Horace A. W. Tabor's mistress, Baby Doe, as an unofficial passenger on the business cars of the Colorado Central to Central City.

But once the name of a Vanderbilt was tarnished when it was testified in court that Alfred Gwynne Vanderbilt had been guilty of dalliance aboard *Wayfarer,* and the Sunday supplements made the most they might of the opportunity to depict the millionaire's private apartments as a love nest of practically Byzantine dimensions. Vanderbilt's wife, the former Elsie French, in filing suit for divorce in New York, stated that the railroad heir had misconducted himself not once but repeatedly in the perfumed recesses of *Wayfarer* with an Agnes O'Brien Ruiz, wife of the Cuban attaché at Washington. Howard Kempster, a former valet of Vanderbilt's, supported the contention and on his evidence divorce was granted. Mrs. French Vanderbilt took with her ten million New York Central dollars. Mrs. Ruiz committed suicide in London and Mr. Vanderbilt married Mrs. Margaret Emerson McKim, of the Bromo-Seltzer Emersons, an alliance which amply repaid the expense of discarding the first Mrs. Vanderbilt.

Another and regrettable association of a member of the private car club with low ways was that of Charlie Gates, son of the barbed wire salesman who had aroused such distaste in the senior J. Pierpont Morgan. It was named *Bright Eyes* after one of its owner's not socially acceptable acquaintances, and feminine lingerie sometimes went to the laundry along with the Pullman linen. Gates also drank. He went to Cody, Wyoming, a remote hamlet on the Colorado & Southern aboard *Bright Eyes* and undertook to drink bottle for bottle with the patron and Western hero for whom the community was named. The encounter was fatal. Buffalo Bill Cody was still on his feet telling about his duel with Yellow Hand when Gates was carried off to the railroad siding to die a day or so later of alcohol poisoning and various complications of the liver and other vitals associated with the bottle.

"Somebody should have told me he was a tenderfoot," said Pahaska when apprised of the tragedy. "We were only in the second case of whisky when his knees buckled."

Many of the improved conveniences that travellers aboard the steamcars came to take for granted had their origins in private varnish whose owners could afford innovations not yet proven in general use. We have seen how the first hot and cold running water appeared on General Palmer's narrow gauge *Nomad*. Many years later the first air conditioning was adapted to the private car of Major Max Fleischman of yeast fame while an even greater service to humanity was evolved when members of the Busch family of St. Louis piped beer under pressure to all compartments of their car, *Adolphus*. Cissie Patterson, publisher of the *Washington Times Herald*, tiring of the identical decor day after day, provided seven complete changes of flowered slip covers for every room in her *Ranger* and her major domo wired ahead for fresh flowers to complete the face-lifting at every considerable stopping point on their travels across the continent. In order that they might eat Thanksgiving dinner under a family roof of sorts, Louis Hill of the Great Northern Railroad made an annual practice of sending his business car to New Haven as long as any of his three sons were undergraduates at Yale. The young men and their friends ate turkey and cranberry in a sort of branch office of the family residence at St. Paul on the private car track provided by the New York, New Haven & Hartford Railroad.

The Pullman *Electric* built for B. F. Yoakum in 1889 was illuminated by the first electric Mazda bulbs ever to be installed in a railroad carriage and twenty years later, when Yoakum was chairman of the board of the St. Louis-San Francisco, the lighting system of his Frisco car was redesigned to eliminate the unshielded bulbs in favor of indirect lighting, also a first for the owner. Next to *Electric*, perhaps the most utilitarian car name was that of *Anthracite*, outshopped by Pullman for the Delaware, Lackawanna & Western, but no such innovations attach to its down-to-earth memory.

A sensationally happy ending can be written to the story of only one narrow gauge private car known to the record. General Palmer's *Nomad,* "the nice house car" of early times on the Denver & Rio Grande amidst the Shining Mountains of Colorado, somehow survived the vicissitudes of time and in 1957 was acquired, on credit as it eventually appeared, by two Texans interested in the promotion of oil properties in the San Juan region. The affairs of the two adventurers, however, shortly came to grief and attachments were issued against the reactivated *Nomad* by decorators, upholsterers and merchants who had supplied pots and pans for its galley. A creditors' committee at Durango was faced with a seemingly insuperable what-to-do.

Happily in this moment of crisis there appeared succor in the person of William M. White, President of the Minnequa Bank of Pueblo and an appreciative antiquarian to boot. Mr. White acquired the venerable *Nomad* and today, running on the occasions of its owner out of Durango, it is not only the only private narrow gauge car in operating condition in the United States, but the only three foot varnish with air conditioning, butane heating and foam rubber upholstery, an ironical end for the car whose hot running water was once a source of outrage and furor.

After the death of Henry Ford his Pullman-built car, *Fair Lane,* became the chief operating executive's business car on the Cotton Belt and the author of these paragraphs had occasion in 1944 to go from St. Louis to Dallas as the guest of the then president of the road, a rock ribbed Texas Baptist with the resounding name of Daniel Upthegrove. Another business car ahead of *Fair Lane* was cut into the consist of the Cotton Belt's only through train at the time and was occupied by the equally resoundingly named Judge Berryman Henwood, receiver for the railroad which was then in bankruptcy. Still further ahead was a third business car temporarily at the disposal of an admiral in the United States Navy in charge of production of war materiel at numerous munition plants located along the Cotton Belt's right of way in Missouri and Arkansas.

Bogged down with heavy wartime passenger traffic, head-end revenue cars and three unaccustomed Pullmans on the rear, No. 7 got further and further off schedule and redball freights piled up whole divisions deep behind it on the road's single mainline track. Somewhere near Paragould as the guests aboard *Fair Lane* were deep in fried catfish and Bourbon, the dispatcher got through to President Upthegrove with the intelligence that millions of dollars worth of wartime freight was cooling its heels behind him all the way to St. Louis. Nobody, of course, wanted the responsibility of ordering the president of the road into a siding so that traffic might run around him, but Mr. Upthegrove himself at once did so and miles of heavy freight commenced thundering past bound for the ports of Texas. The writer remarked jokingly to Mr. Upthegrove that it was the only time he had ever seen a railroad president go in the hole so freight could run around his business car. Mr. Upthegrove waved a glass of Bourbon and branch gracefully, "In the sight of the Lord," he said in Baptist accents, and then added "and the er-stockholders, sir, my time is as nothing."

Even when the owner of a car with a history is professionally interested as a historian of such matters, it isn't always possible to establish with absolute assurance and continuity the record of a private or business car's successive ownership. In the years 1906 and 1907 — the builder's plates bear both dates—the Central Railroad of Georgia outshopped at its Savannah car shops a steel underframe, mahogany finished business car which went into service as the conveyance of the president of the railroad, Car No. 98. Nearly forty years later the car became the property of Charles Clegg and Lucius Beebe who had purchased it from Charles Pidcock, of Moultrie, Georgia, who was President of the Georgia Northern and its connecting railroad in a complex of family owned short lines, the Georgia, Ashburn, Sylvester & Camilla. The new owners rebuilt the working economy of No. 100 as it was listed on the Georgia Northern roster, to their requirements, renamed it *The Gold Coast* and its home road was registered as the then still operating Virginia & Truckee at Carson City, Nevada.

In 1954 *The Gold Coast* was beginning to show its age. It was not air conditioned and carriers whose mainline passenger runs had cardings in some places of eighty and ninety miles an hour were beginning not to appreciate our patronage. *The Gold Coast* went by gift to the Pacific Coast Chapter of the Railway & Locomotive Historical Society at Oakland, California, to end its days like a Roman senator in *otium cum dignitate,* and we purchased from Pullman the car now known as *The Virginia City.*

But of its ownership in the years between the Central of Georgia and the Georgia Northern, the record is at best sketchy. Mr. Pidcock had purchased the car from the Live Oak, Perry & Gulf, a Florida short line celebrated for maintaining the last wood burning locomotives of any common carrier with regular passenger service in the land. There was a report that *The Gold Coast* had once rolled on the lawful occasions of the chief executive of the Georgia & Florida, an important bridge line carrier in the Deep South, but no evidence to support it. To the end, there was a chapter in the case history of *The Gold Coast* which remained a closed book.

Widowed of its No. 100 which had become *The Gold Coast* and its venerable *Moultrie,* as recited elsewhere in this book. C. W. Pidcock, President of the Georgia Northern, tired of borrowing business cars from such carriers as the Atlantic Coast Line, Central of Georgia and the now vanished Atlanta, Birmingham & Coast and purchased from the Chicago & Eastern Illinois its Pullman-built and air-conditioned official car *Mount Vernon* which presently appeared on the Georgia Northern roster as second *Moul-*

trie. The only short line to rival the impressive total of the G. N.'s three business cars is the Nevada Northern whose several p.v. are tallied in the appropriate place.

The trend of ownership from simon pure private cars in the possession of non-railroading individuals was continued by Joseph E. Widener's *Lynnewood* which became No. 27 on the Chesapeake & Ohio, by Franklyn Hutton's *Curleyhut* which turned up as No. 25 on the same carrier, and by *Anoakia* which passed from the hands of Anita M. Baldwin to Union Pacific where it became No. 119. Similarly the car *Californian* built by Pullman in 1912 for the Clara Baldwin Stocker Estate was sold to the Boston & Maine. *Nazu,* the official car of the National Biscuit Company was sold to the Virginian Railway.

Two of the best known private cars of wealthy individuals of all time were destined for ownership by the Pittsburgh & West Virginia in the form of *Hopedale* and *Westmoreland. Hopedale* had been Colonel D. C. Jackling's first *Cyprus,* renamed when it was purchased by Julius Fleischman, while *Westmoreland* went with name and dignity intact from the Estate of Henry Clay Frick.

Crusty old George F. Baker's personal car carried on the Erie Railroad roster as No. 99 was sold to the Delaware, Lackawanna & Western where it became *Pocono.* Mystery surrounds the whereabouts of the younger J. P. Morgan's p.v. which also claimed the Erie as its home line.

In a generation of newspaper reporters not at first hand familiar with private car usage or background, a strange mythology and folklore grows up about almost any business car that is retired to become a roadside diner or private car that finds its way to a museum of railroad antiquities. Many of them are invested with spurious romance as the one time "private car of Diamond Jim Brady." A number of others are assigned to ownership by Jay Gould, Henry Flagler or "the Rockefellers." No Rockefeller, so far as can be discovered, ever owned a private car, but as recently as 1958 and in as ordinarily reliable a journal as *The Atlanta Constitution* a Sunday feature was headed: "Do You Remember Jay Gould's Ornate Palace on Rails?" Closer scrutiny of the story disclosed that it concerned a now retired business car of the Western Railroad of Alabama that had once and briefly been tenanted by Jay Gould's daughter, Helen.

A car whose pedigree is tolerably well assured is *El Fleda* which was outshopped by Pullman in 1901 to the order of John A. Bunting, then known from his humble beginnings as "the millionaire brakeman." When the car changed hands for the last time in 1957 the *Peoria Journal Star* ventured the opinion that, because of its Spanish name, it must once have seen service on a Mexican Railway, which is typical of the inaccuracies which appear in the private car records, some of them gratuitous, some unavoidable. In 1910 Bunting tired of commuting between San Francisco and El Paso in both of which cities he had business interests, and sold *El Fleda* for $17,000 to the Colorado & Wyoming Railway, a Rocky Mountain short line which changed its name to *Sunrise.*

In 1927 the car was substantially rebuilt and a steel underframe built for it at the Colorado & Southern Railroad's shops in Denver and in 1931 the car was sold to the Colorado Fuel & Iron Company, a subsidiary in its early years of General William J. Palmer's Denver & Rio Grande narrow gauge. In the same year the Fuel & Iron Company tired of its acquisition and it passed into the hands of the Burlington Railroad of which the Colorado & Southern was a subsidiary, partly in payment for the repair bills mentioned above. The Burlington used *Sunrise,* ex-*El Fleda* for three years as Business Car No. 98 and in 1934 sold it for $11,520 to the Toledo, Peoria & Western where melodrama entered its until now tranquil, if mobile case history.

On the Peoria line it was assigned to the use of the carrier's President George P. McNear, Jr. Its inlaid mahogany, oak panelling and other rich properties had survived from Bunting's day and there were brass beds in the master staterooms. But the T. P. & W. was having labor troubles and on the night of May 10, 1947, McNear was bushwhacked as he took a stroll near his Toledo home and died of gunshot wounds. The murder never was solved.

The T. P. & W. came into the hands of J. Russel Coulter, a former main line railroader from St. Louis who set about straightening its affairs and eventually restored the badly battered property to operating condition as an important bridge line. But Coulter, a handsome and socially minded executive, wanted nothing of a museum piece as a business car. Besides, he got to thinking about his predecessor's bad end and wanted it even less. The directors bought Coulter a handsome new business car without blood-stains in its background, and in 1957 the once proud *El Fleda* became a diner near the Peoria of its final operating years. With a becoming sense of fitness, its new owner called it *The President's Car.*

The private Pullman of R. T. Crane, New England industrialist, was ordered November 19, 1923, and delivered a year later to a day with the name, *Nituna.* After Crane's death his widow changed the name, which she had never specially admired, to *Lone Tree* and as such it was purchased by the Boston & Maine Railroad in October 1929 to become the B & M's business car No. 333.

Ignominy attended the last days of some p.v. Joshua Cosden's *Roamer* on which the Prince of Wales had toured the continent in 1924 was converted into a stationary dwelling for engineers engaged in coal stripping at Tomhicken, near Hazleton, Pennsylvania. Henry M. Flagler's *Rambler,* later named *Moultrie* when it was the property of the Georgia Northern, came to rest as a summerhouse at Harrisonburg, Virginia. Like Lincoln's military car and the Chicago & North Western's famed Gothic directors' car before it, Arthur Stillwell's No. 100 of the Kansas City, Pittsburgh & Gulf was destroyed by fire. Between its psychic first owner who had ordered the affairs of his railroad on the basis of dreams and visions, and its flaming end it had served the more profane conveniences of Bet-a-Million Gates, the barbed wire king. Jay Gould's *Atalanta* was reported to have seen final service as shelter for a section crew on the T. & N. O. division of the Southern Pacific in Texas. The Carson & Colorado's narrow gauge p.v. *Esmeralda* came to its final rest as a garden gazebo in Lone Pine, California.

Private cars passed from hand to hand in an endless and almost unrecorded saraband of ownership, their status alternating between strictly private maintenance by non-railroad members of the club and the service of division superintendents and chief engineers. The Southern Pacific's Car No. 118, the *Rio Grande,* had been built in 1909 for the Phelps Dodge Copper Company, furnished in burled walnut throughout and assigned for executive use to the company owned El Paso & Southwestern Railroad, and passed into the hands of the Espee in 1924. The one-time Car No. 100 of the Lake Shore & Michigan Southern and occupied by successive presidents of that Vanderbilt affiliate, became No. 22 of the New York Central and served as the stationary office of Edward Hungerford, director of the pageant "Railroads on Parade" at the New York World's Fair in 1939. One of the superintendent's business cars of the Coast Division of the Southern Pacific was purchased as a clubhouse for a group of rail fans at San Jose, California.

Everett De Golyer, Jr., an authority on railroad rolling stock and locomotive rosters everywhere, is of the opinion that many a missing private car, some of them once bearing the most august names, can be traced to service on Mexican carriers and as office cars for mining companies south of the Rio Grande.

"A de luxe example of this special breed of p.v. is the *Arco* which is owned by the American Smelting & Refining Company in Mexico," he says. "In this country almost every important government official and railroad officer has his own car assigned. Many of them were once the property of Goulds and Whitneys in the United States."

A case in point of the double lives frequently led by private cars, especially in the years of transition from the golden age of railroading, was that of the Louisville & Nashville's Business Car No. 362. The Old Reliable was so apprehensive of the implications of private varnish that its business varnish scrupulously avoided even the identification implicit in the conventional numbering from 100 up or down.

The car was originally outshopped by Pullman November 11, 1890, for the use of Austin Corbin, President of the Long Island Railroad and the Elmira, Cortland & Northern. In this ingenuous age there was no invidious distinction between a private car occupied by a railroad president and that occupied by the chief executive of a steel mill, and the car was fastidiously appointed and known without any hesitation as Mr. Corbin's private car, *Oriental*.

Seven years later the *Oriental* passed into the hands of August Belmont, chairman of the board of the Louisville & Nashville, another well born gentleman who saw no stigma attaching to the word, and his private car was rechristened *Louisville* in which style it frequently ornamented private car tracks at Saratoga Springs, Louisville and other resorts of fashion at the purely personal whim of its proprietor.

From Mr. Belmont, the *Louisville* passed through a succession of L. & N. officers and finally in 1933 was rebuilt for the use of W. E. Smith, vice-president and general manager of the Old Reliable. Here, and as a sign of a mildewed time, the car lost its nominal identity and became simply Business Car No. 362, a deplorable demotion for so haughty a conveyance, but times were tough all over in 1933 and Mr. Smith wasn't going to be accused of Babylonish luxury while half the population of the United States was on the dole.

In 1957 the car was retired from active service and after sixty-seven years of the good life generally, was purchased by the Adirondack Historical Association to become a museum piece in the society's railroad exhibit at Blue Mountain Lake, Hamilton County, in Upper New York State. This is a fairly long life span of usefulness for a car in passenger service and the original *Oriental* received such face lifting restorations as a steel underframe, steel siding and air conditioning as these improvements became available. In its final condition it represented a sort of geologic record of American railroading in the six and a half decades of its operative existence.

Unlike automobiles to which family or possessive sentiment is sometimes attached so that vintage Rolls-Royces, Packards and Stanley Steamers are stored in mint preservation against festival occasions requiring period properties or merely against occasional reminiscent inspection, private cars are seldom, apparently, maintained by owners after their hour of obsolescence has struck. A ninety ton, eighty-three foot souvenir of happy times is too massive a memento for convenient storage and no coach houses or stables are repositories of grandfather's Wagner as they still occasionally are of his Beverly Wagon or Brewster opera coach. Now and then, as in the happy case of the Belmont car, a good home is found in a museum of ample dimensions, but all too often the blowtorch or the maintenance gang shelter await even the most lordly varnish.

In the effulgent noontide of travel aboard the steamcars, second hand private varnish was available on the used car lots of the land as Pontiacs and Mercurys were to be advertised in the Sunday classified sections half a century later. Bargains in private cars were on every hand in wonderful

profusion of makes and body styles as witness a 1905 catalogue of The
Males Company of Cincinnati, dealers in locomotives, cars and steam
shovels:

Lot 67. GOOD PRIVATE CAR. Length over body 40 ft. 2½ in., observation room at each end, toilet room, private apartment, kitchen, Baker
heater, 4-wheel trucks, Westinghouse air, automatic couplers. A good
small car.

Lot 68. PULLMAN PRIVATE CAR. Sleeps 15 and seats 25; length over
body 51½ feet, inside finish, mahogany and walnut, upholstered brown
frieze, Baker heater, 6-wheel trucks, 36 in. Allen steel-tired wheels,
Westinghouse air, Janney-Miller combination coupler. A good car. Cheap
for quick sale.

Lot 69. SMALL PRIVATE CAR. Sleeps 6 or more, inside length 49 ft.
3½ in., 2 observation rooms, toilet room, dining room, state room, Baker
heater, oil lamps, Westinghouse air, Janney couplers.

Lot 70. GOOD PRIVATE CAR. Length over body 44 ft. 9 in., 5 compartments, parlor, toilet, 2 staterooms and kitchen, inside finish walnut
and maple, veneer headings, oil lamps, Baker heater, 4-wheel trucks,
Westinghouse air, automatic couplers. Good order.

Lot 71. VERY FINE PRIVATE CAR. Length outside of body 68 ft.,
6 in., 8 compartments, observation room, 3 staterooms, parlor, toilet,
pantry and kitchen, handsomely finished, oak, mahogany, cherry in
various compartments. Baker heater. A most complete and elegant car.

Lot 72. MANN BOUDOIR PRIVATE CAR. About 62 feet long, three
staterooms, sleeps 10 people. Cook's galley and range, new and good
heater. In good general order.

In the year 1905 Colonel Mann was involved in a number of civil suits
with origins in his practice of de luxe blackmail, but his name was still
associated with the word boudoir without its *Town Topics* implications.

That sentiment, while rare beyond the naming of their properties, still
was not altogether absent among members of the private car owners' club
is evidenced by John Hay Whitney who, together with his sister Mrs.
Charles S. Payson, inherited from their father the ancestral Whitney car
Adios.

"It was my idea of heaven," the American Ambassador to the Court
of St. James's wrote the author of this volume, "to ride aboard it when I was
young enough not to care how thick the dirt. It was almost invariably too
hot for human habitation, but in those days what fun to wipe the sweaty
face and exhibit with pride one's black handkerchief! Later, the cleaner air
above became more attractive, if you'll forgive the heresy."

Adios was a pre-air conditioning car and Mr. Whitney went on to
become a flyer of military note as well as one of the country's most amiable
of rich millionaires.

The genealogy of many cars as they shifted from the category of private car to office car and back again in a sort of roller-bearing pavan of continental transport is, of course, clear and available. Henry Ford's *Fair Lane* went directly to the business car track of the St. Louis Southwestern and remains there, so far as is known, to this day. J. B. Duke's *Doris* followed its footsteps and became the presidential business car of Fred B. Whitman of the Western Pacific, where its usefulness in main line service is somewhat inhibited by the circumstance that the W. P.'s only through daily passenger train is the *California Zephyr* which is prohibited from including special equipment in its consist.

Several Southern Pacific cars of noble pedigree were trapped when the Southern Pacific's offices and depot at Third and Townsend were razed during the San Francisco fire of 1906 and other fine Pennsylvania business cars were destroyed in the conflagration and mob violence at Pittsburgh that marked the railroad troubles of 1877. The Nevada Northern's beautifully preserved antiquity *Cobre* upon which assorted Guggenheims, Jacklings and other mining moguls had taken their ease in the bonanza days of copper was burned at the company yards at Ely, Nevada, in 1939, while its trucks were being run out for repairs.

The various patent heaters with which private cars were equipped to make them independent of train line steam probably contributed to their high mortality rate by incineration just as rear end collisions took a heavy toll of cars carried at the far end of the train. There were also potentialities for combustion inherent in the cooking arrangements in private car galleys and, in early times, in the multiplicity of coal oil lamps in staterooms and private apartments where fire could get a start before being detected.

As recently as 1917 two handsome narrow gauge official cars of the Denver & Rio Grande Western figured in a wreck while running over the Silverton Northern Railroad in southwestern Colorado with a party of Eastern bankers representing the United States Smelting & Refining Company on a tour of local mining properties. The train, known as "The Millionaire's Special" comprising six diminutive private cars went into the ditch and, although nobody was injured, fire originating either in the galley or from a Baker heater destroyed two of the varnish cars before it could be extinguished by the primitive methods at hand.

The retreat from ostentation in private rail travel began, as it had been inaugurated, with the Vanderbilt family. Pride of the profane and despotic old Commodore was his personal locomotive *Vanderbilt*, a beautiful American standard eight wheeler with his likeness engrossed on its great headlight. Malicious rumor circulated the report that its trim and fittings, of which there was the usual complement of the period, were of pure gold and the old gentleman's answer was simply to order the engine divested of all ornament of any sort. The ukase extended to all motive power on the New

York Central and since, at the time, the Central was the standard railroad of the world, its example was largely followed by lesser carriers.

The business cars of the Central, while divested of the gold and crimson that had delighted the Commodore, remained handsome if austere examples of the carbuilder's *expertise* for many years to come and their exterior maintenance was strictly in accordance with the status of their occupants. Travelers were able to admire their own reflection in the side-wall panels of the general manager's car when it paused in depots at Syracuse or Buffalo. Mere division superintendents were less fastidiously maintained. The story was a favorite in railroad circles in the eighties of the lowly maintenance superintendent who wired the general manager of the Central in New York for permission to have his far from prepossessing business car attached to a certain down train. "We have some regard for the appearance of the *Albany Day Express*" was the answer.

Ironically, it was the very desirability of the private railroad car that led to its eventual undoing as an exalted property of means and influence. Directors and officials of inconsequential railroads and short line carriers, often at the demands of their wives that they should affect the habit of Goulds and Whitneys, began having private cars assigned to themselves and rolling grandly over the countryside in circumstances of unaccustomed and unwarranted splendor. So long as these gestures of grandeur were confined to the home railroads with which provincial nabobs were associated there was no great complaint, but disaster was latent in the agreement by which private cars of important railroaders were carried without charge as an act of courtesy over connecting lines.

The great Class I railroads of the land found themselves hauling a multitude of private cars belonging to vice-presidents of Arkansas agricultural short lines and one engine streaks of rust in Minnesota, often to the inconvenience of revenue freight and passengers and always as a nuisance value. Important shippers were demanding free handling of varnish filled with their families on crack trains of the New York Central and Atlantic Coast Line. The idea was not only to keep up with the Joneses socially, but to beat their ears back by running around them in passing tracks on the rear of *The Broadway Limited* and the *Florida Special*. What had begun as a gesture of courtesy between princely equals degenerated into an abuse of wholesale proportions. Every nobody and his brother contrived somehow to own, scrounge or assume occupancy of a private railroad car and to assume therewith the airs of Stuyvesant Fish.

Soon after the turn of the century the Interstate Commerce Commission bared its fangs and, with the heartfelt approbation of main line carriers, enacted drastic regulations covering the handling of private varnish. Henceforth, only the business cars of bona fide operating executives were to be handled free on Class I railroads and interchange with connecting lines was to be scrupulously limited to the very highest officials on errands of business urgency. All non-business cars owned by private individuals, with only slightly relaxed tariffs for railroad directors, were to pay eighteen full first class fares for movement and parking charges at set rates in terminals and on private car tracks. Non-railroaders traveling as guests of even the most exalted executives on their business cars must be covered by full fare tickets. Today, if the President of the Pennsylvania or General Manager of the far-flung Union Pacific wishes to have guests aboard his business car who are not members of his immediate family, he buys them full fare tickets for the privilege.

Under these stringent regulations the number of private railroad cars riding for free to Florida and Maine as the season dictated diminished dramatically. Homespun J. P. Morgans and wheatfield Whitneys discovered new agencies of social ostentation such as the up and coming automobile car over which the I. C. C. cast no jaundiced eye. A formidable array of private cars still remained in active operation right down to the market debacle of 1929, but they were the property of Vanderbilts, Huttons, Fricks, McCormicks and Wideners of certified credit ratings.

Sometime after the turn of the twentieth century railroad executives began to develop neuroses about their private cars. The edict went forth that on no account were they to be spoken of as anything but business or office cars. Their occupants took to dining and conducting everything but the more intimate details of their toilets with the window shades up, presumably to dispel the illusion that they were harboring troupes of dancing girls and indulging in licentious revelry at the expense of the stockholders. Presidents and general managers became assiduous in spreading the intelligence that positively no liquor was ever served aboard their cars and a generation of mildewed executives even came into existence among which this was essentially true, although the shades of Joseph Dyer and other notably strong men with a bottle turned in their graves with revulsion.

Just what occasioned this surge of puritanical nonsense has never been specifically established. Evidence is infrequent showing stockholders ever cared two cents worth whether or not division superintendents brushed their teeth with bourbon so long as the carriers paid six percent. Rule G which forbade the use of liquor by train crews and those charged with the actual operations of the system was a sensible enough precaution in the face of evidence that many of the catastrophes of the nineteenth century had their origins in the cup, but how this affected chairmen of the board is difficult to imagine.

Intelligent folk viewed as improbable the claims to almost unearthly virtue among railroad executives as a whole and laughed heartily when the president of one of the great transcontinental systems was found in Denver's Larimer Street in deplorable case and gave a false name to the police when booked for drunk and disorderly.

Whatever its origins, a wave of sanctimoniousness engulfed the conduct of the railroad business in the United States. That much of it was purest hypocrisy on the part of its practitioners did little to recommend its holy ardors. Railroading since its beginning had been a strong man's business calling for the bearded old kings of get and conflict like Jim Hill and Lenore Loree to whom life represented not only subduing mountains and bridges across the abyss, but asserting their vitality among the satisfactions of the flesh. The bagnios that lined the tracks at Dodge City and Abilene derived their trade from cow pokes and railroaders in equal portions. In the golden age of steam and steel a thousand Switch Keys, Caboose Bars and Paycar Saloons vied for the drinking trade of brakemen and president alike.

Whether as cause or result, the decline in the estate of the private car among railroaders coincided almost precisely in its downward graph with the overall decline in the fortunes of railroading. The men who occupied the once glamorous varnish cars with Pintsch lights and capacious cellars of Bourbon and Madeira diminished in stature in exact measure with the diminution of their way of life, and railroading became ensmalled in proportion to the men who conducted its operations.

General managers who dined aboard their business cars with the shades up and presidents who boasted of not drinking became symbolic of all that was mischievous in the operations of the carriers themselves.

In some few cases this parade of subservient morality was a concession to stockholders who somehow confused dividends with church attendance. Lucien Sprague, a notably effective president of the Minneapolis & St. Louis Railway, was unseated from office by shareholders, in part at least, because it was claimed he used his business car to attend harness races of which he was a devotee.

That he had redeemed the M. & St. L. from utter bankruptcy and indeed snatched it from the clutches of the junkman, largely through the agency of business solicited and shippers entertained on these excursions, carried no weight with the stockholders many of whom preferred a decline in earnings to the implications of pari mutuel. It is gratifying to record that promptly on the inaugural of a successor to Mr. Sprague with church affiliations satisfactory to his constituents, the earnings of the carrier declined to almost nothing.

Happily, the twilight of private cars maintained by non-railroad owners suffered no such jaundiced eclipse in their final years. Their disappearance from the high passes and plains was the result of two factors beyond the reach of even their most devoted admirers, the 1941 war and the emergence of the passenger plane. High taxes and the proverbial shortage of servants contributed their part. What the stock market decline of 1929 had commenced, accelerated transcontinental plane service continued. Captains of finance who in other years would have ordered out their private cars now took to the air on affairs of business urgency. It was and will forever be a barbarous and cheerless way of travel but time was on its side. Texas oil men who, had they been possessed of taste or imagination, might have purchased Pullmans in threes and fours maintained private planes instead.

Götterdämmerung, the twilight of private cars, fell quickly. Perhaps the last of the tycoons who arrived at Del Monte amidst the live oaks of Monterey Peninsula as regularly as the seasons was Edward S. Harkness. Colonel Elliott White Springs continued to run Charles Schwab's *Loretto II* over his forty mile Lancaster & Chester Railroad in South Carolina, but its lack of steel underframe barred it from interchange.

The last defenders at the barricades were Bruce Dodson of Kansas City and Palm Beach with *Helma II* and Charles Clegg and Lucius Beebe with *The Virginia City*. In 1958 Dodson resigned from the little club of three. "Mrs. Dodson and I are getting old," he wrote, "and no longer travel as much as we used to."

So drew to a close the age of the most glamorous property of the once glamorous railroads, themselves now fallen upon a blighted age. But for a time the private railroad car all green and gold and glory had carried the nabobs to continental destinies and on far landfarings. They had been incomparably the symbol of an exalted social order and a bold philosophy of acquisition and possession. And they will be a part of the remembered epic of the American way of life forever.

Appendix

(NOTE: Spellings, etc., in this list are those of the Pullman Company's record.)

PULLMAN BUSINESS AND PRIVATE CARS BUILT AT PULLMAN
1882 THROUGH 1930

LOT	CONSIGNEE	DATE	PLAN	NAME
24	E. H. Talbot (Railway Age)	1/ 4/82	117	*Railway Age*
93	Henry Villard	6/ 6/83	175	100
121	Illinois Central	10/16/83	188	95
188	Chicago & Alton	12/19/83	196	500
189	New York, Chicago & St. Louis	12/22/83	193	24
1016	P. L. Cable	8/ 6/84	213	*Aztec* 213
1105	B. Blanchard	5/11/85	247	*Le Paradise*
1198	Houston & Texas Central	12/19/85	312A	45
1231	Chicago, Minneapolis & St. Paul	4/ 5/86	383	*Wisconsin*
1232	Chicago & Illinois Southern	4/ 6/86	392	
1295	David H. Moffat	4/21/86	466	*Mascotte*
1331	Eastern Tennessee, Virginia & Georgia	12/26/86	495A	*Argonaut*
1346	Jay Gould	12/28/86	497C	*Bedford Penola*
1381	Minneapolis, St. Paul & Saulte Ste. Marie	5/25/87	506	99
1384	C. C. Brice	5/30/87	495A	*Marquette* 100
1390	Collis P. Huntington	5/ 5/87		*Oneonta*
1494	General Pullman Service	3/ 8/88	564	*Iolanthe* *Hazelmere*
1541	Savannah, Florida & Western	2/19/89	630A	Plant System 100
1568	Southern Pacific (Edward T. Searles)	3/ 6/89	630A	*San Carlos*
1565	Duluth & Iron Range	4/ 4/89	643	Business Car
1578	San Diego & Aranzas Pass (Yakum)	11/22/89	650	*Electric*
1703	Austin Corbin	12/30/89	716D	*Oriental*
1720		2/ 1/90	817	100
1722	Norfolk & Western	2/ 7/90	798B	1
1758	Inter-Ocean Rwy.	5/13/90	812D	*Isabel*
1770	Missouri-Kansas-Texas Rwy.	6/14/90	838	36
1732	Charles T. Crocker	8/11/90	845C	*Mishawaka*

PULLMAN BUSINESS AND PRIVATE CARS BUILT AT PULLMAN
1882 THROUGH 1930—(Continued)

Lot	Consignee	Date	Plan	Name
1784	James Ben Ali Haggin	9/ 1/90	862B	*Salvator*
1789	A. A. McLeod	9/20/90	836B	*Alexander*
1791	Boston & Maine (Furber)	9/23/90	872A	*Sorrento*
1814	Illinois Central	1/ 2/91	910	1
1877	Chicago & Eastern Illinois	9/11/91	960B	501
1914	Battle Creek & Sturgis (Bacon)	2/ 3/92	980J	*Virginia*
1922	Pecos Valley Rwy.	3/ 8/92	981	*Hesperia*
1923	Minneapolis, St. Paul & Saulte Ste. Marie	3/ 9/92	828B	99
1947	Pencoyd & Philadelphia (McLeod)	6/21/92	863H	*Alexander*
1955	Columbus, Hocking Valley & Toledo	7/27/92	1006F	*Maumee* 43
2011	Atcheson, Topeka & Santa Fe (J. W. Reinhart)	4/11/93	1049G	*Sun Flower State,* 219
2020	Atcheson, Topeka & Santa Fe	4/28/93	1057E	*Bay State* 220
2054	John McLean	3/20/94	1091C	*Ohio*
2080	Baltimore, Ohio & South Western	11/13/94	1111D	*Ohio*
2083	R. C. Kerens	11/30/94	1115A	*Katharyne* (Now *Estelle*)
2101	Selma, Marion & Memphis	3/22/95	1127A	*Ogantz* 712
2113	Illinois Central (Stuyvesant Fish)	9/16/95	1142B	*Marion* 15
2144	Central Railroad of New Jersey	10/ 8/95	1169B	*Atlas* 604
2145	J. M. Hampson	10/12/95	1115C	96
2201	De Beers, Ltd.	8/11/96	1106A	Natl. Only
2246	Mexican Central	5/14/97	1280B	
2247	Mexican Central	5/14/97	1281B	
2251	General Pullman Service	6/18/97	1273A	*Lucania* *Campania*
2265	Kansas City, Mexico & Gulf (Arthur S. Stillwell)	8/19/97	1274B	100
2282	Kansas City, Mexico & Gulf	10/12/97	1294A	98
2286	Southern Railway (Spencer)	10/29/97	1304	100
2333	Colorado Midland	5/23/98	1339B	100
2365	Union Pacific	7/30/98	1367A	100
2362	Chicago & North Western	8/18/98	1375C	60
2403	Pennsylvania	12/19/98	1393G	60
2382	General Pullman Service	11/4/98	1379B	*Glen Eyre*
2425	Edward H. Harriman	2/ 9/99	1406C	*Arden* 1900
2426	Missouri Pacific (Warner)	2/ 9/99	1398B	*St. Louis* 20
2451	General Pullman Service	5/ 4/99	1418C	*Olympia* *Imperial*
2477	Pennsylvania	8/ 9/99	1443C	503
2545	Chicago & Alton (Felton)	1/ 8/00	1512G	*Hadassah* 500

PULLMAN BUSINESS AND PRIVATE CARS BUILT AT PULLMAN
1882 THROUGH 1930—*(Continued)*

LOT	CONSIGNEE	DATE	PLAN	NAME
2557	Pennsylvania (Brooks)	3/ 9/00	1542A	501
2570	Cleveland, Lorain & Wheeling	4/18/00	1550A	10
2591	Mexican Central	8/ 8/00	1591A	18
2627	Chesapeake & Ohio (Stevens)	10/31/00	1651A	5
2722	J. A. Bunting	2/13/01	1659D	*El Fleda*
2744	St. Louis & South Western (Edw. Gould)	4/26/01	1406D	*Dixie*
2745	Southern Railway (Spencer)	4/29/01	1674B	100
2746	General Pullman Service	5/ 1/01	1671C	*Elysian*
2747	General Pullman Service			*Mayflower*
	General Pullman Service			*Colonial*
	General Pullman Service			*Acadian*
2750	C. C. Iron Company	5/18/01		21
2751	Pennsylvania (Green)	5/24/01	1729B	90
2753	Anheuser Busch Co.	6/ 1/01	1702E	*Adolphus*
2772	H. W. Oliver	8/ 1/01	1717E	*Tyrone* 999
2772	Charles M. Schwab	8/ 1/01	1735E	*Loretto*
2774	Hocking Valley Rwy. (Thomas Fortune Ryan)	8/ 1/01	1728E	*Pere Marquette*
2783		8/21/01	1783C	*Cape Giradeau*
2785	William C. Whitney	8/28/01	1730H	*Wanderer*
2791	Mexican Central (H. C. Pierce)	9/13/01	1743B	*Zamora*
2796	Chicago & Eastern Illinois	10/ 4/01	1744B	502
2802	Nashville, Chattanooga & St. Louis	10/30/01	1758D	99
2831	Chicago, Great Western	12/10/01	1776F	101
2851	Elgin, Joliet & Eastern	12/30/01	1367B	40
2886	James Hazen Hyde	2/25/02	1803D	*Bay Shore*
2893	Pere Marquette	3/22/02	1818B	1
2894	El Paso & Northeastern	3/31/02	1822D	*Alamagordo*
2908	Chicago, Rock Island & Pacific (Reed)	5/ 1/02	1849B	
2913	Chicago, Rock Island & Pacific (W. H. Moore)	5/27/02	1839C	*Rockmargo*
2918	Chicago, Rock Island & Pacific (J. H. Moore)	5/27/02	1839C	*Thanis*
2981	Chicago, Rock Island & Pacific (Warren)	9/15/02	1875A	1902
2973	Southern Pacific	11/ 4/01	1095B	*Guadalupe*
2976	Charles Elliott Perkins	11/21/01	1890G	*Black Hawk*
2987	Oregon Short Line	1/ 7/03	1906C	1903
2992	Chicago, Rock Island & Pacific (Leads)	1/22/03	1904E	Rock Island 1901
3021	De Beers, Ltd.	6/10/03	1948B	100
3023	National Railway of Mexico	7/ 1/03	1949C	*Hidalgo*

PULLMAN BUSINESS AND PRIVATE CARS BUILT AT PULLMAN
1882 THROUGH 1930—(Continued)

Lot	Consignee	Date	Plan	Name
3036	Louisiana Exposition	7/28/03	2009	*President*
5121	El Paso & Southwestern	3/16/04	2017D	*Arizona* 104
3124	M. F. Plant	3/29/04	2010B	200
3125	Western Union Telegraph Co.	4/ 5/04	1978A	*Morse*
4180	Pennsylvania (McCrea)	1/26/05	2066D	37
3190	August Belmont	2/ 9/05	2067	*Mineola*
3196	William K. Vanderbilt	2/27/05	2052	*Idle Hour*
3202	Pennsylvania(Pugh)	3/29/05	2080	180
3229	R. I. Imp. Co. (Mudge)	8/30/05	2075	1900
3239	Alfred Gwyn Vanderbilt	6/29/05	2092	*Wayfarer*
3241	William Andrews Clark	6/21/05	2097	2001
3243	Southern (Spencer)	7/10/05	1674F	100
3266	Pensylvania Lines West	8/13/05	2112B	7805
3262	General Pullman Service	8/31/05	2110	*Constitution*
	General Pullman Service	8/31/05	2110	*Republic*
	General Pullman Service	8/31/05	2110	*Commonwealth*
3299	Blair & Company	9/25/05	2124B	*Clinchfield*
	Minneapolis & St. Louis	1/17/06	2168	300
	Buffalo, Rochester & Pittsburgh	2/ 9/06	2161	*Virginia*
	Denver, Northwestern & Pacific	3/ 6/06	2185B	*Marcia*
	General Pullman Service	4/27/06	2203A	*Independence*
	Illinois Central (Stuyvesant Fish)	5/21/06	2178	15
	Sold to Union Pacific			99
	Tidewater Railroad	6/ 7/06	2215B	*Dixie*
	G. C. C. Company (Miller)	8/13/06	2232	*Verde*
	Pittsburgh & Lake Erie (Schoonmaker)	11/ 2/06	2275	99
	Atchison, Topeka & Santa Fe (Edward Payson Ripley)	11/13/06	2248	17
	Southern Pacific (Stubbs)	11/13/06	2251	*Ashland* 120
3539	Chicago & Pacific	11/13/06	2283B	101
3554	B. P. Cheney	4/19/07	2299	25
3574	Vandalia (McKeen)	8/20/07		
3575	Hocking Valley (Monserrat)	10/ 3/07		*Columbus* 25
3701	Daniel C. Jackling	7/19/09	2429	*Cyprus*
3707	Long Island Rwy.	8/ 7/09	2431	30
3714	Chicago, Minneapolis & St. Paul (Earling)	8/28/09	2423	*Wisconsin*
3743	Atlantic Coast Line (Emerson)	9/28/09	2406	300
3763	Chicago, Great Western (Felton)	2/25/10	2463	1910
3768	Pennsylvania (Taylor)	4/24/11	2467	7505
3812	General Pullman Service (St.L.)	1/18/11	2492	*National*
	General Pullman Service (St.L.)		2492	*Federal*
3828	Henry Clay Frick	12/ 3/10	2506	*Westmoreland*

LOT NUMBERS ILLEGIBLE

PULLMAN BUSINESS AND PRIVATE CARS BUILT AT PULLMAN
1882 THROUGH 1930—*(Continued)*

Lot	Consignee	Date	Plan	Name
3829	Norfolk & Western (Johnson)	2/ 1/10		
4115	Yakima & Pacific Coast (Randolph)	1/28/09	2380	*Pocahontas*
3844	New York Central (Brown)	9/22/09	2516	*Herkimer*
3847	General Pullman Service	4/24/11	2305	*Ideal*
3848	General Pullman Service	5/ 1/11	2602	*Advance*
3869	Delaware & Hudson (Lenore Loree)	4/ 4/11	2530	500
3915	Herbert Coppell	8/31/11	2563	
9180	Lehigh & Hudson			*Warwick*
3917	Missouri-Kansas-Texas (E. W. Hawley)	8/11/11	2565	110
3970	Union & Southern Pacific (Lovett)	5/ 4/12	2610	*Overland* 101
	Union & Southern Pacific (Krutschnitt)	5/15/12	2611	*Guadaloupe*
3975	Pennsylvania (Wood)	11/22/12	2606	37
4009	Missouri-Kansas-Texas (Charles E. Schaff)	4/13/12	2857	401
4048	Mrs. C. B. Stocker	5/29/12	2677	*California*
4058	Chicago, Rock Island & Pacific	6/15/12	2878	
4059	Mexican Northwestern (Pearson)	6/24/12		
4073	Baltimore & Ohio (Danl. Willard)	9/ 9/12		
4097	Chesapeake & Ohio (F. Trumbull)	10/29/12	2705	9
4099	McCloud River(J. H. Zural)	10/30/12	2704	100
4129	Pennsylvania	12/17/12	2606	7510
4130	Michigan Central (Ledyard)	12/27/12	2729	1
4161	Chicago, Rock Island & Pacific (Ridgeway)	12/27/12	2734	1911
4182	Delaware, Lackawanna & Western (Truesdale)	1/15/13	2731	*Anthracite*
4158	Chicago & North Western (Gardner)	1/15/13	2733	100
4142	Harry Payne Whitney	1/30/13	1730F	*Wanderer*
4168	Southern (Firley)	4/21/13	2754	1
4194	Norfolk & Western	5/24/13	2785	200
4199	Thomas Fortune Ryan	6/13/13	2783	*Oak Ridge*
4210	General Pullman Service	6/23/13	2492	*New York*
4210	General Pullman Service	6/23/13	2492	*Chicago*
4211	General Pullman Service	6/23/13	2502	*Boston*
	General Pullman Service	6/23/13	2502	*Washington*
	General Pullman Service	6/23/13	2502	*Philadelphia*
4212	Chicago, Milwaukee, St. Paul & Pacific	7/11/13	2787	*Milwaukee*

PULLMAN BUSINESS AND PRIVATE CARS BUILT AT PULLMAN
1882 THROUGH 1930—(Continued)

Lot	Consignee	Date	Plan	Name
4213	Chicago, Milwaukee, St. Paul & Pacific (Bush)	7/11/13	2758	*Walworth*
4214	Chicago, Milwaukee, St. Paul & Pacific (Earling)	7/11/13	2759	*Anaconda*
4219	John S. Cravens	8/13/13	2795	*Nomad*
4220	El Paso & Southwestern	8/21/13	3794	1914
4223	Seaboard Air Line (Warfield)	8/21/13	2792A	*Baltimore*
4224	James Cox Brady	8/27/13	2791	*Adventurer*
4225	Western Maryland (Fitzgerald)	9/ 3/13	2793	203
4241	Daniel C. Jackling	10/ 9/13	2807	*Cyprus II*
4270	Union Pacific (B. L. Winehell)	1/10/14	2818	99
4358	A. K. Macomber	8/ 6/15	2892	*Seminole*
4381	Toledo, St Louis & Western (Ross)	12/ 4/15	2911	400
4378	Nevada Northern	11/30/15	2895	300
4382	Pennsylvania Lines West	12/13/15	2904	7504
ILLEGIBLE	Lehigh Valley	3/ 2/16	2921	353
	Henry E. Huntington	3/ 9/16	2926	*San Marino*
	John Eaton	3/24/16	2927	*Eaton*
	Central Railroad of New Jersey	3/27/16	2936	*Jersey*
4413	James McLean	4/ 5/16	2895A	*Riverside*
4422	General Pullman Service	7/ 5/16	2502B	*New Port*
4422	General Pullman Service	7/ 5/16	2502B	*Manhattan*
4422	General Pullman Service	7/ 5/16	2502B	*Palm Beach*
4429	Duluth, Missabe & Northern (McGonagle)	5/16/16	2928	*Northland*
4432	Canadian Pacific	6/16/16	2948	50
4435	Delaware, Lackawanna & Western	6/10/16	3300	*Scranton*
4436	James B. Duke	8/15/16	3310	*Doris*
4438	Delaware & Hudson	7/10/16	3311	500
4439	Mrs. Henry Flagler	7/13/16	3306	*Whitehall*
4440	John Ringling	7/20/16	3305	*Jomar*
4445	New York, New Haven & Hartford	8/28/16	3309	2
4447	Union Pacific	9/ 7/16	3312	100
4448	Norfolk & Western	9/11/16	3310	300
4450	Charles M. Schwab	10/30/16	3316	*Loretto II*
4466	Illinois Central	11/ 9/16	3317	1
4467	Baltimore & Ohio	11/ 9/16	3334	99
4473	El Paso & Southwestern	11/10/16	3328	*Santa Rosa* 500
4474	New York Central Lines	11/20/16	3323	301
4490	General Pullman Service	1/17/17	2502B	*Patriot*
	General Pullman Service	1/17/17	2502B	*Pilgrim*
	General Pullman Service	1/17/17	2502B	*Pioneer*
4488	Chicago & North Western	1/24/17	3335	66
4512	Edward S. Harkness	3/26/17	3342	*Pelham*

PULLMAN BUSINESS AND PRIVATE CARS BUILT AT PULLMAN
1882 THROUGH 1930—*(Continued)*

Lot	Consignee	Date	Plan	Name
4514	Joseph E. Widener	4/27/17	3343A	*Lynnewood*
4526	Peter W Rouss	6/21/17	2927	*Winchester*
4630	Atchison, Topeka & Santa Fe	10/ 3/17	3349A	30
4580	Henry Ford	2/18/20	3369	*Fair Lane*
4668	New York, Chicago & St Louis	6/10/22		27
4676	Baltimore & Ohio	9/11/22		
4727	Atchison, Topeka & Santa Fe	3/13/23		52
4747	Atchison, Topeka & Santa Fe			
	(Three Cars)	6/26/23		422-423-424
4748	Northern Pacific	7/ 3/23		*Yellowstone*
4749	Copper River & Northwestern	7/10/23		100
4765	R. T. Crane	11/17/23		*Nituna*
4794	Atchison, Topeka & Santa Fe	1/30/24		35-36
4800	Atchison, Topeka & Santa Fe			
	(Four Cars)	2/16/24		420-427-428-429
4756	Wabash (Williams)	8/ 6/23		*Ohio* 400
4750	Seaboard Air Line (Warfield)			*Baltimore*
4838	Nickel Plate	1/14/25		27
4857	J. Pierpont Morgan	10/21/24		*Erie* 400
4883	Atchison, Topeka & Santa Fe			
	(Two Cars)	1/14/25		37-38
4884	Atchison, Topeka & Santa Fe			
	(Four Cars)	1/14/25		400-401-402-403
4893	Missouri Pacific (Hale)	2/11/25		12
4901	Union Pacific	3/20/25		*Overland* 102
4913	Florida East Coast (William F.			
	Kenan)	5/ 8/25		*Randleigh*
4921	William Boyce Thompson	7/ 8/25		*Alder* 63
4927	William F. Kenny	8/12/25		*St. Nicholas*
4934	Southern Pacific (DeForest)	9/ 8/25		*Airslee* 100
4934	Southern Pacific (Sproul)	9/ 8/25		99
4937	Southern Pacific (Scott)			*Alamo* 999
4977	Atchison, Topeka & Santa Fe			
	(Four Cars)	1/26/26		404-405-406-407
	Edward B. McLean	5/20/26		*Inquirer*
	George F. Baker, Jr.	5/14/26		99
	National Railway of Mexico	5/25/26		1-2-3-4-5
	General Pullman Service			Five Cars
	New York Central Lines	12/25/26		1-2-3-4
	National Railway of Mexico	7/24/26		War Dept. Car
	Charles W. Clark	8/19/26		*Errant*
	Chesapeake & Ohio (Harahan)	11/ 1/26		*Richmond*
	Harry Payne Whitney	4/ 6/27		*Adios*
6107	Southern Pacific (Shoup)	5/ 5/27		*Sunset* 140

PULLMAN BUSINESS AND PRIVATE CARS BUILT AT PULLMAN
1882 THROUGH 1930—(Continued)

Lot	Consignee	Date	Plan	Name
6109	New York Central (Four Cars)	5/16/27		1-6-99-400
6113	Atchison, Topeka & Santa Fe (Two Cars)	6/ 6/27		9-10
6116	Southern	6/25/27		*Virginia*
6117	Southern	6/25/27		*Carolina*
6130	Virginian Railroad (Mrs. Vietor)	8/ 4/27		*Vietwood*
R6131	Wabash	7/20/27		400
R6133	Chicago & Eastern Illinois	8/16/27		602
R6134	Fruit Growers Express	9/19/27		*Commonwealth*
R6161	Charles W. Clark	1/12/28		*Errant*
6165	Atchison, Topeka & Santa Fe	2/ 3/28		39
6168	Nickel Plate	2/16/28		1
6175	Bangor & Aroostook	3/ 5/28		*Itsuitsme*
6191	Missouri Pacific	4/ 5/28		4
6169	Mrs. E. Schlesinger	4/ 5/28		*Ranger*
6201	New York Central	4/17/28		99
6204	Kansas City Southern	4/27/28		*Kay See*
6211	Arthur Curtis James	6/11/28		102
6219	Baltimore & Ohio (Daniel Willard)	7/21/28		*Maryland* 100
6225	W. F. Kenny	8/16/28		*Skipaway*
6232	Shedd Aquarium	10/10/28		*Nautilus*
R6236	Nicholas F. Brady	10/26/28		*Adventurer*
6240	E. W. Jones	11/22/28		*Erie I*
6242	Paul Block	11/30/28		*Friendship*
6246	General Pullman Service (2 Cars)	12/19/28		*Ferdinand Magellan*
				Raould Amundsen
6250	Atchison, Topeka & Santa Fe (Two Cars)	1/16/29		408-409
6242	Harry S. Black	3/ 5/29		*Esperanza*
	Sold to A. C. Burrage, Now *Alicia*			
R3670	Anaconda Mining Company			*Anaconda*
6281	W. R. Reynolds	3/10/29		*Winette*
6293	Chesapeake & Ohio	4/30/29		28
6298	R. B. White	3/29/29		99
8320	New York Central (Two Cars)	6/18/29		1-6
R6321	Chicago Great Western	7/ 1/29		1910
6378	Harry Payne Bingham	3/15/30		*Pawnee*
R6382	Harry Payne Whitney	3/24/30		*Wanderer*

Florida East Coast Railway

PRIVATE CARS HANDLED DURING 1894

NAME OF ROAD	CAR	OCCUPIED BY	DATE REC'VD.	MILEAGE
E.T.V.&G.	97	W. A. Vaughan & party	Jan. 7th	322
Pullman	*Wildwood*	Senator Faulkner & party	Jan. 8th	136
Pullman	*Newport*	Eighteen full fares	Jan. 8th	76
C. of G.	12	Clark Howell & party	Jan. 14th	293
Fla. Southern	80	Mrs. F. H. Brown & party	Jan. 15th	60
C. of G.	100	Capt. R. Somers & party	Jan. 28th	76
C.S.&F.	56	Coach	Feb. 7th	
N.E.S.C.	170	C. S. Gadsden & party	Feb. 7th	198
P.W.&B.	21	C. A. Chipley & party	Feb. 7th	66
W. & W.	331	J. R. Kemley & party	Feb. 7th	66
W. & W.	375	W. G. Elliott & party	Feb. 11th	488
St.L.A.&T.H.	*Arab*	G. W. Parker & party	Feb. 10th	198
R.&D.	106	S. Spencer & party	Feb. 10th	76
C. of G.	*Albany*	J. B. Cleveland & party	Feb. 18th	66
C.R.R. of N.J.	*Monmouth*	Pres. Maxwell & party	Feb.17th	354
Pullman	*Wildwood*	Col. Croker & party	Feb. 9th	482
Pullman	**Haslemere*	Senator Quay & party	Feb. 15th	488
E.T.V.&G.	100	S. M. Felton & party	Feb. 20th	487
G.S.&F.	99	Col. Harris & party	Feb. 21st	56
G.S.&F.	100	W. B. Sparks & party	Feb. 24th	412
Lehigh Valley	353	Eighteen full fares	Feb. 21st	76
E.T.V.&G.	97	W. A. Vaughan & party	March 3rd	66
C.C.&C.	99	A. Trapp & party	March 3rd	76
B.&O.	705	G. Patterson & party	March 4th	331
C.&E.I.	501	O. S. Lyford & party	March 5th	488
C.R.I.&P.	300	R. B. Cable & party	March 5th	498
C.C.C.&St.L.	400	Pres. Ingalls & party	March 6th	288
R.&D.	100	R. Foster & party	March 7th	322
P.R.R.	502	J. S. Morris & party	March 5th	354
R.&D.	110	W. K. Ryder & party	March 7th	197
E.T.V.&G.	99	C. H. Hudson & party	March 8th	488
A.T.&S.	220	*Gen. Torrents & party	March 8th	76
L.N.A.&C.	*Monon*	Gen. Howard & party	March 10th	336
Wagner	*Wanderer*	Chas. Miller & party	March 10th	76
R.G.W.	*Nomad*	W. J. Palmer & party	March 14th	408
N.Y.&N.E.	*Alexander*	A. A. McLeod & party	March 14th	76
W.Va.Cent.	*West Va.*	H. S. Davis & party	March 15th	76
C.H.&D.	7	H. F. Shomaker & party	March 16th	488

*Spellings are those of original East Coast records.

12-51 **Private Car**   SOUTHERN PACIFIC LINES   C.S.5460
VIRGINIA CITY   **SUGGESTED ITINERARY**

FOR _Lucius Beebe & Charles Clegg_ FROM _Sparks_ TO _Various Points._

	PLACE	VIA	TRAIN-NO.	TIME	DAY	DATE
Lv	Spa rks	SP	28	6:56PM	Thurs	Feb 2
Ar	Ogden	SP	28	5:20AMPT	Fri	Feb 3
Lv	Ogden	UP	5	7:55AMMT	Fri	Feb 3
Ar	Las Vegas	UP	5	8:05PMMT	Fri	Feb 3
Lv	Las Vegas	UP	5	7:35PMPT	Sun	Feb 5
Ar	Los Angeles	UP	5	5:38AMPT	Mon	Feb 6
Lv	Los Angeles	SP	6	9:00PM	Mon	Feb 6
Arrive	Houston	SP	6	7:15PM	Wed	Feb 8
Lv	Houston	SP	6	8:00PM	Sat	Feb 11
Ar	New Orleans	SP	6	5:45AM	Sun	Feb 12
Lv	New Orleans	L&N	34	5:00PM	Tues	Feb 14
Ar	Jacksonville	SAL	34	8:45AM	Wed	Feb 15
Lv	Jacksonville	SAL	7	9:40AM	Wed	Feb 15
Ar	Miami	SAL	7	6:45PM	Wed	Feb 15
Lv	Miami	SAL	10	9:00PM	Mon	Feb 20
Ar	Washington	RF&P	110	4:25AM	Wed	Feb 22
Lv	Washington	B&O	12	1:00AM	Thurs	Feb 23
Arrive	Jersey City	B&O	12	6:50AM	Thurs	Feb 23

Switching will take approximately 45 minutes from Jersey City to
Weehawken.
Union Terminal at New Orleans have requested that Passengers remain in
Car until after car is switched at approximately 7:00AM.

Above time from current timetables and subject to change without notice.   Arrival, departure and connection of trains as scheduled is not guaranteed.

Phone **charges** and/or **repairs** to car may be billed to this office
for collection from Mr. Beebe & Mr. Clegg. FARE INFORMATION

Collected from Mr. Beebe & Mr. Clegg at Reno----

                Rail Fare $4213.63 Incl Tax.

Parking charges	Las Vegas	$80.00	
" "	Los Angeles	40.00	Total rail and parking
" "	Houston	120.00	charges collected, at
" "	New Orleans	150.00	Reno. $4901.13
" "	Miami	220.00	R. M. Armstrong, T. A.
" "	Washington	40.00	Reno, Nevada.
Switching Charges	Jersey City	37.50	_R. M. Armstrong_